# Hallesche Forschungen

Im Auftrag der Franckeschen Stiftungen zu Halle
herausgegeben von
Veronika Albrecht-Birkner, Mark Häberlein,
Thomas Müller-Bahlke und Udo Sträter

Band 66

Joyce L. Irwin

# In Spirit and in Truth

## Halle Biblical Interpreters on Music in Worship from Francke to Niemeyer

Verlag der Franckeschen Stiftungen Halle
Harrassowitz Verlag in Kommission

Bibliografische Information der Deutschen Nationalbibliothek:
Die Deutsche Nationalbibliothek verzeichnet diese Publikation in der Deutschen National-
bibliografie; detaillierte bibliografische Daten sind im Internet über https://dnb.de abrufbar.
Bibliographic information published by the Deutsche Nationalbibliothek:
The Deutsche Nationalbibliothek lists this publication in the Deutsche Nationalbibliografie;
detailed bibliographic data are available on the Internet at https://dnb.de.

ISSN 0949-0086
ISBN 978-3-447-12098-2
eISBN 978-3-447-39449-9

© Verlag der Franckeschen Stiftungen Halle 2024

http://www.francke-halle.de und http://www.harrassowitz-verlag.de

Das Werk einschließlich aller seiner Teile ist urheberrechtlich geschützt. Jede Verwertung außer-
halb der engen Grenzen des Urheberrechtsgesetzes ist ohne Zustimmung des Verlages unzulässig
und strafbar. Das gilt insbesondere für Vervielfältigungen, Übersetzungen, Mikroverfilmungen
und die Einspeicherung und Verarbeitung in elektronischen Systemen.

Gedruckt auf alterungsbeständigem Papier.

Printed in Germany.

Satz: Nicola Willam, Berlin
Druck: Beltz Grafische Betriebe GmbH, Bad Langensalza

# Contents

Acknowledgements ................................................. IX

Introduction: German Pietism and Music ............................ 1
    1    Philipp Jakob Spener (1635–1705) ........................... 4
    2    Johann Anastasius Freylinghausen (1670–1739) ................ 6

Chapter One: "Not forsaking the assembling of ourselves together":
August Hermann Francke (1663–1727) on Worship and Music .......... 13
    1    Internal vs. External Worship .............................. 15
    2    Christ as the Kernel of Scripture .......................... 16
    3    Music in the Old Testament ................................. 19
    4    Music as Harmony........................................... 25
    5    The Song of Glory.......................................... 27
    6    The Joy of Salvation ....................................... 30
    7    Summary.................................................... 32

Chapter Two: "Whatever you do, do everything for the glory of God":
Music in the Bible Commentaries of Joachim Lange (1670–1744) ......... 35
    1    The Bible as Prophecy...................................... 36
    2    Mosaic Light and Justice ................................... 38
    3    Ceremonies of the Old Testament ............................ 41
    4    The Historical Books ....................................... 42
    5    Prophetic Music............................................ 44
    6    The Psalms ................................................ 47
    7    The Gospels................................................ 52
    8    The Epistles............................................... 53
    9    Music in the Book of Revelation ............................ 57
    10   Excursus on Music and Morality ............................. 60
    11   Summary ................................................... 65

Chapter Three: A Heart Tuned for Praise:
Johann Jakob Rambach (1693–1735) as Preacher, Professor, and Poet ..... 67

    1   Old Testament Passages on Music .......................... 69
    2   New Testament ......................................... 76
    3   On the Value of Hymns .................................. 81
    4   Affections ............................................. 83
    5   Poetry and Style ....................................... 85
    6   Selected Themes in Rambach's *Geistliche Poesien* ............. 90
        6.1   The Joy of Heartfelt Praise ........................... 91
        6.2   The Struggle between Good and Evil ................... 93
        6.3   The Word Incarnate and the Troubled Soul ............. 94
        6.4   The Majesty of God .................................. 97
    7   Summary .............................................. 99

Chapter Four: Old and New Wine Blended: A Period of Transition ....... 101

    1   Siegmund Jakob Baumgarten (1706–1757) ................... 101
    2   Johann Salomo Semler (1725–1791) ........................ 113
    3   Summary ............................................... 120

Chapter Five: Elevating Religion through Poetry and Music:
August Hermann Niemeyer (1754–1828), Literary Theologian .......... 121

    1   On the Interpretation of the Bible ........................ 121
    2   Genesis: On the Origin of Music .......................... 125
    3   Job .................................................... 126
    4   David .................................................. 128
    5   Prophecy .............................................. 134
    6   The Book of Revelation ................................. 135
    7   Poetry, Music, and Religion ............................. 137
    8   Summary .............................................. 144

Chapter Six: Love, Trust, Constancy, and Humanity in Biblical Characters:
Niemeyer's Oratorios, or Religious Musical Dramas .................. 145

    1   *Abraham auf Moria* (1776) ............................... 147
        1.1   Abraham and Sarah .................................. 147
        1.2   Isaac ............................................... 150
        1.3   Literary Themes ..................................... 152

2  *Lazarus* (1778) .......................................... 154
      2.1  Mary and Martha ................................... 155
      2.2  Jemina ............................................ 158
      2.3  Simon the Sadducee ................................ 159
      2.4  Nathanael ......................................... 160
      2.5  Lazarus ........................................... 161
   3  *Thirza und ihre Söhne* (1779) ............................ 163
      3.1  The Story and its Themes .......................... 163
      3.2  Dramatic Exposition ............................... 165
      3.3  Chryses ........................................... 165
      3.4  Joel .............................................. 167
      3.5  Selima ............................................ 167
      3.6  Thirza ............................................ 168
   4  *Mehala* (1781) ........................................... 169
      4.1  Interpreting the Story ............................ 170
      4.2  Developing the Drama .............................. 172
   5  *Die Feyer des Todes Jesu* (1783) ......................... 175
   6  Pietism and Niemeyer's Musical Views .................... 178
   7  Summary ................................................. 180

Postscript: Into the Nineteenth Century ....................... 181

Summary ....................................................... 185

Bibliography .................................................. 189
   Primary Sources ............................................ 189
   Secondary Sources .......................................... 193

Index of Names ................................................ 201
Index of Biblical References .................................. 205

# Acknowledgements

With the support of the Alexander von Humboldt Foundation, I began this study in Halle in the summer of 2018. Professor Wolfgang Hirschmann graciously agreed to act as supervisor for my research, and he enabled me to affiliate with the Interdisciplinary Centre for European Enlightenment Studies (IZEA) of Martin-Luther-Universität Halle-Wittenberg. Professor Daniel Fulda and Research Coordinator Andrea Thiele provided not only study space but also a very supportive and welcoming atmosphere for my time there. I am also grateful for the assistance of the staff of the Francke Foundations library and the various branches of the university library.

When the COVID-19 pandemic hit and all the libraries in Princeton and elsewhere were closed, I gained new appreciation for all the efforts of anonymous workers who had digitized so many 18th-century books and made them available on the internet. For one book that was not yet available, I am grateful to Karsten Labahn of the Rostock University Library for filling the gap. Although I was sometimes discouraged by the lack of access to secondary materials, the primary sources available through the Verzeichnis Deutscher Drucke des 18. Jahrhunderts (VD 18) made possible my continued progress through those times of isolation. In fact, having this project underway motivated me to spend pandemic time profitably, perhaps even enjoyably.

After finishing some chapters, I asked scholarly friends Dr. Richard Sturm, retired from New Brunswick Theological Seminary, and Dr. Karl Reichl, emeritus professor at the University of Bonn, to offer comments, and I thank them for their helpful responses. Professor Hirschmann read the final draft and encouraged me to submit it for consideration in the Hallesche Forschungen series. From that point, my gratitude extends to Metta Scholz, Head of Publications of the Francke Foundations, who efficiently guided the manuscript through the evaluation and review process. She and her colleague Lukas Nils Regeler offered useful editorial suggestions but were willing to let me override them when I so chose. For that reason, any remaining faults of the book are entirely my own.

Joyce L. Irwin
Princeton, New Jersey
September 2023

Introduction
# German Pietism and Music

Anyone writing on the subject of Pietism and music has to deal first with the definition of Pietism. Does it include Johann Arndt and other devotional writers of the seventeenth century? Did it emerge out of the Reformed tradition of English Puritans and Dutch Calvinists? Or do we define it as beginning with Philipp Jakob Spener's publication of *Pia Desideria*? Then we must make distinctions among the groups to whom we apply the label. One way of distinguishing is to look at whether they remained within the Lutheran confessional church or set up alternate communities. Even with such a guideline, strict categories may become blurry. The Herrnhuters, for instance, tried to rise above sectarian differences by finding common ground but then developed a spirituality that offended most other Pietists.

One recent attempt to summarize the place of music in Pietism took a very inclusive approach. Christian Bunners, in volume four of *Geschichte des Pietismus*,[1] began with Arndt and the devotional movement of the seventeenth century, then proceeded to the musical subjects *Lied* and *Aria* and to the composer Dietrich Buxtehude. Sections on theologians and groups (Spener, Separatists and Inspired, Francke, Freylinghausen and Porst) are followed by thematic sections—criticisms of Pietist singing and the struggle surrounding opera. There are sections on the Zinzendorf community, on J. S. Bach, and on the course of Pietist influence on music into the twentieth century. Clearly, with a broad definition of Pietism, the subtopic of music in Pietism becomes quite multi-faceted.

Tanya Kevorkian, in a similar "state of research" article, opts for a narrower definition of Pietism, stating that the broad view leads to identifying as early or proto-pietists those who advocated for ideas that were actually common tendencies of the age. All Lutheran clergy and many laypeople, she observes, emphasized pedagogical clarity and accessibility as well as "a richly felt emotional attachment to Christ." Against Bunners' designation of Pietist hymnals as those that "promoted an individualization of faith, a privatization of worship, and the reception of new hymns," Kevorkian argues that these were also characteristics of Orthodox hymnal editors and text writers.[2] Addressing the question of whether Pietism was hostile to the arts, she discusses the theological issues raised in critiques of church music and recognizes that many Orthodox writers expressed similar critiques. The opening

---

[1] Christian Bunners: Musik. In: Glaubenswelt und Lebenswelten. Ed. by Hartmut Lehmann. Göttingen: Vandenhoeck & Ruprecht, 2004, 428–455. Bunners also wrote the article "Gesangbuch" in the same volume, pp. 121–142.

[2] Tanya Kevorkian: Pietists and Music. In: A Companion to German Pietism, 1660–1800. Ed. by Douglas H. Shantz. Leiden: Brill, 2015, 171–200, here 176.

sentences of her article aptly sum up the complexity of the subject: "Pietists had a complex, diverse, ambivalent, and sometimes even contradictory relationship with music. Different groups of Pietists had highly distinctive musical cultures, so there was actually no one set of Pietist attitudes toward music."[3]

In an earlier article entitled "German Pietists and Church Music in the Baroque Age,"[4] I attempted to resolve some of the apparent contradictions by pointing out that musicologists often worked with an overly simple view of Pietism as subjective and individualistic.[5] In fact, many Pietists or pre-Pietists were seeking a greater degree of community and communal worship than they experienced in churches that featured highly artistic choir and organ music. If subjectivity is defined as mystically inclined poetry expressing the believer's union with God, this could be found in either Orthodoxy or Pietism. The subjectivity that most characterizes Pietism is the concern for the moral standing of the musician; hence, the Pietists could regard those church musicians as individualistic who seemed to be performing to demonstrate their own skills rather than to express their devotion. For the most part, Pietists were focused on practical problems of engaging the congregation musically, and many of their objections to the church music of the day were shared by respected church musicians within Orthodoxy.

While my book *Neither Voice nor Heart Alone*[6] pursued these issues at greater length, it continued to examine the differences that separated Pietists from Orthodox in the context of particular controversies. For my current study, I began with the hope of finding a theology of music among Pietists not in controversial literature but in biblical commentaries. Knowing that Halle professor Joachim Lange had written lengthy biblical commentaries, I decided to limit my study to the writings of Halle university academicians insofar as they addressed musical topics. I soon found that it would not be solely through biblical commentaries that I would find this material. Lange's colleagues did not attempt such a thorough commentary on the Bible and often published studies of single books of the Bible. In many cases these are exegetical works that explain the meaning of the Hebrew or Greek with minimal commentary. For an understanding of the thought of such theologians

---

[3] Kevorkian: Pietists and Music, 171.
[4] Joyce Irwin: German Pietists and Church Music in the Baroque Age. In: Church History 54, March 1985, Issue 1, 29–40.
[5] Udo Sträter comments that these general terms are not sufficient to define Halle Pietism: "Der hallesche Pietismus seiner klassischen 'Blütezeit' (ca. 1690–1730) kann also nicht verstanden werden auf der Grundlage eines allgemeinen geistesgeschichtlichen Konzepts von pietistischer Religiosität, Innerlichkeit, Subjektivismus, etc. sondern nur, wenn man seine Wurzeln in der innerlutherischen Kirchenkritik- und Reformbewegung des 17. Jahrhunderts und sein eschatologisch qualifiziertes Selbstverständnis als einer religiös-sozialen Reformbewegung mit gesamtgesellschaftlichem Anspruch ernst nimmt." Udo Sträter: Halle als ein Zentrum des Pietismus. In: Musikkonzepte – Konzepte der Musikwissenschaft. Ed. by Kathrin Eberl and Wolfgang Ruf. Vol. 1: Bericht über den Internationalen Kongress der Gesellschaft für Musikforschung Halle (Saale) 1998. Kassel: Bärenreiter, 2000, 214–225, here 218.
[6] Joyce L. Irwin: Neither Voice nor Heart Alone: German Lutheran Theology of Music in the Age of the Baroque. New York: Peter Lang, 1993; reprint Eugene, OR: Wipf & Stock, 2018.

on musical questions, it was necessary to turn to other genres such as sermons and meditative essays. Some of the leading academicians were also active hymn writers and authors of cantata or oratorio texts; when these treat biblical themes or personages, such hymns and oratorios are themselves an indirect form of biblical commentary.

While deciding to focus on Halle academicians, I also decided not to limit my study to the main period of Pietism. At some point about midway through the century, Pietism ceased to be the dominant stance of Halle theologians, and yet I hope to show that the core of their musical attitudes remained consistent even while biblical interpretations changed. In the course of the eighteenth century, Halle professors turned increasingly to a focus on biblical hermeneutics and dramatically changed the approach to the study of the Bible. These new approaches to the Bible were accompanied by new developments in German poetry and a more literary approach. As a result, my sources came to include essays on the role of music and poetry in religion in addition to studies of biblical characters and methods of biblical study.

Readers knowledgeable in the history of the university of Halle may question the choice of theologians to study. The first few should be obvious. Any history of theology in Halle would have to include August Hermann Francke, the dominant leader throughout the peak period of Halle Pietism. Joachim Lange, though less famous in our day except for his role in ousting the philosopher Christian Wolff from Halle, was a formidable figure and prolific scholar who might well be called the academic defender of Pietism. Johann Jakob Rambach, who did not live long enough to be as prolific, was highly respected in his own day and also active in hymnody and poetry. In a study involving biblical interpretation, Siegmund Jakob Baumgarten and Johann Salomo Semler could not be ignored; they represent the transition from Pietism to the Enlightenment or what has been called Neology as a new approach to theology in the latter half of the eighteenth century. From this later period, the extensive attention devoted to August Hermann Niemeyer may seem out of proportion to his importance as a theologian. To be sure, he was not an intellectual innovator, but his ability to blend biblical scholarship, theology, and poetry into a form set to music by a noteworthy composer marks the culmination of Halle developments in theology and music. There were, to be sure, many professors of theology in Halle who do not appear in my study, Joachim Justus Breithaupt, Paul Anton, and Johann Heinrich Michaelis, to name a few. Those I chose for this study contributed the most, so far as I have determined, to the biblical perspective on music among Halle theologians, either through biblical commentaries or through literary interpretations. This cannot pretend to be a history of theology in Halle, therefore, but rather a glimpse into that history and into one aspect of the history of Pietism.

As is clear from the above, the subject "Pietism and Music" must be examined in discrete units before any comprehensive survey will be possible. By restricting my study to the Halle university faculty of the eighteenth century, my purpose is not to offer a definitive description of Pietist attitudes toward music but to observe transitions in theology and hermeneutical method that result in changing attitudes toward the arts. At the same time, I see a consistent emphasis throughout the century on inward appropriation of religion and simplicity of outward expression. Like the attempt to distinguish Pietist from Orthodox in the seventeenth century, the boundaries between Pietism and literary movements such as Empfindsamkeit and Romanticism are blurry. Isaiah Berlin, for instance, regarded Pietism as the root of Romanticism, seeing a continuity from one to the other.[7] Mark Gignilliat endorsed this view in tracing the history of Old Testament biblical criticism, citing Berlin's statement to the effect that while science had removed the certainties of faith, the intense spirituality of Pietism remained.[8] This is true of Friedrich Schleiermacher, the pivotal theologian of the early nineteenth century, whose Pietist background is frequently mentioned as a factor in his emphasis on affective experience in religion.[9] While Schleiermacher spent most of his career in Berlin, he did study and teach for a time in Halle, which legitimates a short concluding chapter about him here.

## 1 Philipp Jakob Spener (1635–1705)

No study of Pietism can bypass its founding father, Philipp Jakob Spener (1635–1705), even if he does not fulfill the other criteria for this study as a Halle professor and biblical theologian. Nor did he comment systematically on the role of music in church. Still, as the revered leader of the movement, he influenced all those who are considered Pietists.

Others, most notably Martin Geck and Christian Bunners, have studied Spener's views on music so that a summary of their findings will suffice for our purposes.[10] Those who wish to consult the primary sources should turn first to Geck, whose plenteous citations from Spener draw from a variety of Spener's writings.

Both Geck and Bunners identify edification as the primary goal of singing in worship for Spener. Geck uses the Latin term *aedificatio hominis*, saying that for Spener there is no worship service, no liturgy, no worship music "in itself" without people's active participation.[11] Bunners uses the German word "Erbauung", which, in a citation from Spener related to singing, is defined as "increase of grace, strengthening of belief, growth in spiritual joy, foretaste of eternal life." Both the Latin and the German words have as their root the connotation of building, as does

---

[7] Isaiah Berlin: The Roots of Romanticism. Ed. by Henry Hardy. 2nd ed. Princeton: Princeton University Press, 2013, 43.

[8] Mark S. Gignilliat: A Brief History of Old Testament Criticism from Benedict Spinoza to Brevard Childs. Grand Rapids, MI: Zondervan, 2012, 87.

[9] See, for instance, Tenzan Eaghll: From Pietism to Romanticism: The Early Life and Work of Friedrich Schleiermacher. In: The pietist impulse in Christianity. Ed. by Christian T. Collins Winn et al. Eugene, OR: Pickwick 2011, 107–119.

[10] Martin Geck: Ph. J. Spener und die Kirchenmusik. In: Musik und Kirche 31, 1961, 97–106, 172–184; Christian Bunners: Philipp Jakob Spener und die Kirchenmusik. In: Philipp Jakob Spener—Leben Werk, Bedeutung: Bilanz der Forschung nach 300 Jahren. Ed. by Dorothea Wendebourg. Tübingen: Niemeyer, 2007, 241–265.

[11] Geck: Ph. J. Spener und die Kirchenmusik, 180.

the English cognate "edification," defined in Webster's *Third New International Dictionary* as "a building up of the mind, character, or faith: intellectual, moral, or spiritual improvement." In succeeding chapters, I will translate "Erbauung" as "edification," even though in ordinary English usage the sense is more of intellectual than spiritual improvement. In recent years, the term "spiritual formation" has become widely used in Christian denominations, denoting a process of growth in relationship to God by shaping of the heart, will, and spirit. This might be a better way to understand what eighteenth-century writers meant by "edification," but it would be anachronistic to translate "Erbauung" as "spiritual formation."

Spener's requirement that all music be edifying meant that artistic concerted music, particularly texts sung in Latin and/or in the imported Italianate style, was not appropriate for ordinary worshippers. Nor was elaborate organ-playing that often served to feed the organist's ambition more than the congregation's spiritual hunger. Music influenced by secular styles could too easily divert the mind and senses; some such music was more suited for dancing than for sacred worship. While music is a gift of God, it should be used to promote devotion to God and should be characterized by *simplicitas* and *gravitas*. Older polyphonic choral music sometimes achieved the requisite simplicity and seriousness, but even then it was often difficult to understand the words. Because not everyone could appreciate or benefit from such motets, it is best not to tax the congregation's attention with long, prominently placed concerted music. Even more fruitful would be to hold separate services where the figural music would be featured as the main content for those who are receptive to it.

Singing by the congregation, on the other hand, played an important role for Spener. Not only does music have a natural power to move the affections, but furthermore the combination of music and poetry in hymns has an almost mysterious power to make hearts receptive to the Word. When the text of the hymn conveys the biblical message, the indwelling of the Word is strengthened. Geck notes that while Spener recognized three functions of hymns—for honoring God, for calling upon God, for one's own edification—, in practice the first two receded almost completely behind the third.[12] His psychological view of music as an "art of the affections" is similar to the contemporaneous music-theoretical doctrine of the affections, which Geck presumes was unfamiliar to Spener. Rather than blaming Spener for breaking with Orthodoxy, Geck sees the Enlightenment as the common source of a new mentality.[13]

Bunners pointed out the connection of congregational singing to the Reformation teaching on the priesthood of all believers, which took a more central place in the theology of Spener than it had with the Orthodox. Not only did the professional choirs and soloists perform music that people in the pews did not understand, but they also decreased the participation of the congregation as a whole. The small group gatherings or *collegia pietatis* that Spener promoted were one means of

---

[12] Geck: Ph. J. Spener und die Kirchenmusik, 103.
[13] Geck: Ph. J. Spener und die Kirchenmusik, 180–181.

promoting leadership among the laity, and these explicitly included the singing of hymns. Spener also encouraged the writing of new hymns and the publishing of new hymnals, but for the hymnals to be used in public worship he advocated retaining the familiar treasured hymns without alterations. He was sensitive to the possibility of confusing parishioners with innovations or pressuring them to purchase too many new hymnbooks. Moreover, he found great value in many seventeenth-century hymns, particularly those of Paul Gerhardt, which, in Spener's opinion, excelled all other hymns in spirit and power. He also considered it important for the texts to accord with pure doctrine and not simply to stir the emotions.

Because Spener's reflections on music and hymnody are scattered in hymnal prefaces, funeral sermons, and practical reform statements, there is no biblical commentary that might provide us with a more comprehensive picture of his biblical theology of music. The earliest singing of the Hebrews, he believed, was characterized by *gravitas*, but with Jubal's discovery of musical instruments, their music took on a more frivolous and sensual tone while also striving for artistry. The temple music of later times was merely outward observance lacking in faith and devotion, provoking the outcry of Amos against the noise of their songs. One positive comment by Spener on the temple music was that the people actively participated in the singing. It is the singing of psalms that carries over into the New Testament when all the external ceremony is removed. This did not mean for Spener, as it had for Calvinists, that all instrumental music should be excluded, but the purpose of using instruments should be for accompaniment and enhancement of congregational singing. He recognized that the meaning of the word *psalm* itself connoted a song accompanied by strings.

In the following study we will encounter many of these same themes again in the writings of the Halle Pietists. To what extent Spener may have influenced their thoughts on church music is difficult to determine. Spener himself drew to some extent on Theophilus Großgebauer, whose biting criticism of church music practices was far more notorious than any of Spener's comments.[14] Spener's greatest influence for church music was arguably in the encouragement of hymn writing. As Bunners writes, "His affirmative vote for new hymns contributed to the blossoming of a pietistic 'springtime of hymns'."[15]

## 2 Johann Anastasius Freylinghausen (1670–1739)

The hymnodic springtime burst forth in Halle with the publication of the *Geist= reiches Gesangbuch* in 1704, edited by Johann Anastasius Freylinghausen (1670–1739), assistant to August Hermann Francke in pastoral duties in Glaucha as well as in the organization of the orphanage and Glaucha Foundations. Freylinghausen

---

[14] See my chapter on Großgebauer in Irwin: Neither Voice nor Heart Alone, 79–88.
[15] Bunners: Spener, 262.

had been involved in some predecessor hymnal publications in the 1690s,[16] but this hymnal was so successful that it was republished nineteen times over the next five decades and spread throughout the Halle mission field. The hymnal has been studied from many perspectives in three volumes of essays edited by Wolfgang Miersemann and Gudrun Busch,[17] and a critical edition with commentaries has been published in multiple volumes by Miersemann and Dianne Marie McMullen.[18]

Not everyone in the early eighteenth century was pleased with the hymnal, however. A decade after the publication of the first edition, the theological faculty of Wittenberg issued a very critical evaluation of the Halle hymnal.[19] With Wittenberg as the stronghold of Lutheran orthodoxy, their theologians' negative appraisal of a hymnal issuing from Francke's circle is hardly surprising. Resentment over the favoritism of the Prussian rulers toward Francke increased the theological rivalry between the two camps.

In discussing the Wittenberg criticisms, musicologists tend to focus on issues of musical style. The Wittenberg theologians had said that both the meter and the notes of hymns should be "serious, devotional, and godly but not in the lewd, frivolous, very trivial manner of secular songs."[20] The hymnal in question, according to Wittenberg, has "very many hopping, jumping dactylic songs that are for the most part provided with unspiritual, quite lewd melodies that are not in the least suited to the seriousness of the lofty mysteries that they should contain."[21] Ulrike Harnisch examined the melodies and found that the number of truly dactylic tunes was not so large as the Wittenbergers implied but that indeed triple meter was so unusual for hymns at the time that its presence was striking. Even though small in number, the dancelike characteristic of the new tunes is a legitimate basis,

---

[16] See Beate Besser: Art. "Hallesches Gesangbuch 1704". In: Komponisten und Liederdichter des Evangelischen Gesangbuchs. Ed. by Wolfgang Herbst. Göttingen: Vandenhoeck & Ruprecht, 1999, 128.

[17] Gudrun Busch and Wolfgang Miersemann, eds.: "Geist=reicher" Gesang: Halle und das pietistische Lied. Tübingen: Niemeyer, 1997; Pietismus und Liedkultur. Tübingen: Niemeyer, 2002; and "Singt dem Herrn nah und fern": 300 Jahre Freylinghausensches Gesangbuch. Tübingen: Niemeyer, 2008.

[18] Johann Anastasius Freylinghausen: Geistreiches Gesangbuch: Edition und Kommentar. Ed. by Dianne Marie McMullen and Wolfgang Miersemann. Tübingen: Franckesche Stiftungen, Niemeyer, 2004–2020.

[19] Dated 17 September 1714, the document appeared in print in 1716: Der Löblichen Theologischen Facultæt zu Wittenberg Bedencken über das zu Glauche an Halle 1703. im Wäysen=Hause daselbst edirte Gesang=Buch. Frankfurt/Main and Leipzig: Zimmermann, 1716. The 1703 date is based on the September 1703 dating of the dedication and preface, but the date on the title page is 1704. Cf. Freylinghausen: Geistreiches Gesangbuch: Edition und Kommentar, Vol. 1, pt. 3, 15.

[20] "daß die Gesänge [...] etwas ernsthafftes / andächtiges / und gottseeliges in sich fassen / nicht aber auf eine üppige / leichte / und fast liederliche Art der weltlichen Gesänge hinaus lauffen." Der Löblichen Theologischen Facultæt zu Wittenberg Bedencken, 7.

[21] "finden wir in erwehntem Gesang=Buche sehr viel hüpffende / springende dactylische Lieder / welche mehrentheils mit ungeistlichen und fast üppigen Melodeyen versehen sind / und insonderheit sich zu der Gravität der hohen Geheimnisse / die sie in sich halten sollen / im geringsten nicht reimen." Der Löblichen Theologischen Facultæt zu Wittenberg Bedencken, 25.

according to Harnisch, for labelling them "pietistic hymns."[22] Dianne McMullen, on the other hand, pointed out examples of dactylic rhythms in Lutheran hymnals as early as 1640, though these were intended originally for house devotions. By the time the Halle hymnal was published, she argues, such rhythms were not unknown even in church hymns, supported by the Baroque doctrine of the affections.[23] Similarly, Gudrun Busch placed the Freylinghausen hymnal in the larger context of stylistic shifts from Baroque to galant in both secular and sacred song. She identified various dance rhythms in different hymns but found them sometimes hidden within the text rather than the melody.[24] In another article she viewed the lively rhythms as a means of enabling the spiritual awakening that lay at the core of the Pietist movement. By means of music that touches the emotions, the heart is prepared for the workings of the Spirit. Busch thus saw Francke, an opponent of all worldly dancing, as endorsing the expression of joy through dance for the awakened, the inspired, and the regenerate.[25]

If Busch meant to imply that Francke wanted to introduce dancing as a spiritual act, after the manner of King David or as the Shakers would later do, that would be inaccurate.[26] Her comment does, however, highlight the seeming inconsistencies in Pietists' views of the arts that have puzzled many scholars. Manfred Bukofzer, for instance, found that the songs of the Pietists resembled the styles of music that they had opposed in principle: "Paradoxically enough, these songs were more often than not derivatives of shallow operatic airs and betrayed the very same secular influence that the Pietists attacked so vehemently in theory."[27] Bunners noted that Freylinghausen's use of triple meter and large melodic intervals did not accord with Spener's ideals of simplicity and gravity, concluding that "Pietism had a completely

---

[22] Ulrike Harnisch: Die "ungeistlichen und fast üppigen Melodeyen" des Gesangbuches von J. A. Freylinghausen Halle 1704. In: Musikkonzepte: Konzepte der Musikwissenschaft. Ed. by Kathrin Eberl-Ruf. Vol. 2. Kassel: Bärenreiter, 2000, 246–252.

[23] Dianne Marie McMullen: Melodien geistlicher Lieder und ihre kontroverse Diskussion zur Bach-Zeit: Pietistische contra orthodox-lutherische Auffassungen im Umkreis des Geist=reichen Gesang=buches (Halle 1704) von Johann Anastasius Freylinghausen. In: Geist=reicher Gesang, 197–210. See also McMullen and Miersemann: "Ungeistliche" und "leichtsinnige" Weisen? Zur Eigenart "Hallischer Melodien" anhand ausgewählter Beispiele. In: Singen, beten, musizieren: Theologische Grundlagen der Kirchenmusik in Nord- und Mitteldeutschland zwischen Reformation und Pietismus (1530–1750). Ed. by Jochen M. Arnold et al. Göttingen: V&R unipress, 2014, 211–231.

[24] Gudrun Busch: Lieder in "liederloser Zeit," oder: der "Freylinghausen" (1704/14) als wiederentdeckte Klammer zwischen zwei Jahrhunderten deutscher Liedgeschichte. Versuch einer Bestandsaufnahme. In: "Singt dem Herrn nah und fern", 1–53.

[25] Gudrun Busch: "Der Geist hilft unsrer Schwachheit auf". Das Geist=reiche Gesang=Buch Johann Anastasius Freylinghausens von 1704 auf dem Wege zur Erweckung. In: Alter Adam und neue Kreatur. Pietismus und Anthropologie. Beiträge zum II. Internationalen Kongress für Pietismusforschung. Ed. by Udo Sträter. Tübingen: Niemeyer, 2009, 621–644, esp. 640.

[26] See Joyce L. Irwin: Dancing in Bach's Time-Sin or Permissible Pleasure? Bach Perspectives 12. Ed. by Robin Leaver. Champaign, IL: University of Illinois Press, 2018, 24–25.

[27] Manfred Bukofzer: Music in the Baroque Era: From Monteverdi to Bach. New York: W. W. Norton, 1947, 272.

pluralistic conception of hymns."[28] Rainer Bayreuther approached this issue by drawing a distinction between Orthodox and Pietist views of the relationship between form and content. For the Orthodox, he maintains, the musical form itself has implications for the content: if the form is too "üppig"—a word I have translated above as "lewd" but also has connotations of lavishness and extravagance—,[29] it fails in its intended purpose, no matter how devout and appropriate the text. The Pietist view of hymnody, according to Bayreuther, breaks apart this connection between form and content, applying the category of "üppig" solely to the content, not to the form, thus removing the hymn melody from any accusation of "Üppigkeit."[30] In other words, Pietists attribute any sinfulness in relation to music not to the music itself, which is neither good nor bad, but to the particular context of its use. Accordingly, Pietists were free to make use of any musical style or genre that enabled them to express their personal experience of faith. From a music history perspective, this aligns Pietist music more closely with Empfindsamkeit and the early classical period in their individualistic expression of the affections than with the stylized Baroque use of musical figures and rhetoric to connote affections.[31]

Bayreuther's explanation from a musicological perspective of the alleged inconsistencies in the Pietist position on music is in keeping with the explanation I presented from a theological perspective in my article on German Pietists and church music. Gottfried Vockerodt (1665–1727), a leading Pietist spokesman on issues of ethics and the arts, was not interested in distinguishing musical styles according to their moral value but in judging the musicians themselves according to their spiritual motivation. Even musical instruments or styles normally associated with godlessness might be put to godly use by a musician of deep faith. Music in itself is morally neutral; it is sinful only when practiced for self-glorification, lustful pleasure, or any other purpose than to glorify God.[32] As both Bayreuther and I have concluded, musical style is not a helpful criterion by which to distinguish between Orthodox and Pietists.

Of the criticisms by the Wittenberg theologians of the Freylinghausen hymnal, stylistic objections in fact accounted for only a small number of their points, most of which were theological. The Wittenbergers offered detailed criticisms of numerous texts from the hymnal, labelling many as "fanatical" or "enthusiastical," the latter term having none of the modern English connotation of eager or excited but rather the claim of direct spiritual revelation. They identified certain expressions as

---

[28] Bunners: Spener, 253: "Der Pietismus hat also eine durchaus plurale Liedauffassung gehabt."

[29] The complex meaning of the word in the eighteenth century is noted in *Grimm's Wörterbuch*: "und zwar ist dem neueren wort oft eine eigenthümliche mehrdeutigkeit eigen, indem sich verschiedene bed. mischen." (Jacob Grimm and Wilhelm Grimm: Deutsches Wörterbuch. Leipzig: Hirzel, 1854–1961. Vol. 24, col. 2340. URL: https://www.woerterbuchnetz.de/DWB?lemid=U13488 [accessed: August 8, 2023]).

[30] Rainer Bayreuther: Pietismus, Orthodoxie, pietistisches Lied und Kunstmusik. Eine Verhältnisbestimmung. In: Pietismus und Liedkultur, 134.

[31] Bayreuther: Pietismus, Orthodoxie, pietistisches Kunstlied und Kunstmusik, 136–137.

[32] Irwin: German Pietists and Church Music, 36–37.

mystical, as expressing a belief in the indwelling of God in the soul or an essential union of the person with God. This represented for them an erroneous belief that human nature can be changed to the point of deification where none of the sinful nature remains. Another charge is that of chiliasm or belief in the thousand-year reign of Christ on earth, especially in the section of the hymnal labelled "On the hope of Zion." This, of course, was one of the major points of division between the Orthodox and Pietists, though even among the Pietists different views of the end times were expressed. Several of the hymns, the Wittenbergers pointed out, were taken from Gottfried Arnold's *Liebes=Funcken* and exhibited his radical Pietist theology. Though they were able to identify these, they objected to the lack of attribution of the hymns in general. It seemed they were prepared to judge the merit of the hymn text based on the moral or theological reputation of its author. More egregiously, Wolfgang Herbst points out, they criticized the hymnal on the basis of a hymn, the "Geheimniß=volle Triumph=Lied," that was not even included in the hymnal at issue but appeared in Arnold's *Liebes=Funcken*. Even Arnold admitted in his preface that this long esoteric poem was not easily comprehensible, but the fact that he did publish it was sufficient for Wittenberg to find fault with the Halle hymnal through guilt by association.[33]

Further analysis of the Wittenberg criticisms is beyond the scope of this study, though it would be a worthwhile project. Dianne McMullen made a good start in a section of her 1987 dissertation where she explained some of the theological differences between Pietists and Orthodox in relation to the hymns.[34] The scholar who has devoted most attention to the theology of the *Geist=reiches Gesangbuch*, Suvi-Päivi Koski, has compared it to Freylinghausen's dogmatic theology in his *Grundlegung der Theologie*, seldom viewing it through the lens of Orthodoxy.[35] In a footnote Koski does defend the biblical basis of the idea of deification and Luther's endorsement of the same, recognizing that it was long considered as foreign to Lutheranism,[36] as indeed it was to the Wittenbergers in their critique. Like Koski, we must leave the analysis of Freylinghausen's relationship to Luther or to the orthodox Lutherans of his time to other scholars. I would only say that the word "geistreich," which has been at the forefront of much scholarship surrounding this hymnal, is not specific to Pietism. The Wittenbergers also regarded many hymns of poets such as Becker, Rist, Gerhardt

---

[33] Wolfgang Herbst: Pietismus und Dadaismus. Das "Geheimniß=volle Triumph-Lied" aus Gottfried Arnolds zweitem Teil der *Göttlichen Liebesfunken* von 1701. In: Jahrbuch für Liturgik und Hymnologie 56, 2017, 186–239, esp. 188–190.

[34] Dianne Marie McMullen: The Geistreiches Gesangbuch of Johann Anastasius Freylinghausen (1670–1739): A German Pietist Hymnal. Diss. phil. University of Michigan, 1987.

[35] Suvi-Päivi Koski: "Und sungen das lied Mosis deß Knechts Gottes/ und das lied deß Lamms – Apoc. XV:3": Zur Theologie des Geist=reichen Gesang=Buches (Halle 1704) von Johann Anastasius Freylinghausen. In: "Geist=reicher Gesang", 171–196; also: Zur theologischen Anthropologie der Freylinghausenschen Gesangbücher. In: Alter Adam, 597–610.

[36] Koski: Zur theologischen Anthropologie, 600, fn. 17.

and others as "geistreich"[37]; the use of the word as applied to hymns goes back at least as far as Cyriacus Spangenberg in 1582.[38]

For the present study of Halle theologians' biblical interpretation on musical questions, an examination of the theology expressed in Freylinghausen's hymnal preface rather than the hymns themselves must suffice. His preface to the 1708 edition assembles numerous biblical references to singing in both Old and New Testaments.[39] Only a thorough study of hymnal prefaces before and during Freylinghausen's time could determine whether his selection of biblical references is unusual. Certainly, many citations are fairly standard and predictable. The songs of Moses and Miriam praising God for deliverance from the Pharoah are the earliest song texts recorded in the Bible, followed by the songs of Deborah with Barak and Hanna. The psalms of David are a strong precedent and basis for Christian singing, and Paul's instructions in Ephesians and Colossians to sing psalms and hymns serve as an endorsement for singing in church. Isaiah's vision of the Lord surrounded by singing angels is recalled in John's vision in the Book of Revelation. Angelic singing also accompanied the birth of Jesus as narrated in the gospel of Luke. A few other references cited by Freylinghausen were slightly less common, such as to Wisdom 10 or Sirach 47, but all of these can be found in other hymnal prefaces or treatises on music.

The most noteworthy aspect of Freylinghausen's treatment is perhaps the manner in which he views the biblical examples as an integrated picture through the lens of promise and prophecy. The deliverance from Egypt was evidence of the promise God had made to the patriarchs. The song that Moses sang shortly before his death (Deut 32) was, according to Freylinghausen, given to him by God as testimony of the future reign of the church and the Messiah. The spirit of God *awakened* the prophetess Deborah to sing a song to the Lord following the victory over the Canaanites. Freylinghausen's twofold use of the word "erweckte" here seems significant against the backdrop of Pietist view of an awakened heart as one that is receptive to the movement of the Spirit. To the Old Testament prophets, he attributes an awareness of the ultimate fulfillment of God's promises in the glorious reign of Christ; thus, not only Isaiah's vision in chapter 6 but also other references to singing in Isaiah 26 and Jeremiah 31 prefigure the glory of the church triumphant, as do David's many prophetic "Hallelujahs."

There was, to be sure, nothing new about seeing the Old Testament as a prefiguring of the New, but, as we will see, this was a central interpretive principle for the Halle theologians. Freylinghausen quotes Sirach 47,9–12 as if it were a clear instance of Jesus' application to himself of references in the law, prophets, and the psalms (Luke 24,44). After citing Psalms 89 and 101, he writes, "Thus

---

[37] Der Löblichen Theologischen Facultæt zu Wittenberg Bedencken, 5.
[38] See Grimm and Grimm: Wörterbuch, Vol. 5, col. 2790. URL: https://www.woerterbuchnetz.de/DWB?lemid=G05877 (accessed August 2, 2023).
[39] Only this edition was available to me, as it was chosen as the basis for the modern edition. Johann Anastasius Freylinghausen, preface to Geist=reiches Gesang=Buch. 4th ed. Halle, 1708. In: Freylinghausen: Geistreiches Gesangbuch, Vol. 1, Pt. 1, 13–20.

in the fullness of time the previously prophesied grace and truth likewise had to be proclaimed as present in psalms and songs of praise."[40] This approach seems especially strained when he connects the song of Moses to the song of the Lamb by way of new and old fruit in the Song of Solomon (7,13) and new and old treasure in Matthew (13,52).[41] The issue of Old Testament prophecy and foreshadowing in relation to the New Testament will be a recurring theme among the Halle theologians we will study.

Another question Freylinghausen addressed was whether it was appropriate for a congregation comprised of both spiritual and unspiritual persons to sing together. Pietists believed that an unrepentant person of the flesh cannot sing in a way that pleases God, and some felt that for this reason it might be preferable to do away with singing in public worship. Freylinghausen responded, however, that God can use hymns to move hearts in a better direction; a person who sings along in worship out of mere habit may nevertheless experience a pang of conscience that could lead toward conversion. Faithful servants of God should carefully point out to such persons the truths of which they are singing and the importance of singing "in spirit and in truth." Such singing—and only such singing—is pleasing to God. This, in sum, is the biblical view of music for the Halle theologians throughout the eighteenth century.

---

[40] "Also muste in der Fülle der Zeit die vorher geweissagete Gnade und Wahrheit als gegenwärtig in Psalmen und Lobgesängen gleichfals ausgeruffen werden." Freylinghausen: Geistreiches Gesangbuch, Vol. 1, Pt. 1, 15.

[41] Freylinghausen: Geistreiches Gesangbuch, Vol. 1, Pt. 1, 17.

Chapter One

# "Not forsaking the assembling of ourselves together": August Hermann Francke (1663–1727) on Worship and Music

As the founder of the Glaucha Anstalten, influential pastor in Halle, and university professor, August Hermann Francke was uncontestably the major shaper of the phenomenon we know as Halle Pietism. Much has been written about his life and accomplishments, but little specifically about the role of music in his life and thought. He wrote instructions for musical education in his schools, encouraged the publication of hymnals, and wrote some hymns himself. One can assume that Francke fully supported the efforts of his colleague Johann Anastasius Freylinghausen that were discussed in the introduction. The so-called "Sing=Stunden" that took place in his parsonage may have begun as practice sessions for learning the new hymns included in these hymnals. Yet in writing later of these gatherings, Francke said they should not have been called "singing hours" because the singing occurred only at the beginning and end of the sessions that were primarily devoted to instruction. A more appropriate name—if there had to be a label at all—would have been "hours of edification or admonition" ("Erbauungs= oder Ermahnungs=Stunden").[1] Undoubtedly, Francke ranked theology higher than music, but does this objection to the term "Sing=Stunden" indicate that music was of little importance to him?

It may be no surprise, given the Pietist reputation of antipathy to music, that Francke cautioned parents and tutors against turning to music instruction as a means of combating idleness in children. In schools and universities, music has often been the occasion, Francke claims, for "liederliches Wesen" ("dissolute conduct") that leads more to "üppige Welt-Lust" ("wanton sensual pleasure") than to the honor of God. Early musical instruction could entangle children in a web from which they could later not free themselves.[2] This warning should not be interpreted as a general statement about music but as applying to secular activities that Francke considered unwholesome. He also wrote rather adamantly against

---

[1] August Hermann Francke: Idea Studiosi Theologiae, oder Abbildung eines der Theologie Beflissenen. Halle: Waisenhaus, 1712, 224–225. For a thorough study of the origins of the Singstunden, see Friedrich de Boor: Von den privaten "Singestunden" im Glauchaer Pfarrhaus (1698) zu den öffentlichen "Ermahnungs=Stunden" im Waisenhaus (1703): Forschungsbericht und Quellenüberblick. In: Pietismus und Liedkultur, 1–46.

[2] August Hermann Francke: Kurzer und einfältiger Unterricht, wie die Kinder zur wahren Gottseligkeit und christlichen Klugheit anzuführen sind (1702). In: A. H. Francke: Werke in Auswahl. Ed. by Erhard Peschke. Berlin: Evangelische Verlagsanstalt, 1969, 140.

dancing customs of his time, even though the orthodox Lutheran position on dancing was much more tolerant.[3] As I wrote regarding the debates about music in the late seventeenth century, "It was not religious music but recreational or theatrical music which aroused the greatest controversies involving Pietists and most clearly pitted Pietism against Orthodoxy."[4]

Music in church was a different matter, and in that context Francke recognized its great pedagogical potential. Singing was, of course, part of the school curriculum and a means of teaching children. Beyond that, hymns that churchgoers had been singing all their lives without true understanding could be a means of catechization. In his introduction to the sermons on the psalms, Francke tells of a pastor who was disturbed by the ignorance of his congregants and found no better way of educating them in the faith than to point out the truths that they could recognize from hymns they had known since their youth. The songs became a "blessed aid" in bringing them to greater knowledge.[5] For the illiterate, songs are helpful tools and were used in the early days of the Reformation for spreading the gospel. The fact that songs are repeated means that their content remains in memory longer than reading a story or hearing a sermon once.

Beyond the pedagogical value for individuals, singing serves to create and strengthen community. If many people were to speak at the same time, it would sound strange, but thousands of individuals can join together in song at the same time and produce a "harmony, symphony and melodious sound."[6] The communal experience of singing is the greatest benefit of music for Francke, and harmony is a recurrent theme in his thinking. This should serve to counteract those depictions of Pietism that define it as individualistic and subjective. To be sure, Francke's insistence on the rebirth of the heart through the Holy Spirit is central to his theology, and his account of his conversion experience is well known. One cannot deny that individual conversion is subjective, but it does not, in Francke's thinking, lead to isolation and withdrawal, even from an unregenerate church community. While there is tension between the two that sometimes is unresolved, Francke seeks a balance of individual and corporate worship, or inward appropriation and outward expression of the message of salvation.[7] The following is an examination of his comments on music and worship as found in his sermons on the Psalms, published posthumously by his son Gotthilf August Francke in 1730–1731 from transcripts of talks at the weekly "Sing=Stunden" from 1704 to 1707.[8]

---

[3] August Hermann Francke: Was von dem weltüblichen Tanzen zu halten sei? (1697). In: Francke: Werke in Auswahl, 383–391. See also Irwin: Dancing in Bach's Time, 17–35.
[4] Irwin: Neither Voice nor Heart Alone, 117.
[5] August Hermann Francke: Erklärung der Psalmen Davids. Vol. 1. Halle: Waisenhaus, 1730, 28.
[6] Francke: Psalmen Davids, Vol. 1, 27.
[7] Peter James Yoder explores this dual aspect of Francke's theology through the lens of the sacraments, in: Peter James Yoder: Pietism and the Sacraments: The Life and Theology of August Hermann Francke. University Park, PA: The Pennsylvania State University Press, 2021.
[8] The first volume encompassed Psalms 1 through 89 plus five introductory chapters. Vol. 2, published in 1731, covered Psalms 90 through 150. In future references, citations will be

## 1 Internal vs. External Worship

At various points in his sermons on the psalms, Francke advocates for a combination of inward and outward worship, recognizing the insufficiency of each alone. Discussing Holy Week in connection with Psalm 64, he gives attendance at Holy Week services a half-hearted endorsement; one may attend such services "out of a good heart," but they are often "a gathering of the wicked," as expressed in Psalm 64,2. One should not think that these public services are all that is required; rather, one should also spend time in meditation on the suffering and death of Jesus. "We should do the one but not omit the other; we should not withdraw from public gatherings, as Paul reminds us in Hebrews 10,25, but contemplate in our hearts the great and precious benefactions that are proclaimed to us in these days, namely the crucifixion of our Lord and Savior Jesus Christ and his victorious resurrection."[9] (I, 952)

In reflecting on Psalm 119,41–48, Francke sets up patriarchal worship as a model of devotion and balance that should be imitated. The example he cites is admittedly not about corporate worship but rather a union with God that is not limited to specified hours of prayer or public worship. Isaac went out to pray in the field in the evening (Gen 24,63), not following a prescribed practice. Most importantly, the patriarchs prayed to God from the heart, not merely reading an evening blessing from a prayer book and saying a blessing before and after meals or just going to church, "as so-called Christians do today, which for most of them is in fact pure hypocrisy. [The ancients] sought rather to unite the external with the internal."[10] (II, 499)

The same theme continues with later verses of Psalm 119 where the psalmist says he praises God seven times a day (v. 164). Francke does not take this literally as indicating seven specific times of prayer during the day but rather a constant mindfulness of God. It is as if David is saying, "I do not restrict myself only to the morning and evening blessings, but your praise flourishes and blossoms the whole day long, all the time I am working, constantly in my heart."[11] (II, 698) If one has not made a temple for God in one's heart in this way, no outward worship will suffice. Still, attendance at public worship is of some value and should not be omitted. Against those who claim superior knowledge of God as if they have

---

given in parentheses within the text, the first number indicating which of the two volumes, the second the page number.

[9] "Vielmehr sollen wir das eine zwar thun, aber das andere nicht lassen; uns zwar nicht von den öffentlichen Versammlungen entziehen, nach der Erinnerung Pauli, Ebr. 10, 25. aber auch unsere Meditationen im Hertzen über diejenigen hohen und theuren Wohlthaten, welche uns in diesen Tagen verkündigt werden, anstellen, und zwar zuerst über den Creutzes=Tod unsers Herrn und Heylandes Jesu Christi, und denn auch über seine siegreiche Auferstehung."

[10] "wie das heut zu Tage die Hauptsache der so genannten Christen, und in der That bey den meisten lauter Heucheley ist. Sie [die Alten] haben vielmehr das äussere mit dem innern zu vereinigen gesuchet."

[11] "Ich binde mich nicht an den Morgen= und Abend=Segen allein, sondern dein Lob grünet und blühet den gantzen Tag, unter aller meiner Arbeit, immerdar in meinem Hertzen."

no need of the church, Francke charges: "It would certainly be better if they went to church and heard a good exhortation than that they spend the time badly and yet want to be regarded as superior because they know that Christianity does not consist in externals and that it does not depend just on going to church. What, then, is better? To go to church and let oneself be chastised for one's sinfulness or to spend the time at home in idleness?"[12] (II, 698)

Those who rejected public worship as mere external formality, however, might find support in other parts of Francke's Psalm commentaries. In commenting on Psalm 27, where David expresses the wish to remain in the house of the Lord all his days, Francke recognizes David's attachment to the place where God made his covenant with Israel but credits David also with an awareness through God's Spirit of the time to come when God will be worshipped not in a particular location but, as Jesus said (John 4,24), in spirit and truth. David saw beyond the building of physical temples, Francke believes, and understood, when he yearned to remain always in God's house, that it was not a house built with hands but one whose builder was God (Heb 11,10), a habitation of God in the Spirit (Eph 2,22). (I, 384–385) David, according to Francke, understood that the heart was the true temple of God, and he desired that his heart be the temple where he might behold the beauty of the Lord. (I, 385)

## 2    Christ as the Kernel of Scripture

In order to understand this view of David, it is necessary to look at the hermeneutical framework that makes such a view of an Old Testament figure possible. While it had been customary among Lutherans to read many passages of the Old Testament as referring to Jesus, Francke explicitly applied this to all of Scripture. In his 1702 publication *Christus Der Kern heiliger Schrifft*, Francke asserts that everyone recognizes that Christ is the kernel of the whole sacred scripture, but few understand what this means, and even fewer make an effort to find this kernel so that they can truly eat it for their nourishment.[13]

To help those who want to make the effort, Francke offers some procedural guidance. Those just beginning to understand scripture may find many chapters obscure and unclear, especially in the Old Testament. In such cases they should not

---

[12] "Es wäre gewiß besser, daß sie in die Kirche gingen, und eine gute Vermahnung anhöreten, als daß sie die Zeit so übel anwenden, und dennoch dafür angesehen seyn wollen, als hätten sie vor andern eine mehrere Erkäntniß, daß das Christenthum nicht im äusserlichen bestehe, und daß es nicht daran liege, daß man nur in die Kirche gehe. Was ist denn besser, in die Kirche gehen, und sich wegen seines sündlichen Wesens bestrafen lassen, oder zu Hause die Zeit mit Müßiggang zubringen?"

[13] August Hermann Francke: Christus der Kern heiliger Schrifft. In: A. H. Francke: Schriften zur biblischen Hermeneutik. Vol. 1. Ed. by Erhard Peschke. Berlin: De Gruyter, 2003, 216. For more on Francke's imagery of shell and kernel as a distinction between cognitive/external and experiential/internal understanding of the Bible, see Erhard Peschke: Studien zur Theologie August Hermann Franckes. Vol. 2. Berlin: Evangelische Verlagsanstalt, 1966, 45–56.

rack their brains trying to make sense of the passages but should just absorb the easier parts and build on those. It is best to begin with the preaching of Christ in the New Testament, where one encounters his person, his teachings, his deeds, and his suffering. The gospels also contain Jesus' own citations from the Old Testament. By looking up these citations, one begins to come to an understanding of Moses, the prophets, and the psalms. In this way, Jesus and his apostles themselves become guides to interpreting scripture with Christ as the key to the whole. A "diligent and attentive pupil" will then see that Jesus is the same person of whom Moses and the prophets wrote, namely the "Son of God and true Savior of the world."[14] With this key, one is able to unlock the Old Testament, comparing the shadows with the reality, the prophecies with their fulfillment.

Although Francke frequently refers to the Old Testament as a shadow, an image that seems to denigrate it, he is by no means dismissive of its value and meaning. There is a reciprocal relationship between the two parts of scripture, as they point to one another. Knowledge of one part increases understanding of the other. There is a harmony and agreement between the two.

> The more practiced you are in consideration of the New Testament, the more easily and swiftly you will progress in the Old Testament. And as you have been previously introduced through the New Testament into the understanding of the Old, in the same way Moses, the prophets, and the psalms must serve for you to understand the New Testament more thoroughly and deeply. And the invariable harmony and agreement of the Old and New Testaments will give you a great certainty or plerophory of faith or else will indescribably increase and strengthen the certainty you have attained.[15]

The final purpose of studying the Bible in this way was in fact "to observe with pleasure the lovely harmony and connection of all divine truths."[16] There is no indication that Francke was making any implicit reference to music when he used the term "lovely harmony," and it is a metaphor he frequently used to indicate the unity of the Bible. When referring to the harmony of the gospels, Francke followed in a long tradition of seeking to reconcile the apparent differences in the narratives of Matthew, Mark, Luke, and John. While some of these attempts were called synopses, others, such as Andreas Osiander, Martin Chemnitz, and Johann Gerhard, used the term "harmony." Thus, while there was a recognized theological use of the term, even the synonym Francke chooses for "harmony," i.e. "Einstimmung," has a musical implication of "with one voice" or "in unison," though, admittedly, the

---

[14] Francke: Christus der Kern, 220–221.
[15] Francke: Christus der Kern, 222: "Je geübter du nun bist in der Betrachtung des Neuen Testaments / je leichter und hurtiger wirst du im Alten Testament fortkommen; Und wie du vorhin durch das Neue Testament in den Verstand des Alten bist eingeleitet worden / also werden dir nun Moses / die Propheten und Psalmen hinwiederum dienen müssen / das Neue Testament so viel gründlicher und tiefer zu verstehen; Und die beständige Harmonie und Ubereinstimmung des Alten und Neuen Testaments wird dir eine grosse plerophorie oder Gewißheit des Glaubens geben / oder doch die erlangte Gewißheit unbeschreiblich stärken und vermehren."
[16] Francke: Christus der Kern, 218: "die liebliche harmonie und Verbindung aller Göttlichen Wahrheiten mit Lust zu beschauen."

common usage of the word was a more general "consensus" or "agreement."[17] Not only the gospels but also the epistles show the "splendid harmony or connection of the whole Christian teaching."[18] The most musical terminology for the agreement of all of scripture occurs in Francke's Latin text on hermeneutics, *Manuductio ad lectionum scripturae sacrae*, where he writes, "hic vero etiam spectamus harmoniam, & symphonicum oraculorum divinorum concentum" ("Here indeed we also observe the harmony and symphonic concord of holy utterances").[19]

Despite the deepened understanding that is to be gained by studying Moses, the psalms, and the prophets, the religious practice of the ancient Hebrews was characterized by external observance that became obsolete with Jesus. The fact that Francke finds this higher level of religious consciousness in the Psalms indicates the way in which the Old Testament agrees with the New, but it also raises doubts about the sincerity of Francke's support of outward worship. At least in his commentary on Psalm 96,6, he finds the sanctuaries of the ancient Hebrews superseded by the sanctuary of the heart. The conversation with the Samaritan woman at the well, already mentioned above in connection with Psalm 27, promotes the ideal of worship as located not in a physical place but in the sanctuary of the heart:

> This sanctuary should be our heart. For God no longer has the tabernacle that was in the desert, for it has been abolished. He also no longer has the temple of Solomon, for it has also been destroyed and thrown into a heap. He also does not have the second temple [...]; rather, after Christ came into the second temple, and the prophecy of Haggai 2,7–8 was fulfilled, that temple was also destroyed. Where, then, is the sanctuary of the Lord now to be found? Should we run into the desert and seek the tabernacle there? Or should we go toward Jerusalem and seek the temple there? We are no more likely to find it in one place than the other. Well, then, where should we see the sanctuary of the Lord now? We can let Christ Jesus himself teach us, as he told the Samaritan woman in John 4,21–24 [...]. God is a spirit, and those who worship him must worship him in spirit and in truth.[20] (II, 98–99)

---

[17] August Hermann Francke: Einleitung Zur Lesung Der H. Schrifft Insonderheit Des Neuen Testaments. In: Francke: Schriften zur biblischen Hermeneutik, Vol. 1, 139: "Daß man auch die Harmonie oder Einstimmung der Evangelisten nicht verachte / so wohl in der Sache selbst / als in der historischen Ordnung."

[18] Francke: Einleitung Zur Lesung Der H. Schrifft, 143: "und also auch die treffliche Harmonie oder Verknüpffung der gantzen Christlichen Lehre desto besser fassen." See also p. 170: "daß man die Harmonie und rechte göttliche Übereinstimmung der Apostolischen Lehre desto besser erkenne."

[19] August Hermann Francke: Manuductio ad lectionum scripturae sacrae. In: A. H. Francke: Schriften zur biblischen Hermeneutik, 65.

[20] "Dis Heiligthum soll unser Hertz seyn. Denn Gott hat nicht mehr die Hütte des Stifts, welche in der Wüste gewesen ist; sondern dieselbe ist abgethan. Er hat auch nicht mehr den Tempel Salomonis: derselbe ist gleichfalls zerstöret und über einen Haufen geworfen. Er hat auch nicht den andern Tempel [...]; sondern, nachdem Christus in den andern Tempel gekommen ist, und an ihm die Weissagung Hagg. 2, 7.8. erfüllet worden, so ist derselbe auch zerstöret. Wo ist denn nun das Heiligthum des Herrn zu finden? Sollen wir in die Wüste laufen, und daselbst die Hütte des Stifts suchen? Oder sollen wir gen Jerusalem gehen, und daselbst den Tempel suchen? Oder sollen wir gen Jerusalem gehen, und daselbst den Tempel suchen? Wir würden eines so wenig finden, als das andere. Wohlan denn! Wo soll doch nun das Heiligthum des Herrn seyn? Das laßt uns von Christo Jesu selbst lernen. Denn also sagt er Joh. 4, 21=24. [...] **Gott ist ein Geist, und die ihn anbeten, die müssen ihn im Geist und in der Wahrheit anbeten.**"

## 3 Music in the Old Testament

This view that the Old Testament prefigures with outward images what will come to be understood more fully in New Testament times is the key to Francke's view of musical references in the Bible. Commenting on Psalm 81, Francke says, "From this example we have to learn what the image, the shadow, the prefiguring of the Old Testament with its music, psalteries, harps, trumpets, drums, and the like were supposed to mean and represent—namely that it pointed to the New Testament and depicted how the hearts of people should be moved through the Holy Spirit, and the powers of their souls should be made active toward the praise and glory of God."[21] (I, 1184) If the heart is not tuned to God's spirit, the outward sound of music has no value: "We must not think that God is served by outward drums, trumpets, and the like; these are certainly of as little value to him as the howling of a dog, if the heart is not present and awakened to his praise."[22] (I, 1184)

The Old Testament prefigurings, nevertheless, do have value for Francke as seen through his hermeneutical principle of biblical unity. The role of musicians in the tabernacle and the temple prefigures the role not of church musicians but of apostles and teachers:

> The shadow work of the Old Testament points to the truth of the New. Just as the children of Korah were engaged as singers, guards, and custodians of the tabernacle and later in the temple, so also they signify the chorus of apostles and of all those who afterward were awakened through the Spirit of God to carry out the office of the New Testament, not of the letter but of the spirit (2 Cor 3,6). The Holy Spirit foresaw how the apostles and teachers of the New Testament would, through the power of the Spirit, proclaim the gospel to all creatures, trumpet out the splendor of Jesus Christ and encourage people to the praise and glory of God.[23] (I, 692 on Psalm 47)

Not just the function of the children of Korah but also the content of the psalms they sang served to carry the message of Jesus' sacrificial death, even though the singers may not have fully understood it. Francke believed that David received knowledge of the Cross and was inspired to write psalms that conveyed this

---

[21] "Aus diesem Exempel haben wir zu lernen was die Figur, der Schatten und das Vorbild des Alten Testaments mit seiner Music, Psalter, Harfen, Trommeten, Paucken und dergleichen, habe bedeuten und vorstellen sollen, daß es nemlich auf das Neue Testament gegangen, und abgebildet habe, wie durch den Heiligen Geist die Hertzen der Menschen solten beweget, und die Kräfte ihrer Seelen in ihnen zum Lobe und Preis Gottes rege gemacht werden."

[22] "Denn da dürfen wir nicht gedencken, als ob Gotte mit dem äusserlichen Paucken, Trommeten, und dergleichen, was gedienet sey; welches gewiß eben so wenig vor ihm gilt, als ein Hunde=Geheule, wenn das Hertz nicht dabey und zu seinem Lob erwecket ist."

[23] "Es deutet aber das Schattenwerck Altes Testaments auf die Wahrheit des Neuen. Wie die Kinder Korah im Alten Testament zu Sängern, Wächtern und Hütern im Stifts=Hütte, und hernach im Tempel, bestellet waren: also bedeuteten dieselben den Chor der Apostel und aller derjenigen, welche nachmals durch den Geist Gottes erwecket worden **das Amt zu führen des Neuen Testaments, nicht des Buchstabens, sondern des Geistes.** 2 Cor. 3, 6. Der Heilige Geist hat vorher gesehen, wie die Apostel und Lehrer des Neuen Testaments in der Kraft des Geistes das Evangelium allen Creaturen verkündigen, die Herrlichkeit Jesu Christi ausposaunen, und die Menschen zum Lobe und Preise Gottes ermuntern würden."

knowledge. It was then the duty of the sons of Korah to transmit this message. Francke finds this role indicated in the superscript of those psalms such as Psalm 44, where the German reads, "Eine Unterweisung der Söhne Korah, vorzusingen."

> Because then these descendants of Korah, in service to Samuel and David, were engaged partly as gatekeepers and partly as singers in the tabernacle, such psalms were transmitted to them [...] to instruct them correctly concerning the secret of the cross and the kingdom of the Messiah, our Lord Jesus Christ. The singers thus employed had to make music and sing about this openly until the time that such teaching about the secret of the cross would be truly revealed and fulfilled in Christ, our highly blessed head, and in his members, who would have to be led along with him through the cross to glory.[24] (I, 611–612)

In relation to Psalm 47, which most Christians of Francke's time read as referring to Jesus' Ascension, Francke asked how the ancient Israelites could sing this joyous message without experiencing the Ascension. He responded by saying that the Holy Spirit inspired them by putting the words in their mouths to proclaim the grace that would come with Jesus Christ. The ancient Jews were the only ones who could rejoice in this way, for the other peoples did not have knowledge of God. If the Jews were able to sing so joyfully, how much more should Christians rejoice:

> The Holy Spirit in the Old Testament and in the shadow work of Levitic worship employed singers who had to trumpet out and sing with joyous sound, "Clap your hands, all you peoples, etc.," when at that time there was no other people under the sun except the Jewish people who could rejoice in this way; all the others were stuck in idolatry, and none of them worshiped the God of Abraham. So we should rightly be ashamed, when we are also called by God at these ends of the earth, if we do not want all the more to clap our hands and sing with joyous sound because of the great mercy that has been bestowed on us in Christ Jesus.[25] (I, 692)

Clearly, Francke is not rejecting the audible music in itself, for the absence of joyous singing is cause for shame and evidence of insufficient gratitude. In the case of Psalm 47, the sense of prefiguring is eliminated in favor of a direct application to Jesus' Ascension, even if this is not the view of Jewish interpreters:

---

[24] "Weil nun diese Nachkommen Korah, durch den Dienst Samuelis und Davids, theils zu Thorhütern, theils auch zu Sängern in der Hütte des Stifts bestellet waren; wurden ihnen solche Psalmen übergeben. [...] sie vom Geheimniß des Creutzes und von dem Reiche des Meßiä, unsers Herrn Jesu Christi, recht zu unterrichten; welche durch die dazu bestellte Sänger öffentlich hat müssen vorgesungen und musiciret werden, bis auf die Zeit, da solche Unterweisung von dem Geheimniß des Creutzes an Christo, unserm hochgebenedeyeten Haupte, und an seinen Gliedern, welche samt ihm durchs Creutz zur Herrlichkeit müsten geführet werden, recht offenbaret und erfüllet würde."

[25] "Da nun der Heilige Geist im Alten Testament und in dem Schattenwerck des Levitischn Gottesdienstes Sänger bestellet hat, die dergestalt haben posaunen, und mit fröhlichem Schalle singen müssen: **Frohlocket mit Händen, alle Völcker, u.s.w.** da doch damals noch kein Volck unter der Sonne war, als das Jüdische Volck, so frohlocken konte, die andern alle aber in der Abgötterey steckten, und keines unter ihnen den Gott Abrahams anbetete; so sollten wir uns ja billig schämen, da wir an diesen Enden der Erden auch von Gott herzu berufen sind, wenn wir nicht vielmehr mit Händen frohlocken, und mit fröhlichem Schalle singen wolten, wegen der grossen Gnade, die uns in Christo Jesu wiederfahren ist."

## 3 Music in the Old Testament

"God goes up with a shout and the Lord with the sound of a trumpet." [Ps 47,5] It does not make sense when some superstitious Jews interpret this as the giving of the law or something similar. But it does make sense that Christ should first come down from heaven and then go up again to his heavenly father in the choir of holy angels.[26] (I, 695)

In an interesting twist, Francke turns attention away from the trumpet to angelic singing. Reasoning that Jesus' birth was accompanied by the glorious song of angels, as testified by the shepherds (Luke 2,13–14), Francke is convinced that angels must also have sung at Jesus' ascension. If the song of the angels happened in fact at his birth, how should it not also have happened when he ascended, even if no mention was made in the account and perhaps was not even heard by those present?

And even though the same angelic song was not reported or heard by the people, we should have no doubt about the matter itself. If the angels ministered to him in his humbled state and stood by him in the wilderness when he was tempted by the devil (Matt 4,11), why should they not have also accompanied him and ministered to him with joyous shouts and songs of praise when, having overcome all his suffering, he went up victorious and triumphant to take up the throne of glory and sit at the right hand of majesty in the heights?[27] (I, 695)

Continuing to focus not on the trumpet but on the singing that accompanied it, Francke turns to the following verse, "Sing praises to God, sing praises; sing praises to our king, sing praises." This, he claims, is to be regarded as a song of the angels, and it is quite lovely and fitting that the angels recognize Jesus as their king, for this is in keeping with 1 Peter 3,22, where angels are said to be subject to Christ. Further, when verse 8 of the psalm declares that God is king over the whole earth, it is just as the angels sang at Jesus' birth: "Peace on earth, good will to all." The second half of the verse, "sing with understanding," means, Francke says, to sing a psalm in which the salvation that is in Christ Jesus is proclaimed. The message of the psalm is summed up in verse 9 with God as king over the nations, sitting in majesty on his sacred throne.

Thus, says Francke, this psalm points to agreement of the Old and New Testament in the whole divine economy or dispensation. (I, 696) In fact, it points beyond the past and present to the future, when God will be recognized over the whole earth. This is not idle speculation for Francke but a goal for an ambitious missionary program that he laid out and in great part carried out. He believed that the early successes of his social and educational programs were already a sign of

---

[26] "**Gott fähret auf mit Jauchzen, und der Herr mit heller Posaune.** Es reimet sich gar nicht, wenn es einige abergläubische Juden auf die Gesetz=Gebung, oder auf etwas anders dergleichen, gedeutet haben. Wohl aber reimet sichs darauf, daß Christus erst vom Himmel hernieder kommen, und denn wieder zu seinem himmlischen Vater im Chor der heiligen Engel auffahren solte."

[27] "Und obgleich derselbe Englische Gesang nicht aufgezeichnet, noch von Menschen gehöret worden: so dürfen wir doch an der Sache selbst keinesweges zweifeln. Haben die Engel Christo im Stande der Erniedrigung gedienet, und sind sie zu ihm getreten in der Wüsten, da er von dem Teufel versuchet worden war: Matth. 4, 11. wie solten sie nicht auch zu ihm getreten seyn, und ihm mit fröhlichem Schalle und Lobgesang gedienet haben, als er nun alle sein Leiden überwunden, siegend und triumphirend aufgefahren, den Thron der Herrlichkeit eingenommen, und sich zur Rechten der Majestät in der Höhe gesetzet hat?"

God's favor and a basis for spreading the knowledge of God into the entire world.[28] Based on this psalm, he could envision various peoples offering their hearts to Jesus and rejoicing with glad sounds, raising their hands in praise, encouraging their descendants with the same shouts of joy. (I, 697) The joy of release from sin to the service of God as King moves outward from the heart and soul to bodily expression and audible sound:

> Oh, what a great thing that is! Heart and soul should certainly shout for joy at this, and each person should clap with delight and rejoice with a glad sound if God has granted such grace and bestowed such mercy on him that he can say in truth: I belong to Jesus Christ, I belong to the Lord of all Lords and am a part of him. In this way everyone should make a point of singing such a psalm properly.[29] (I, 697)

While Francke's interpretation of Psalm 47 seems fully to endorse singing, though not necessarily trumpet playing, as an outward expression of a joyful heart, other psalms lead back to a disjunction between the internal and the external. Again it is the musical instruments that give rise to a spiritualizing interpretation of Psalm 81. The festival of the new moon, as other Israelite festivals, was a testimony, Francke believes, to the future coming of the Messiah, and musical instruments were used to awaken the spirit and encourage praise, but the outward music was not of value in itself:

> Therefore it reads: "Take the psalms, and bring on the timbrel, the pleasant harp with the psaltery." This cannot be understood as if what matters to our dear God are the outward sounds of the timbrel, harp, and psaltery. No! Following this same outward depiction, the hearts of the believers should be awakened to the genuine lovely harmony of the spirit, and the faculties of their souls should be stirred to praise God and glorify the Lord for the overwhelming mercy he has bestowed on them.[30] (I, 1182)

Furthermore, the literal meaning of some verses in Psalm 81 is not applicable to Francke's listeners. He recognizes that the exodus from Egypt is the foremost cause for the rejoicing of the Hebrew people and that it is repeatedly mentioned in the psalms as a reason for praising God. For people of the New Testament, however, it is the release not from bondage in Egypt but from bondage to sin that is cause for joy. The physical deliverance from Egypt is of no lasting advantage and was in the end not so successful, for, according to Francke, six hundred thousand

---

[28] August Hermann Francke: Projekt zu einem Seminario universali, 1701. In: Francke: Werke in Auswahl, 108–115.

[29] "O! wie ein grosses ist das! Darüber soll gewiß Hertz und Seele jauchzen, und ein ieder soll billig mit den Händen frohlocken, und mit fröhlichem Schalle jauchzen, wenn ihm Gott solche Gnade gegeben, und ihm diese Barmhertzigkeit wiederfahren lassen, daß er mit Wahrheit sagen kann: Ich gehöre Jesu Christo zu, ich gehöre dem Herrn aller Herren zu, und bin seines Theils. So soll denn ein ieder derselben solchen Psalm ihm lassen angelegen seyn, daß er denselben recht singen möge."

[30] "Darum hieß es: **Nehmet die Psalmen, und gebet her die Paucken, liebliche Harfen mit Psalter**; welches ja nicht so kan verstanden werden, als sey es dem lieben Gott um den äusserlichen Klang der Paucken, Harfen und Psalter zu thun gewesen. Nein! Die Hertzen der Gläubigen solten nach demselben äusserlichen Bilde zu der rechten lieblichen Harmonie des Geistes erwecket, und die Kräfte der Seelen in ihnen zum Lobe Gottes aufgemuntert werden, die überschwengliche Gnade, die Gott der Herr an ihnen gethan hatte, zu preisen."

## 3  Music in the Old Testament

Hebrews died in the wilderness, and even those who made it to the promised land died there. The purpose of the Exodus is as a symbol that points to the truth of the New Testament: "God did it only as witness that we should believe in him and recognize that he is the same one who can help us to eternal life."[31] (I, 1189) The joyous song of Miriam becomes our song when we experience spiritual deliverance:

> When we are saved through Jesus Christ, when he seizes our heart through his Holy Spirit, when he leads us through the Red Sea of his blood, when he first seals the forgiveness of sins in our hearts, then we can take up the tambourines and harps with Miriam, Aaron, and Moses; then we can sing to him a joyous song and praise him for saving our soul. Only then does one begin to understand what it is to rejoice and triumph in the Lord.[32] (I, 1189)

It is difficult to know whether Francke is actually imagining a musical sound emitted by joyous redeemed persons. He had just chastised those who confess Christ with the mouth but whose hearts "have not yet sung to him with psaltery, tambourines, and sweet harps and have not exulted and rejoiced." (I, 1188) Musical instruments always seem to be metaphors for Francke, but it seems natural that the exuberance of the heart would issue forth in joyous singing.

Francke's focus on figurative meaning is more explicit in his discussion of another important Old Testament passage relating to music, namely the account of Levitic temple musicians in 2 Chronicles 5,12–13. Much has been said about Johann Sebastian Bach's marginal note to verse 13 of his Calov Bible: "Bey einer andächtig Musig ist Gott allezeit mit seiner Gnaden Gegenwart" ("Where there is devotional music, God with His grace is always present").[33] It is significant that Bach includes the word "devotional," but there is little doubt that he believes in the value of audible music. Francke, by contrast, reads these verses as a figurative counterpart to the spiritual meaning found in the New Testament. The counterpart, he finds, is in the account of Pentecost in Acts 1 and 2. The parallels are that there were 120 priests blowing trumpets at the altar and 120 persons gathered in the upper room. That was no mere coincidence but the Holy Spirit's intention of foreshadowing in the Old Testament what was to happen in the truth of the New Testament. "There it was outward priests and Levites, but here it is those whom Jesus Christ made his spiritual priests through faith in him."[34] (I, 1183) Most important, however, was not the number but the unity of voice. In Chronicles the singers and instrumentalists made what seemed to be a single sound in praising God; after the Ascension, the disciples were of one accord in prayer and supplication (Acts

---

[31] "Jenes hatte Gott nur zum Zeugniß gethan, auf daß wir an ihn glauben, und erkennen solten, daß er derselbige sey, der uns zum ewigen Leben verhelfen könne."

[32] "Wenn wir aber von Jesu Christo errettet werden, wenn derselbe unser Hertz durch seinen Heiligen Geist ergreifet, wenn er uns durchs rothe Meer seines Blutes führet, wenn er erst die Vergebung der Sünden in unsern Hertzen versiegelt: alsdenn können wir die Paucken und Harfen mit Mirjam, Aaron und Mose ergreifen; alsdenn können wir ihm ein frölich Lied singen, und ihn loben, daß er unsere Seele errettet hat. Alsdenn erfähret man erst, was es sey, dergestalt in dem Herrn jubiliren und triumphiren."

[33] Robin A. Leaver: J. S. Bach and Scripture: Glosses from the Calov Bible Commentary. St. Louis, MO: Concordia, 1985, 97.

[34] "Dort waren äusserliche Priester und Leviten, hier aber dieselbigen, welche Jesus Christus zu geistlichen Priestern gemacht hatte durch den Glauben an ihn."

1,14), and on the day of Pentecost, they were with one accord in one place (Acts 2,1). "There it was an outward unity of voices and music; here, however, the hearts harmonized in prayer, and the spirits sounded so lovely together through the Spirit of God."[35] (I, 1183) The true music is not the external sound but the concord of hearts: "That was the true music of God and it is still the true music of the New Testament that God wants to have, namely that hearts truly become one and flow together to his praise through the Holy Spirit."[36] (I, 1183) The contrast between the two testaments is further observed in the mode of divine presence in the two accounts. In Chronicles the house of the Lord was filled with a cloud that so filled the house that the priests could not stand and minister; in Acts the fiery tongues lit up each person, and they received power to preach. "There the house, or the outward temple, was filled with smoke and fog, here, however, the hearts are filled with light and joy of the Holy Spirit."[37] (I, 1184)

In his exposition of Psalm 92, Francke takes up the theme of harmony and refers again to these same biblical passages. He cites Augustine on the significance of the ten-stringed psaltery, thus carrying on a long-standing tradition of allegorical interpretation. On Psalm 92,4, Augustine had written, "Speak rightly and act rightly if you want to sing to the accompaniment of the lyre."[38] Like Augustine, Francke interprets the ten-stringed instrument as the Ten Commandments; these must not only be known in words but sung in deeds. As if to say that God plays the human heart as an instrument, Francke writes, "When the finger of God, that is, the Holy Spirit, writes these on the tablet of the heart, then the heart is properly tuned. And when one practices them in thought, word, and deed, then these are to our dear God the ten strings, psaltery, and playing on the harp."[39] (II, 44) He then proceeds to make the connections with Acts 1–2 and 2 Chronicles 5, saying that this lovely agreement of the strings is like the unity and agreement of the believers when their hearts were filled with the Holy Spirit and like the beautiful harmony that sounded when the glory of God filled the temple. This unity of hearts and minds in the Holy Spirit is well expressed, he comments, in the first verse of Psalm 133: "Behold, how good and how pleasant it is for brethren to dwell together in unity." (KJV)

---

[35] "Dort war eine äusserliche Einigkeit der Stimmen und der Music: hier aber harmonirten die Hertzen im Gebet, und die Gemüther stimmeten durch den Geist Gottes so lieblich zusammen."

[36] "Das war die rechte Music Gottes, und ist noch die rechte Music des Neuen Testaments, die Gott haben will, daß nemlich die Hertzen durch den Heiligen Geist zu seinem Lobe recht eins werden und zusammen fliessen."

[37] "Dort war das Haus oder der äussere Tempel, mit Rauch und Nebel, hier aber werden die Hertzen mit Licht und Freude des Heiligen Geistes erfüllet."

[38] Augustine: Expositions of the Psalms: 73–98. In: The Works of Saint Augustine: A Translation for the 21st Century III/18. Trans. by Maria Boulding. Hyde Park, NY: New City Press, 2002, 350 (numbered Psalm 91,4 following the Vulgate).

[39] "Wenn der Finger Gottes, das ist, der Heilige Geist, dieselben auf die Tafeln des Hertzens geschrieben hat, so ist das Hertz recht gestimmet. Und wenn sich der Mensch darin in seinen Gedancken, Worten und Wercken übet, das sind dem lieben Gott dieselbigen zehen Säyten, Psalter und Spielen auf der Harfen."

## 4 Music as Harmony

The theme of unity in community is a recurrent emphasis in Francke's interpretation of music in the Bible. Other writers often discussed the most explicit New Testament passages about music—the Pauline exhortations of Colossians 3,16 and Ephesians 5,19—either as endorsements of congregational singing or as admonitions to inward devotion. Francke blends these approaches into a vision of a whole community united by the Holy Spirit. Music becomes an image for persons with different gifts and tasks working toward a common goal, as Paul expressed in other passages concerning the church. Writing about the superscript to Psalm 46, "A Song to sing to the children of Korah," Francke interprets the children of Korah as those among whom, according to Col 3,16, the Word of Christ is to dwell richly and in all wisdom, teaching with psalms, hymns and spiritual songs, singing and playing in their hearts to the Lord:

> Included in this figure is the community of members of Christ in their lovely harmony of divine love and strength that is brought about through the Holy Spirit; in this they flow together in childlike and brotherly love and community to the praise and service of God. These many functions, in accordance with the many attributes of the members of Jesus Christ, who all harmonize and agree with one another through the same one Spirit who works in them, are the true and most beautiful music to the ears of God, of which Paul speaks in Eph 4,3.14–16, in 1 Cor 12,4–11, and in other places.[40] (I, 672)

Lest we take this metaphorical interpretation as indicating a rejection of actual singing, we must consider another point at which Francke specifies that this is not his intention. The words "in their hearts" of Col 3,16 do not mean in the heart alone:

> When it says, "in your hearts," that should not be taken to mean that it would be incorrect to sing with the mouth, as if only the internal were demanded. For "in the heart" means that it should not happen only with the mouth; rather, the heart especially should be employed so that everything truly proceeds from the heart and out of the heart.[41] (II, 1447)

Still, he is clearly less interested in the audible music than in the spiritual effect. Even in the next paragraph where he cites Ephesians 5,19, Francke moves immediately away from music itself:

---

[40] "Es ist zugleich in diesem Vorbilde mit begriffen die Gemeinschaft der Glieder Christi in ihrer durch den Heil. Geist Gottes lieblich gewirckten Harmonie der göttlichen Liebe und Kräfte, darin sie in kindlicher und brüderlicher Liebe und Gemeinschaft zum Lobe und Dienste Gottes zusammen fliessen, welche mancherley Geschäfte, nach den mancherley Eigenschaften der Gliedmassen Jesu Christi, die alle mit einander harmoniren und übereinstimmen durch denselbigen einigen Geist, der in ihnen wircket, die rechte und schönste Music in den Ohren Gottes seyn; wovon Paulus Eph. 4, 3.14–16, I Cor. 12, 4–11. und an andern Orten mehr redet."

[41] "Wenn es heißt: **in eurem Hertzen**; so hat man solches nicht dahin zu deuten, als obs unrecht wäre, mit dem Munde zu singen, und hier nur bloß das inwendige erfordert würde. Denn, **in dem Hertzen**, heißt so viel, als, daß es mit dem Munde nicht allein geschehen, sondern das Hertz vornehmlich sein Geschäfft dabey haben solle, so, daß alles recht aus dem Hertzen und von Hertzen gehe."

> That which is said about outward instrumental music in the Old Testament points to the true worship in spirit and in truth where people are moved to prayer and praise of God through the Holy Spirit and where believers unite with one another for prayer and praise of God.[42] (II, 1447)

Again Francke compares musical instruments playing together in harmony to the parts of a human body in the manner that Paul used the image to refer to the variety of gifts of the Spirit.

> At the same time all these instruments indicate the different gifts that are distributed among the members of Jesus Christ. For just as each member of the human body has its own gift by which it provides assistance to the body and the other members, so also the Holy Spirit distributes his gifts to the living members of Jesus Christ in such a way that the whole body provides assistance to one another, as Paul teaches in 1 Cor 12 and 14. And the many instruments that make lovely harmony in music point to the spiritual harmony that is brought about through the Holy Spirit.43 (II, 1447)

Through these comparisons, Francke shows an appreciation of musical harmony, even if spiritual harmony is a higher value. Had he not been moved by the beauty of congregational singing, he would not have used such a comparison. Had he opposed audible singing, he would have used another biblical locus classicus, namely Amos 5,23, to express his opposition. Rather, he admonishes Christians not to let their singing become mere noise or howling that displeases God but to be a harmony of loving hearts that is pleasing to God. (II, 45) In seeming contrast to passages cited earlier where Francke implied that outward music was of no value to God, his interpretation of Psalm 33 implies otherwise. The three instruments of Psalm 33,2, harp, psaltery, and an instrument of ten strings, require three players playing at the same time, and, as the words of Matthew 18,20 promised, if they are gathered in Jesus' name, he is in the midst of them. This, then, is a choir or a gathering of believers using their voices and instruments to praise God. To be sure, music can be misused when it serves the lusts of the flesh and is then an abomination to God. On the other hand,

> when [music] is properly consecrated to God, when people sing and play music and at the same time praise God in their hearts, outward music also arouses and kindles hearts to the praise of God. Thus it may well please the Lord when people are gathered in the name of the Lord Jesus and rejoice in the Lord, as it says here. There he is in the midst of us.[44] (I, 460)

---

[42] "Was im Alten Testament von äusserlicher Instrumental=Music gesagt wird, das wird da auf den rechten Gottesdienst im Geist und in der Wahrheit geführet, da der Mensch durch den Heiligen Geist zum Gebet und zum Lobe Gottes beweget wird, und da sich die Gläubigen mit einander zum Gebet und zum Lobe Gottes vereinigen."

[43] "Es deuteten aber alle diese Instrumente zugleich auch die unterschiedenen Gaben an, welche unter die Glieder Jesu Christi vertheilet sind. Denn gleichwie ein iegliches Glied an dem menschlichen Leibe seine eigene Gabe hat, dadurch es dem Leibe und den übrigen Gliedern Handreichung thut; also hat auch der Heilige Geist seine Gaben in die lebendigen Gliedmassen Jesu Christi vertheilet, so, daß der gantze Leib einander Handreichung thut; wie Paulus I Cor. 12. und 14. Cap. lehret. Und wie viele Instrumente in einer Music eine liebliche Harmonie machen: also wird damit die geistliche Harmonie, so durch die Gaben des Heiligen Geistes gewircket wird, angedeutet."

[44] "Wenn sie Gott recht geheiliget wird, wenn man da singet und klinget, wenn zugleich die

## 5   The Song of Glory

The psalms are not to be interpreted solely as foreshadowing the coming of Christ into the world and the preaching of the gospel to all nations, that is, the kingdom of grace, but also as pointing to the end times, or the kingdom of glory. Francke frequently refers to passages from the book of Revelation as another application of the meaning of the psalms. In Psalm 29, for example, he writes that we have on one level a prophecy of Jesus and how his mighty voice and the thunder of his Word will proclaim the gospel to all creatures under heaven; at the same time, the psalm enables us to look "as through a spyglass or telescope" at the kingdom of glory as envisioned in John's Revelation. (I, 409) In relation to Psalm 46, Francke says that the children of Korah were indicating not only the kingdom of grace but also the kingdom of glory; to demonstrate this connection, Francke cites in full Revelation 5,11–13, 14,1–5, and 15,3–4. The verses of Psalm 46 lead Francke to focus more on destruction of the world than on future glory, but he does see David's confidence in God's strength as a song of triumph and victory that will be sung to the Lamb. (I, 675)

When the term "new song" appears in the psalms, it is for Francke a reference not only to the coming of the Messiah but also to the new song that is sung to the Lamb in Revelation 5 and 14. In his exegesis of Psalm 33, he connects these levels of meaning through reference to the common elements in the texts:

> [Ps 33] v. 3. "Sing to him a new song; play skillfully on the string, with loud shouts." (NRSV) When he speaks here of a new song, he does not understand this only as that new song that is often sung by believers when the Lord God has rescued them from a particular danger (for then they always sing new songs and praise him joyfully [...]). Rather, scripture speaks also with a very special purpose of a new song, namely of the song of the Lamb. [...] For [in Revelation] the new song appears again. [...] From this we may learn what this new song is about and that it actually applies to the day of the Messiah and the last days.[45] (I, 460–61)

That Francke does not think of the musical references solely as metaphors seems evident in the following paragraph, where his usual insistence on the renewal of the heart is connected to mention of a new hymnal, possibly the *Geistreiches Gesangbuch* edited by Freylinghausen and published in Halle in 1704. While he was undoubtedly pleased to have the new hymnal, he also finds value in the older hymns, for they also can speak to the heart:

---

[45] Hertzen Gott loben, und also auch durch äusserliche Music zum Lobe Gottes erwecket und entzündet werden: so mags Gott dem Herrn wohl gefallen, daß man im Namen des Herrn Jesu versammlet ist, und sich im Herrn freuet, wie hier stehet. Da ist er mitten unter uns." "**Singet ihm ein neues Lied; machets gut auf Säitenspielen mit Schalle**. Wenn er hier von einem neuen Liede redet, so verstehet er nicht allein dasjenige neue Lied, das bey Gläubigen oft gesungen wird, wenn sie Gott der Herr aus einer besondern Noth errettet hat; (denn da singen sie immer neue Lieder, und loben ihn frölich [...]). Sondern die Schrift redet auch in einer gantz besondern Absicht von einem neuen Liede, nemlich **von dem Liede des Lammes**. [...] Denn [in der Offenbarung Johannis] kommt das neue Lied wieder vor. [...] Daraus mögen wir lernen, was dieses neue Lied auf sich habe, und daß es sein Absehen eigentlich auf die Tage des Meßiä, und auf die letzten Zeiten habe."

> But when the heart has first become alive in God, and God's Spirit rules and governs therein, so that one can praise God with cheerful spirit—that is what it means to sing a new song. If one were to sing all the new songs and yet keep the old heart while singing the new song, the Lord God would not be served in any way at all. Nowadays many rejoice that they have a new hymnal in their hands but do not see whether they are able truly to sing to the Lamb the new song and whether they also have a new heart. One should be truly concerned about this; in this way the new songs might also be sung quite agreeably. Even when singing the old songs, a new heart must also be present. Then the old songs always become new again. For, whenever they are sung, one receives new strength and new life from them.[46] (I, 461)

Another psalm where Francke sees the three levels of meaning—historical, prophetic, and eschatological—is Psalm 150. After discussing how God was praised in temple worship and how the outward temple is superseded by the temple of the Holy Spirit, he proceeds to the third aspect, namely how the psalm "points to the future and eternal glory." (II, 1448)

> Thus we must also recognize how this psalm deals not only with the Old Testament, and not only of the situation of the New Testament, as of the church militant, but also points to the community of the elect and the perfected righteous ones who will one day be with Jesus Christ in his glory [...]. The psalm also leads us further into the 4th and 5th chapters of Revelation.[47] (II, 1449)

The Hallelujah that begins and ends Psalm 150, Francke notes, occurs four times in Revelation. If we are to prepare to sing Hallelujah to the Lamb, we must put on the proper garb for the marriage of the Lamb by purifying our heart to become the temple of the Holy Spirit where God is praised unceasingly. (II, 1450) Praise of God is, after all, the eternal occupation of the elect, as it is the actual business of the angels; thus, it is not merely a major element of Christianity but also a true foretaste of eternal life. (II, 322)

The Psalms, according to Francke, offer a complete message of the path of suffering, redemption, and eternal glory. When Psalm 61 ends with "I will sing praise to your name eternally," this corresponds to the eternal Hallelujah of which Revelation speaks.

---

[46] "Wenn aber das Hertz erst in Gott recht lebendig worden ist, und Gottes Geist darinnen regieret und herrschet, daß man Gott mit frölichem Muth loben kan; das heißt denn, ein neu Lied singen. Sünge man sonst gleich alle neue Lieder, und behielte das alte Hertz bey dem neuen Liede; so wäre damit Gott dem Herrn gantz und gar nicht gedienet. Also freuen sich anietzo zwar viele darüber, daß sie ein neu Gesangbuch in Händen haben, sehen aber nicht, ob sie dem Lamme das neue Lied recht singen können, und ob sie auch ein neu Hertz haben. Darum solte man recht bekümmert seyn; so liessen sich denn auch die neuen Lieder recht lieblich singen. Ja wenn man auch die alten Lieder singet, so muß doch auch dabey ein neu Hertz seyn. Alsdenn werden die alten Lieder immer wieder neu. Denn, so oft man sie singet, empfängt man neue Kraft und neues Leben davon."

[47] "So haben wir nun auch von diesem Psalm zu erkennen, daß derselbe nicht allein vom alten Testament, auch nicht allein von dem Zustande des neuen Testaments, als der streitenden Kirche, handelt, sondern daß er auch in die Gemeine der Auserwählten und vollendeten Gerechten hinein weiset, wie dieselben dermaleinst mit Jesu Christo in seiner Herrlichkeit seyn werden [...]. Weiter führt uns dieser Psalm auch in das 4te und 5te Capitel der Offenb. Joh. hinein."

## 5  The Song of Glory

This is directed to the same Sabbath and the eternal Hallelujah of which John speaks so much in Revelation. Therefore, those psalms that deal with the suffering and death and also the glory of Christ as well as the suffering of his believers and of their entrance into the eternal kingdom of our Lord Jesus Christ also generally close with such a lovely Hallelujah.[48] (I, 909)

We cannot here trace the interpretation of the book of Revelation in the Lutheran tradition, but the contrast between Francke and Luther on this topic is worth noting. It is commonly known that Luther wrote disparagingly of the book of Revelation. Early in his career, when he was first translating the New Testament, Luther wrote that Christ is not to be found therein.[49] In a detailed study of Luther's use of Revelation, Hans-Ulrich Hofmann writes that it is a mistake to take this comment as Luther's consistent view of the book. In succeeding years Luther did cite passages from Revelation referring to the Lamb as confirming the eternity of Jesus, his sacrifice and his mediatorial role. He also frequently cited Rev 5,10 in support of the priesthood of all believers, and he used the image of the Antichrist to refer to the pope.[50] In a new and much more extensive introduction to Revelation in 1530, Luther treated the book primarily as an exposition of historical events. In its time, of course, it was a book of prophecy, but Luther identifies figures of the intervening time where the prophecies were fulfilled. The lesson to be learned is that the church has undergone tribulation and suppression but has endured and will endure. Luther finds here a message both of comfort and of warning:

> With this kind of interpretation we can profit by this book and make good use of it. First, for our comfort! We can rest assured that neither force nor lies, neither wisdom nor holiness, neither tribulation nor suffering shall suppress Christendom, but it will gain victory and conquer at last. Second, for our warning! [We can be on guard] against the great, perilous, and manifold offense that inflicts itself upon Christendom.[51]

In spite of the message of consolation, the prevailing image in Luther's interpretation of Revelation is of struggle against the Antichrist represented by the pope and the Church of Rome. It was not, as it was for Francke, an image of the glorious community of the elect and heavenly beings.

---

[48] "Diß zielet demnach auf denselbigen Sabbath und auf das ewige Halleluja, wovon in der Offenb. Joh. so viel geredet wird. Darum schliessen sich auch solche Psalmen, die von dem Leiden und Sterben, und von der Herrlichkeit Christi, wie auch von dem Leiden seiner Gläubigen, und von ihrem Eingange in das ewige Reich unsers Herrn Jesu Christi handeln, insgemein mit einem so lieblichen Halleluja."

[49] "das Christus drynnen wider gelert noch erkant wird." Martin Luther, WA DB 7, 404, 27.

[50] Hans-Ulrich Hofmann: Luther und die Johannes-Apokalypse. Dargestellt im Rahmen der Auslegungsgeschichte des letzten Buches der Bibel und im Zusammenhang der theologischen Entwicklung des Reformators. Tübingen: J. C. B. Mohr, 1982, esp. 343–346. Hofmann cites Luther's 1528 treatise *Vom Abendmahl Christi* and his sermon on John 18:4 from 1528.

[51] Luther's Works (LW), vol. 35, 409. "Nach dieser auslegung, können wir dis buch uns nutz machen, und wol brauchen, Erstlich zur tröstung, das wir wissen, wie das keine gewalt noch lügen, keine weisheit noch heiligkeit, kein trübsal noch leid, werden die Christenheit unter drucken, sondern sie sol endlich den sieg behalten und obligen. Zum andern zur warnung, widder das grosse ferliche manchfeltige ergernis, so sich begibt an der Christenheit." Luther, WA DB 7, 418, 5–10.

## 6  The Joy of Salvation

In recent years there has been an effort especially by Scandinavian scholars to emphasize the element of joy in Luther's thinking in contrast to the traditional picture of a combative, ink-throwing polemicist. While the latter side of his personality may prevail in his identification of the pope as the Antichrist, a persuasive case can be made that the belief in salvation by grace alone was for him a joyous, liberating experience.[52] A similar re-imaging needs to take place for Francke. An article by Peter Damrau on "godly sadness" among Pietists implies that Francke regarded the sadness of repentance to be a permanent condition.[53] To be sure, Francke was a strict disciplinarian who opposed activities he regarded as frivolous. He did not waste time, did not like jokes, and probably did not engage in anything we would label "fun," but he did find joy in his faith and in the life of Christian community. He frequently speaks of joy ("Freude") and peace ("Friede") together, an indication that the believer moves beyond the turbulent emotions of the struggle against sin to the release and comfort of forgiveness. Francke specifies with a citation from Luther that true joy comes from a good conscience:

> Now everyone surely wants to have peace and joy or to possess a cheerful heart, but a cheerful heart arises only from the certainty that one has a gracious God. To the words of Sirach 50,23, "May God give us a cheerful heart," blessed Luther placed as a gloss, "a good conscience." For when a person has a good conscience before God, he also has the right kind of cheerful heart. All other joys that the world offers are regarded by the children of God as foolish and not as genuine joy.[54] (I, 998 on Psalm 67)

Even a time of fasting and praying can be a time of joy. Francke scolds his contemporaries for their passivity in the season of Advent. In the early church, he claims, people came together, encouraged one another, praised God, fasted, and prayed, all with joyful singing in preparation for the coming of the Savior. If inspiration is

---

[52] See Birgit Stolt: "Laßt uns fröhlich springen!"; Gefühlswelt und Gefühlsnavigierung in Luthers Reformationsarbeit. Berlin: Weidler, 2012; and Miikka E. Anttila: Luther's Theology of Music: Spiritual Beauty and Pleasure. Berlin: De Gruyter, 2013.

[53] Peter Damrau: Tears That Make the Heart Shine? "Godly Sadness" in Pietism. In: Edinburgh German Yearbook, Issue 6: Sadness and Melancholy in German-Language Literature and Culture. Ed. by Mary Cosgrove and Anna Richards. Rochester, NY: Camden House, 2012, 19–33. Erhard Peschke, on the other hand, noted that Francke explicitly rejected the thought that the Bußkampf leads to melancholy or despair, and he explained that for Francke joy is a virtue (Francke: Studien, Vol. 1, 46, 85). Gary Sattler also takes a balanced approach, writing, "We find within Francke a mixture of severity and grace, a very moralistic approach to life and behavior tempered with a gentleness of spirit." Gary R. Sattler: God's Glory, Neighbor's Good: A Brief Introduction to the Life and Writings of August Hermann Francke. Chicago, IL: Covenant Press, 1982, 89.

[54] "Nun will ja iederman gern Friede und Freude haben, oder ein fröhliches Hertz besitzen: aber das allein ist ein recht fröhliches Hertz, welches aus der Gewißheit entstehet, daß man einen gnädigen Gott habe, wie der selige Lutherus in der Rand=Glosse bey die Worte Sir. 50, 25. **Er gebe uns ein fröhliches Hertz**, gesetzet hat: **ein gut Gewissen**. Denn wenn ein Mensch ein gut Gewissen vor Gott hat, so hat er auch das rechte fröhliche Hertz. Alle andere Freude, die die Welt hat, wird von Kindern Gottes für eine thörichte, und nicht als eine wahrhaftige Freude angesehen."

not coming from others, people should take the initiative to encourage themselves to pray, read the psalms, and come before God, who will then pour a transforming power into the soul, as happened with Jesus himself:

> It says in Luke 9,29, "When Jesus was praying, the appearance of his face changed." In this way we would also soon be changed. If we only prayed diligently, our heart and appearance would be changed, the joy of the Lord would fill our soul, and his power would be felt strongly among us.[55] (II, 102)

While this results in an individualistic devotional practice, it is, as Francke presents it, a substitute for the collective practice of the early church. Only the lack of fervor among Christians of his age makes this individualism necessary. It is shameful when those who profess belief in Jesus do not rejoice heartily because of the salvation they received through him:

> We should rightly be ashamed that we have confessed Christ with the mouth and yet our heart has not sung to him with psaltery, tambourine, and pleasing harp, nor has it exulted and shouted for joy. That is, the faculties of our souls have not yet been stirred to praise and glorify him, and we have not yet truly rejoiced in our Savior.[56] (I, 1188)

We have already cited references to Psalm 47 about how Christians are to rejoice at Jesus' Ascension. In that context, Francke chastises those who do not rejoice but let their hearts be filled with sadness rather than joy.

> Since Christ Jesus has deigned to make your heart into a kingdom of heaven and a hall of joy where you should clap your hands and shout with a joyous sound, offering him one song of praise after another, why would you then disgrace him by letting your heart be sad and filled with darkness and gloominess?[57] (I, 698)

Even in times of suffering or tribulation when one is tempted to succumb to discouragement, there is cause for joy that one is worthy of suffering with Christ, knowing that through suffering he entered into glory. Joy, then, is not an emotional state or a temporary response to sensory stimuli but an enduring consequence of the peace that comes through the Holy Spirit. This is far removed from ordinary experiences of happiness:

> For that reason, Paul, when he was sitting in shackles in Rome, wrote to the Philippians, "Rejoice in the Lord always, and again I say, rejoice." (Phil 4,4) He wants them to rejoice in the Lord just as he does. He is exhorting them, however, not to a joy of the flesh or a joy in

---

[55] "Es heißt: Luc. 9, 29. **Da Jesus betete, ward die Gestalt seines Angesichts anders**. Also würden wir auch bald anders werden. Beteten wir nur fein fleißig, so würde das Hertz und Angesicht bald anders werden, so würde die Freude des Herrn unsere Seele einnehmen, und seine Kraft würde sich herrlich bey uns äussern."

[56] "Wir haben uns also billig zu schämen, daß wir Christum zwar mit dem Munde bekannt haben, und dennoch unser Hertz ihn noch nicht mit Psaltern, Paucken und lieblichen Harfen besungen, und ihm nicht gejauchzet und gefrohlocket, das ist, daß unsere Kräfte der Seelen noch nicht zu seinem Lobe und Preis erreget worden, und wir uns noch nicht recht dieses unsers Heylandes gefreuet haben."

[57] "Da Christus Jesus dein Hertz gewürdiget hat, dasselbe zu einem Himmelreich und zu einem Freuden=Saal zu machen, darinnen du mit Händen frohlocken, mit fröhlichem Schalle jauchzen, und ihm ein Loblied nach dem andern bringen solst: warum wolltest du denn ihm die Schande anthun, dein Hertz trübe machen, und mit Dunckelheit und Finsterniß erfüllen lassen."

the five senses or even just to a joy that one might always have as a sensation in the heart, but rather to that joy by which the peace of God is maintained and not interrupted.[58] (I, 698)

For those who define Pietism as a subjective approach to faith, this passage is worthy of special attention. With all his insistence on participation of the heart, Francke distinguishes between an intense religious experience that may fade over time and an ongoing commitment to a life of religious practice. Erhard Peschke pointed out that Francke criticized ancient philosophers for classifying joy only as an affect or emotion, whereas in the New Testament it is also classed as a fruit of the Spirit and is, accordingly, a Christian virtue rather than a sensual experience.[59] The latter may provide a valuable impetus, but it has to be continually renewed through devotional exercise such as reading the Psalms.

> Therefore one should fortify oneself with a psalm like this and use it to avoid what often happens at the beginning of conversion: one senses great joy and peace in the heart because of the great mercy that has been granted in the gospel, but right after this the ashes fall on the coals and cover their glow in such a way that one cannot either see or feel them, and finally the fire is totally extinguished.[60] (I, 698)

With the observation that religious zeal waxes and wanes, this view of conversion is clearly not "once saved, always saved." Francke's own dramatic conversion has sometimes been considered normative, but Jonathan Strom has shown the variety of Pietist conversion narratives, including those that are not concluded until the time of death.[61]

## 7 Summary

Just as it is important not to oversimplify the Pietist understanding of conversion, it is crucial to avoid reducing Pietist theology to individual rebirth. While Pietists may have viewed reform of individuals as the path to reform of the church, it was the church as a community of believers that they were seeking to reform. As Peter

---

[58] "Darum schrieb Paulus, als er zu Rom in den Banden saß, an die Philipper: **Freuet euch in dem Herrn allewege, und abermal sage ich, freuet euch**. Phil. 4, 4. Da will er, daß, wie er sich freue, also solten auch sie sich in dem Herrn freuen. Er ermahnet sie aber nicht zu einer Freude im Fleisch, zu einer Freude in den fünf Sinnen, oder auch nur zu einer Freude, die man allezeit in seinem Hertzen empfindlich hätte; sondern zu derselbigen Freude, durch welche der Friede Gottes erhalten, und nicht gestöret wird."

[59] Peschke: Studien, Vol. 1, 85–86, citing August Hermann Francke: Kurtze Anweisung Zur wahren / lautern und Apostolischen Erkenntniß Jesu Christi. Halle: Waisenhaus, 1714, 35–36.

[60] "Darum soll man sich mit einem solchem Psalm recht rüsten, und denselben dazu brauchen, daß es nicht einem nicht also gehe, wie es insgemein zu geschehen pfleget, daß, wenn man im Anfang der Bekehrung über der grossen Gnade, die einem im Evangelio aufgegangen ist, Freude und Friede im Hertzen empfindet, man doch darnach gleich wird den Kohlen, über welche die Asche fällt, und ihre Glut so bedecket, daß man dieselbe nicht sehen noch spüren kann, bis endlich wol gar das Feuer verlöschet."

[61] Jonathan Strom: German Pietism and the Problem of Conversion. University Park, PA: Pennsylvania State University Press, 2018, esp. 55–58.

## 7 Summary

James Yoder writes, "Francke's theology cannot be understood outside of this Pietist commitment to rebirth in all areas of the church, and attempts to construct his religious thought without the framework of church reform inevitably fractures the cohesiveness of his theology."[62] Martin Schmidt recognized on the one hand that Pietism was the forerunner of modern individualism as it appeared in the time of Goethe and Romanticism, yet he regarded that as only a partial truth. The reborn person, he observed, does not stand alone but seeks interaction and is dependent on the community that validates his or her experience. Writing about Pietists in general, Schmidt says that they sought the true church not where the Word of God was preached but where the reborn children of God came together.[63] With all the faults of the institutional church, they often looked to the invisible church as the place of community, and we have seen how Francke turned to the apostolic church or the eschatological community as an ideal that contrasted with the visible church. Yet he worked within the church of his day and stretched the boundaries by creating new institutions to reform the body of Christ. As Jonathan Strom states, while older scholarship has focused on the "individual, subjective, and otherworldly nature of Pietists, [...] one of the hallmarks of Pietism from its inception has been the creation of groups and experimentation with new forms of religious association [...]."[64] It is understandable if observers sometimes focus only on one of these themes, for Francke struggled to integrate the two. The tension between individualism and community, between subjective experience and outward expression, pervades Francke's theology, including his theology of music. At times, his stress on the music of the heart nearly drowned out the music of the voice. Whether or not he succeeded in maintaining a harmonic balance, it is clear that his intention was that both should be heard.

---

[62] Yoder: Pietism and the Sacraments, 145.
[63] Martin Schmidt: Der Pietismus und die Einheit der Kirche. In: Der Pietismus als theologische Erscheinung, Gesammelte Studien zur Geschichte des Pietismus. Vol. 2. Ed. by Martin Schmidt. Göttingen: Vandenhoeck & Ruprecht, 1984, 84–85.
[64] Pietism and Community in Europe and North America, 1650–1850. Ed. by Jonathan Strom. Leiden: Brill, 2010, 2.

Chapter Two

# "Whatever you do, do everything for the glory of God": Music in the Bible Commentaries of Joachim Lange (1670–1744)

Based on the percentage of space devoted to music in Joachim Lange's thousands of pages of biblical commentary, there would be little reason to focus on his view of music. While he expresses appreciation for music, he reveals no particular personal interest in the subject. What warrants the study of his theology of music is the very fact that, as a leading Halle theologian from 1709 to 1744 who wrote several lengthy commentaries covering the entire Bible, he offers the opportunity to describe the Pietist view of music apart from the polemical writings that have dominated most studies.

Lange shares much in his attitude toward music with other Pietists who placed greater value on the inward state of the person singing or playing music than on the music itself. Yet he by no means rejects music, which he calls "very noble," saying its harmony comes from God himself, though its basis is almost incapable of investigation; it should be used to arouse the frame of mind that has the praise of God as its purpose.

> As far as the nature and effect of music are concerned, it is on the one hand the case that it contains a true ϑεῖον, something truly godly or something springing from divine wisdom and goodness; and also, what is truly amazing, that it has a quite special natural power to influence and move the human spirit.[1]

Similar statements recur in different places in his commentaries, as we will see. In the following, I will first discuss Lange's interpretation of the Bible in general and then look at passages that relate to music, arranging the material roughly in the order of the books of the Bible as we know it today. Though that is not the order in which Lange wrote his commentaries, there is no observable change in his views that would merit a chronological ordering principle.

---

[1] "Was nun die Eigenschaft und Wirckung der Music betrifft, so ist es zwar eines theils allerdinge an dem, daß darinnen ein rechtes ϑεῖον, recht etwas göttliches, oder das, was von göttlicher Weisheit und Güte herrühret, lieget, und wie recht verwunderns würdig, also auch von einer natürlichen gantz sonderbaren Krafft zum Eindruck und zur Bewegung des menschlichen Gemüths ist." Joachim Lange: Biblisch-Historisches Licht und Recht, Das ist, Richtige und Erbauliche Erklärung Der sämmtlichen Historischen Bücher Des Alten Testaments, Von dem Buche Josuä an bis auf das Büchlein Esther, Mit hinzugethanem Buche Hiobs. Halle, Leipzig: [n.p.] 1734, 305 (commentary on 1 Samuel 16,15–23).

## 1 The Bible as Prophecy

Lange's belief in the unity of the whole Bible is symbolically indicated in the titles of his biblical commentaries, all of which include the phrase "Licht und Recht" ("Light and Justice"). In the preface to the last of his commentaries, *Prophetisches Licht und Recht* (1738), Lange looked back on the twelve years since he started his project, grateful that he had lived long enough to bring it to completion. In the first volume, *Apostolisches Licht und Recht* (1729), he recognized that, as he was already nearing 60, he might not live to finish it, in which case he had entrusted his son-in-law, Johann Jakob Rambach, with carrying it out. However, as Lange noted, "Man proposes, God disposes" ("der Mensch denckts, Gott lenckts"), and Lange survived to finish the final volume, whereas Rambach died in 1735 at the age of 42. The other volumes, covering all the canonical books of the Bible, were *Apocalyptisches Licht und Recht* (1730), *Mosaisches Licht und Recht* (1732), *Biblisch-Historisches Licht und Recht* (1734), *Evangelisches Licht und Recht* (1735), and *Davidisch-Salomonisches Licht und Recht* (1737). As most of these were about 1500 folio pages long, this was an enormous undertaking; even the considerable repetition and overlap can be excused as Lange's attempt to explain the uniform message of all parts of the Bible.[2]

That message is summarized on the title page of *Prophetisches Licht und Recht*, where Lange explains that he will treat the Old Testament prophetic books primarily as prophecy of Christ's person, his mediatorial role, and his kingdom. More specifically in regard to the kingdom of Christ, he will show how, "after the foundation and spread that has already occurred, it will be expanded much more in the last times among all peoples for their conversion and the glorification of the name of God."[3] In addition, the volume includes an introduction to the Revelation of John (*Offenbahrung Johannis*) with a hermeneutic key to the more difficult places in the psalms and prophets. Among those most difficult passages, he observes in his introduction, are those that deal with the last days and the great changes that the church on earth will undergo in the end times. Other interpreters, he finds, have

---

[2] Lange apparently did not think he was prolix. In his preface to the *Prophetisches Licht und Recht*, he remarked that others had thought he should make two volumes out of the prophet commentaries, but he felt he had a gift from God to be able to say much with few words: "vermeine von Gott die Gabe empfangen zu haben, daß ich mich kurtz fassen, und mit wenigen viel sagen, und doch, wie ich hoffe, deutlich schreiben kann." Joachim Lange: Prophetisches Licht und Recht, Oder Richtige und erbauliche Erklärung Der Propheten. Halle: Francke, 1738, 6.

[3] The full title reads, *Prophetisches Licht und Recht, Oder Richtige und erbauliche Erklärung der Propheten: Darinnen nach dem Grundtext, aus eigener Betrachtung, unter andern Materien vornehmlich die Weissagungen von Christi Person, Mittler=Amte und Reiche abgehandelt sind: Und zwar die vom Reiche Christi also, Wie dasselbe, nach der schon geschehenen Gründung und Ausbreitung, in der letzten Zeit unter allen Völkern, zu ihrer Bekehrung und Verherrlichung des Namen Gottes, noch vielmehr wird erweitert werden. Mit einer Einleitung in die Offenbahrung Johannis zum hermeneutischen Schlüssel In die schweresten Stellen der Psalmen Davids und der Propheten: und mit einem Anhange von der allgemeinen Gnade in Christo.*

lacked insight into these matters, and he does not demand that everyone agree with his interpretation, because it is impossible to know exactly how the prophecies will be fulfilled. Nevertheless, even if the hope of better times, as it was labeled by Philipp Jakob Spener, cannot be regarded as a fundamental doctrine, it is for Lange correct, certain, and important.[4]

The future that Lange finds prophesied throughout the Bible is that one day light will triumph over darkness and justice will triumph over injustice. When this happens, there will be what Lange calls a Sabbath period on earth. This will be ushered in by the Fall of Babylon and the Realm of the Antichrist, at which time the church of Christ will spread throughout the world through the conversion of Jews and pagans.[5] Against a common belief that biblical prophecies had already been fulfilled, Lange was adamant that the Sabbath period was yet to come. The seventh trumpet of Revelation 10,7 has not yet sounded; when it does, it will bring an end to the "present depraved condition of the church on earth."[6] The angel of Rev 14,6 that proclaimed the gospel to all peoples and nations was not, Lange asserts, the evangelical voice that was heard at the time of the apostles or of the Reformation; it is rather the time foreseen by Jesus in Matt 24,14 when the gospel is proclaimed throughout the world just prior to the end of time.[7]

This hermeneutic key to the Bible dominates Lange's exegesis to an extent not true of Spener or Francke. While Spener's view of the hope of better times was an important influence, the prophetic theology of Reformed theologians provided Lange with a more systematic framework. In the introduction to his *Apocalyptisches Licht und Recht*, Lange pays tribute to Johannes Cocceius but even more so to Campegius Vitringa (1659–1722), whose hermeneutical system was in Lange's view more successful. Lange happily reports that in matters of prophecy there is no conflict between Reformed and Lutheran teaching. Wanting to give credit where credit is due, Lange recognizes that these Reformed thinkers were earlier in coming to this understanding of prophecy, but their works have now gained a strong following in Germany, according to Lange. Vitringa's *Anakrisis Apocalypsios Joannis Apostoli* was first published in the Netherlands early in the century, but because of its popularity in Germany, it was published again in

---

[4] Lange: Prophetisches Licht und Recht, 6. The doctrinal debates about eschatology are beyond the scope of this study, though the issue itself pervades his biblical commentaries. In *Antibarbarus* (1711), Lange's polemical response to Valentin Ernst Löscher, he recognized that the hope of better times was a secondary teaching, not essential to salvation, but he defended Spener against the charge of contradicting Article XVII of the Augsburg Confession. For a study of Spener's eschatology and the resulting controversies, see Heike Krauter-Dierolf: Die Eschatologie Philipp Jakob Speners: Der Streit mit der lutherischen Orthodoxie um die "Hoffnung besserer Zeiten". Tübingen: Mohr-Siebeck, 2005. For an overview of Lange's theology, see Rolf Dannenbaum: Joachim Lange als Wortführer des Halleschen Pietismus. Diss. phil. Universität Göttingen 1951.

[5] Joachim Lange: Apocalyptisches Licht und Recht, Das ist, Richtige und erbauliche Erklärung Des Prophetischen Buchs Der heiligen Offenbahrung Johannis. Halle: Francke, 1730, fol. B$^{vo}$.

[6] Lange: Prophetisches Licht und Recht, 19.

[7] Lange: Prophetisches Licht und Recht, 20.

Weißenfels in 1721 and, according to Lange, had been widely recognized.[8] Also influential was Vitringa's commentary on the book of Isaiah,[9] which Vitringa interpreted in light of the book of Revelation. Because of the enormous length of this two-volume work, Lange offered his readers a summary of Vitringa's system in his own commentary on Revelation, though he also added his critique of the points where he found Vitringa to be in error.[10] In his *Prophetisches Licht und Recht*, following his commentary on the book of Ezekiel, Lange also included a summary of Vitringa's earlier book on the temple as understood by Ezekiel.[11] While Lange did not accept all of Vitringa's interpretations uncritically, his overwhelmingly positive view of the Franeker theologian might be symbolized in the index to Lange's *Prophetisches Licht und Recht*, where one entry is given for a page where Vitringa is contradicted and 21 pages where he is praised.[12]

This orientation to prophetic theology explains the striking prevalence of the theme of prophecy in Lange's discussion of biblical passages regarding music. Whenever music appears in a positive light in the Old Testament, Lange sees it as the result of a prophetic spirit. Beginning with Miriam, who led a song of praise for the deliverance from Egypt, through Hannah, who sang when she offered her son Samuel to God's service, to the Levitic temple singers, and above all, to David, songs of praise proceeded from a prophetic spirit. Though these pre-Christian singers may not themselves have had insight into the full course of history, the Christian reader of their stories sees in them the prefiguring of the Messiah and the ultimate victory of good over evil. Lange's hermeneutic principle is to see Christ throughout the Old Testament, finding "types" or foreshadowings of New Testament images, which are then labeled "antitypes."

## 2   Mosaic Light and Justice

The invention of musical instruments is ascribed to Jubal by most biblical commentators on the basis of Genesis 4,21. For orthodox theologians who wanted to find an ancient biblical basis for organs, the verse could be used as support. Translators' attempts to find equivalents for Hebrew names of instruments sometimes gave direct encouragement for this, as the King James Version actually rendered the terms as harp and organ. Lange uses Luther's translation of "Geiger und Pfeiffer,"

---

[8]   Lange: Apocalyptisches Licht und Recht, fol. B. The first edition of Vitringa's *Anakrisis Apocalypsios Joannis Apostoli* was published in Franeker in 1705, the second edition in Amsterdam in 1719. The Weißenfels publication in 1721 was the third edition.
[9]   Campegius Vitringa: Commentarius in librum prophetiarum Jesaiae. Leeuwarden: Halma, Pt. 1: 1714; Pt. 2: 1720. The second edition that Lange used was published in Herborn, Pt. 1: 1715; Pt. 2: 1722.
[10]  Lange: Apocalyptisches Licht und Recht, 1–48.
[11]  Campegius Vitringa: Aanleiding tot het recht Verstant van den Tempel, die de prophet Ezechiel bezien en beschreeven heft. Franeker: Gyselaar, 1687. Lange's "Recension, Oder Kurtzer Auszug" was published in Pt. 2 of Lange: Prophetisches Licht und Recht, 180–216.
[12]  Lange: Prophetisches Licht und Recht, Pt. 1, [620], Register.

terms that have no sacred connotations, for which an English translation might be "fiddlers and pipers." Indeed, in his commentary he uses the German term *Musicanten*, which has connotations of street musicians, and notes that Jubal and his ilk misused music for their worldly pleasure and thus were a contributing cause of the Flood as punishment for their sins.

With the surrounding verses, this passage is an attempt to identify the origin of agriculture and industry as well as music, and Lange accordingly reflects on the invention and multiplication of so many arts and sciences. Some he regards as useful, others not, but he does not further elaborate on the relative value of different skills. The message for him is that these were invented at certain points in time, evidence that the world and its inhabitants are not eternal. His thoughts at this point are directed against any philosophical claim that the world is eternal.[13]

The 15th chapter of Genesis presents a more favorable view of music. Moses and the children of Israel sang a song of thanksgiving for their release from captivity. Lange comments that the singing of this song doubtless occurred in an orderly manner, which he supposes to have had these characteristics:

a. Moses, as a prophet, first uttered this song of praise through the inspiration ("Eingebung") of the Holy Spirit.
b. Next, he either dictated it to the elders of all the tribes and families or else it was communicated to them by a special collaboration with God, so that they made it known to the whole community in many choirs.
c. Moses then gave the sign for the song to begin, and all joined in singing together in good order and harmony. The Holy Spirit had to have worked among them in an extraordinary manner to keep them in good order and harmony, for if Moses had sung alone, not one percent of the many hundred thousand people in the camp could have heard him, much less taken part.
d. What Moses and Aaron undertook with the men, Miriam and her sisters did with the choirs of women.[14]

Recognizing that this is the first song recorded in scripture, Lange nevertheless speculates that the patriarchs going back to Adam must have praised God with singing. This would have been a reasonable manner in which to carry out their obligation to praise God. Though Jubal, as a descendant of Cain, misused musical instruments, the descendants of Seth, the godly son of Adam and Eve, undoubtedly used them appropriately. Lange had noted in commenting on Genesis 4,26 that public worship in the family of Adam was instituted anew with Seth and his line after it had been either neglected or hindered in some way.[15]

Noteworthy in this commentary is the emphasis on order and regularized worship. The song of triumph is not a spontaneous outburst of a crowd but a divinely

---

[13] Joachim Lange: Mosaisches Licht und Recht, Das ist, Richtige und erbauliche Erklärung Der fünf Bücher Mosis. Halle, Leipzig: Walther, 1732, 92.
[14] Lange: Mosaisches Licht und Recht, 445.
[15] Lange: Mosaisches Licht und Recht, 93.

inspired, well-organized collective act of praise and thanksgiving. It occurs within an established tradition of worship that included singing and musical instruments, going back at least to Seth. There is also continuity into the future: reasoning on the basis of Jewish tradition and some textual calculations, Lange says that the crossing of the Red Sea took place on the seventh day of the Israelites' departure from Egypt; the New Testament counterpart is found in Revelation 15,1–5 when the song of Moses will be sung after the last of the seven plagues is overcome and those who had conquered the beast stand beside the sea of glass.

Noteworthy also is the observation that the genders were separated. The singing of women under Miriam's leadership, which is recorded in Exodus 15,20–21, occurred in alternation with the singing of the male choirs. Here Lange provides alternate connotations to Luther's Bible based on his understanding of Hebrew. Rather than *Reigen* Lange gives *Singe-Chören* as the Hebrew meaning, and for *sang ihnen vor*, he reads *antwortete*, explaining it as the choirs of women answering the choirs of men. Again, though Miriam led the choirs and was a prophetess through whom God spoke, she did not sing alone but with all the female singers. The most appropriate parallel that Lange finds for this form of worship is in Philo's description of the Egyptian Therapeuts in *De vita contemplativa*, who also separated the women from the men but in such a way that they could hear one another. The most inappropriate use of this passage, Lange insists, is for a defense of dancing. He correctly notes that some church leaders and biblical interpreters have regarded this passage as a basis for the respectability of dancing. This and David's dancing before the Ark of the Covenant lead to the support of worldly and unreasonable dancing by persons of both sexes. To Lange this is a perversion by fleshly-minded people who are unable to recognize things as spiritual. Even the drums are not seen by Lange as a worldly instrument, for Miriam "had brought several of them out of Egypt for spiritual use."[16]

Toward the end of the book of Exodus, Bezaleel is called to build the tent of meeting and all the furnishings of the tent. The name Bezaleel means, according to Lange, either "in the shadow of God" or "in the shadow is God." The whole of Levitic worship is for Lange the shadow or type to which Christ is the body or antitype. As Bezaleel was said to be filled with the spirit of God and with wisdom and understanding, the shadow image should not be taken to belittle his accomplishments. His constructions were arranged with the most perfect proportion and symmetry, and that is what qualifies them to serve as a counterpart to the perfection and highest wisdom of the Christian religion.[17]

As an introduction to Part 2 of *Mosaisches Licht und Recht*, which contains his commentary on Leviticus, Numbers, and Deuteronomy, Lange states his position on ceremonial law. Its foundation was in God himself and specifically in God's two main characteristics of justice and grace. Justice would have required God to carry out his threat of death for eating the forbidden fruit, but grace allows for animal

---

[16] Lange: Mosaisches Licht und Recht, 448.
[17] Lange: Mosaisches Licht und Recht, 569.

sacrifice for reconciliation. Thus, through external symbols, the ceremonial law contained the basis of the moral law and of prophecy. It is, Lange says, "not mere law but at the same time also a bodily gospel."[18] As excellent as this dispensation was, it was also incomplete and not suited to the kingdom of the Messiah. First, Levitic worship was external, sensual, deficient, and very tiresome, and God, as spirit, could take no pleasure therein. Second, the form of worship was tied to a single place and people, from whom the Messiah should come; but it is unsuited to the kingdom of the Messiah, which should extend to all peoples, and thus it had to be abrogated. The advantage of the new dispensation is contrasted with the old:

> What was a shadow there is the true body here; there promise, here fulfillment; there servitude under the Mosaic yoke of statutes, here adoption in evangelical freedom; there, as it were, the night with the light of the moon, here the bright day of the sun of righteousness and such a light as is also full of strength. [19]

Nevertheless, Lange strongly believed that the Mosaic law was given by God, and any changes were to be introduced by God, not humans. When God added books to the Bible after the Mosaic books, he did not introduce any new teachings or new rules for living; he merely continued to expound upon his advice for our salvation.[20]

## 3  Ceremonies of the Old Testament

Throughout Lange's commentaries on the Old Testament, the thesis is that everything has its counterpart in the time of the gospel. As the culmination of history, the Book of Revelation provides the counterparts in many instances, particularly in the image of seven trumpets that were played by seven angels after the opening of the seventh seal (Rev 8–11). Lange notes that the number seven was already significant in the days of creation, and not only was the week divided into seven days but also the years were measured in sevens. The Sabbath year was a reminder of God's orderly processes, and the Jubilee year followed upon seven periods of Sabbath years. In his commentary on Leviticus 25, where the year of Jubilee is introduced, Lange makes explicit the parallels with Revelation and the important role of trumpets in both. He strives to explain the complex and uncertain etymology of the word "jubilee," whether it implies the role of a blown instrument,

---

[18]  Lange: Mosaisches Licht und Recht, 613: "Daher es denn nicht ein blosses Gesetz, sondern auch zugleich ein leibliches Evangelium war."

[19]  Lange: Mosaisches Licht und Recht, 614: "War dort **Schatten**, so ist alhier der rechte **Cörper**; dort **Verheissung**, hier **Erfüllung**; dort **Knechtschaft** unter dem Mosaischen Joche der Satzungen, hier Kindschaft in Evangelischer Freyheit; dort gleichsam die **Nacht** mit dem Schein des Monden, hier der **helle Tag** mit der Sonne der Gerechtigkeit und ein solches Licht, welches auch voller Kraft ist."

[20]  Lange: Mosaisches Licht und Recht, 1053: "Wenn Gott zu den Mosaischen die übrigen Bücher der heiligen Schrift hinzu gethan hat, so hat er damit nicht etwas neues, oder neue Glaubens=Lehren, und Lebens=Regeln geoffenbahret und vorgeschrieben, sondern seinen Rath von unserer Seligkeit nur immermehr dadurch erläutert."

and whether it was a ram's horn that was blown, but the important point for him is that the trumpet is a true "Sabbath instrument" and was used to announce not only the Sabbath but also the new moon and new year.[21]

Trumpets were used also for practical purposes of calling together the tribes in the wilderness and notifying them to break camp, described in Numbers 10. Lange interprets the blowing of the trumpet as the equivalent of the spiritual sound of the gospel as it would go throughout the land. Because only the Levitic priests were to blow the trumpet, that is an indication that no one other than a spiritual priest anointed by God is worthy and capable of proclaiming the gospel. Lange sees this passage in Numbers as connected to the overall musical duties of the Levites described in 1 Chronicles 25. The use of trumpets to announce festivals has its equivalent in Christian festivals, he says, and vocal and instrumental music in general is associated with joyous occasions. This is a holy joyousness that should be approved by all, and it was such joy that caused David to dance as the Ark of the Covenant was brought home. The dedications of both the first and second temples were such occasions also, as was the reform of music under Hezekiah (2 Chr 29). Because the trumpets were "Sabbath instruments," their greatest significance for Christians is the parallel to the World Sabbath that is to come, the seventh of the historical periods, which will, according to Revelation 10,7 and 11,15, be announced by the blowing of the trumpet by the seventh angel. The music that will accompany the entrance to the heavenly Jerusalem will also be glorious, an image of the heavenly joy of those who surround the Lamb (Rev 14–15). Believing Christians, however, should not wait until this future glory but should already now join their voices and spirits in the exercise of "sanctified musical joy of the heart" ("geheiligte musicalische Hertzens=Freude"), as instructed by Paul in Ephesians 5 and Colossians 3. Predictably, though, Lange does not leave this treatment of the joyous use of music without warning against the all-too-common abuse of music for "earthly and fleshly worldly joy" ("bey aller irdischen und fleischlichen Welt=Freude").[22]

## 4 The Historical Books

Another aspect of Levitic worship that Lange appreciated was its orderliness. This is described in the book of First Chronicles, beginning with chapter 23, and ascribed to David, whose earlier life will be discussed later. But while David was able to arrange the classes of musicians so well as a result of his well-developed musical skill,[23] the orderly system was divinely ordained, as God is a God of order.[24]

---

[21] Lange: Mosaisches Licht und Recht, 752–754.
[22] Lange: Mosaisches Licht und Recht, 873–874.
[23] Lange: Biblisch-Historisches Licht und Recht, Vol. 2, 378.
[24] The concept that God is a God of order was also central to Francke's theology. See Peschke: Studien, Vol. 1, 18 and Peter Menck: Die Erziehung der Jugend zur Ehre Gottes und zum Nutzen des Nächsten: Die Pädagogik August Hermann Franckes. Tübingen: Niemeyer, 2001, 95–98.

Without proper organization and with so many people, Israelite worship might have resulted in great confusion. Even with the simpler forms of worship in the New Testament, God is said to prefer good order (1 Cor 15,40).[25] The number 24 figures prominently in the division of the different classes of priests and musicians and prefigures the perfect worship depicted in Revelation 5, where the 24 elders kneel before the Lamb. Multiples of 24 are seen in the number of musicians in each class and in the 144,000 blessed ones who sing the new song in Revelation 14–15.[26] In commenting on 1 Chronicles 25, where the names of all 24 music leaders are given, each of whom had twelve singers, Lange lists other biblical appearances of the number 12: twelve patriarchs of the sons of Jacob leading to twelve tribes of Israel and twelve parts of the land, twelve apostles, and the many mentions of twelve or its multiples in the book of Revelation.[27]

It is not only the orderliness of the musical personnel and organization that pleased God but, even more, the beauty of the music. When Solomon's temple was completed and dedicated (2 Chr 5), the music played by the large group of musicians was "quite outstanding and most marvelous" ("recht vortreflich und höchst verwundernswürdig"). The occasion was one of great importance, as the completed temple caused great wonder and reverence. The excellent musical gifts and skill of these many vocalists and instrumentalists could only have come about, Lange believes, through a special influence of God, which resulted in the most perfect harmony. In response, God himself showed his pleasure by filling the temple most gloriously with the pillar of cloud. This was the pinnacle of music on earth: "Accordingly, one can say that never, either before or after, was a more glorious musical performance held."[28] Furthermore, the content of the music was completely evangelical, as the text was "For the Lord is gracious and his mercy endures forever." The spiritual counterpart of this event is identified by Lange as the first apostolic community which grew to 5,000 people and stood together in such harmony that "they were all of one heart and one soul (Acts 4,24.32)."[29]

Lange admits that no one, not even the Jews of his day, knows how the ancient Hebrew music sounded or how the music was structured. Yet if God gave the prophetic gift to his lead musicians and added supernatural awareness to their natural insights, as he did for the workers and designers of the temple, the music must have been as marvelous as the temple building. The music of the temple, as ordained by God, was most noble and capable of arousing the senses by its harmony and variation in sounds. Lange bemoans again the misuse of music for all kinds of sinful pleasure and extravagance. Music appealing to the senses is not to be rejected, however, because Christians have both body and soul, but the best music is spiritual music that joins the hearts of believers in harmony directed to

---

[25] Lange: Biblisch-Historisches Licht und Recht, Vol. 2, 377.
[26] Lange: Biblisch-Historisches Licht und Recht, Vol. 2, 379.
[27] Lange: Biblisch-Historisches Licht und Recht, Vol. 2, 385.
[28] Lange: Biblisch-Historisches Licht und Recht, Vol. 2, 414: "Daß man demnach wohl sagen kan, es sey niemal, weder vorher, noch nachher in der Welt ein herrlicherer actus musicus gehalten worden."
[29] Lange: Biblisch-Historisches Licht und Recht, Vol. 2, 414.

God.³⁰ Lange credits the believers of the Old Testament with having maintained this bond between body and soul. Levitic music had as its purpose the glorious praise of God, and this will be a part of the perfect worship that is to come in the Kingdom of Glory, along with the most perfect harmony. Reminding the reader again of the ultimate goal toward which Hebrew temple worship was leading, Lange inserts all of his favorite verses from Revelation describing the glorious worship of the future final Sabbath period.³¹

## 5   Prophetic Music

In the previous sections, it was made clear that Lange did not separate Law from Gospel in a disjunctive manner but saw them as integrally related. If Christ was the theme of the entire Bible, then certain specially gifted persons in the times before Christ must have had some understanding of him. This prophetic gift enabled them to write and to sing of the Messiah to come. This prophetic spirit is seen in the song of Hannah who, Lange claims, was awakened to her song by the Holy Spirit.

Hannah sang her song when offering her son Samuel in the temple to the service of God. It was a song of praise to God for giving her a son after years of barrenness. Her prophetic spirit, Lange said, can be seen from the style in which she sang. Her song has much in common with Mary's song in Luke 1. Also the name Hannah, meaning "grace," was shared with the elderly widow, better known today as Anna, who lived as a prophetess in the temple in Jerusalem and saw in the baby Jesus the fulfillment of the Messianic promise.³²

With these connections it follows naturally that the song of Hannah ("I rejoice in your salvation") is interpreted as referring to the Messiah. In fact, the last line of her song (1 Sam 2,10) is the first use of the Hebrew word משיח, the anointed one, rendered, as Lange notes, by the Greek translators of the Septuagint as χριστος. The surrounding context with its references to king and judgment confirms for Lange that the prophecy is of the final judgment and the future reign of Christ in glory.³³ Lange analyses the symbolism within Hannah's song, relates it to similar images in various other biblical passages, and concludes that its content "stands in the most precise agreement with the writings of the prophets and apostles."³⁴

Some poetic aspects of Hannah's song also receive Lange's attention. He is pleased that she uses the phrase "in the Lord" rather than "from the Lord," for it expresses the union and communion ("Vereinigung und Gemeinschaft") of her relationship with the Lord. In addition, her alternation between "his" and "your" in addressing the Lord expresses "the fullness of affect" by which the heart is

---

30   Lange: Biblisch-Historisches Licht und Recht, Vol. 2, 378.
31   Lange: Biblisch-Historisches Licht und Recht, Vol. 2, 379.
32   Lange: Biblisch-Historisches Licht und Recht, Vol. 1, 232–233.
33   Lange: Biblisch-Historisches Licht und Recht, Vol. 1, 237.
34   Lange: Biblisch-Historisches Licht und Recht, Vol. 1, 237: "Es stehet demnach das bisher erläuterte Gebets=Lied der gläubigen Hanna mit den Schriften der Propheten und Apostel, seinem Innhalte nach, in der genauesten Uebereinstimmung."

## 5 Prophetic Music

directed toward God. Hannah is filled with the Spirit in such a manner that her joy necessarily overflows into vocal expression: "my mouth has opened wide" (1 Sam 2,1) is equivalent to David's "I believe, therefore I speak" (Ps 116,10). Lange emphasizes that believing children of God have true joy already in this world, though it is not "according to the world, but rather directed to God and in accordance with his holy will, and therefore it is enjoyed also in God, namely in the blessed community with God, just as it is given by God."[35] Her second expression of rejoicing is directed to "your salvation," and, with the little word "your," Hannah shows her enjoyment of the truth of her salvation. The same poetic impact is found in the song of Mary with the words, "My soul magnifies the Lord, and my spirit rejoices in God my Savior."

The story of Samuel's boyhood call from God in the temple is well known (1 Sam 3). With his response, "Speak, for your servant is listening," Samuel showed his openness to God, and when in verse 19 it reads that God was with him, Lange explains that God was **in him**, filling him with his prophetic spirit. Furthermore, when God is said in verse 21 to reveal himself to Samuel, that indicates for Lange that Samuel had the "grace of revelation."[36] Later in 1 Samuel, after Samuel had anointed Saul, he told him that he would meet a band of prophets, the spirit of God would come upon him, and he would prophesy. Noteworthy for our discussion of music is that the band of prophets would be accompanied by psaltery, drum, flute, and harp. Lange makes the following points about these "music-making" prophets:

a. Prophets were men who had been awakened by God in an extraordinary and immediate way and held an exceptional teaching office (apart from the regular offices of priest and Levite) by virtue of the visions or secret revelations they received through the power of the Holy Spirit. They might admonish, encourage, or console the people, but they also foretold certain future matters, of which the Messiah and his kingdom were the foremost.
b. These prophets formed schools in which they instructed the youth in the Mosaic words and the works of God, especially the prophecies concerning the Messiah. Part of the instruction, in keeping with the Jewish love of vocal and instrumental music, was to teach the great songs of praise, such as that of Exodus 15 about the crossing of the Red Sea.
c. Because this was very pleasing to God, he blessed the students and often gave the gift of prophecy also to them, enabling them not only to sing and play the music that was passed down but also from the fullness of the Spirit to express all sorts of spiritual and edifying matters along with their instrumental music, including the future promise of the Messiah.

---

[35] Lange: Biblisch-Historisches Licht und Recht, Vol. 1, 233: "aber sie ist nicht nach der Welt, sondern nach Gott eingerichtet, und seinem heiligen Willen gemäß; und daher wird sie auch in Gott, nemlich in der seligen Gemeinschaft mit Gott, genossen, gleichwie sie von Gott gegeben wird."
[36] Lange: Biblisch-Historisches Licht und Recht, Vol. 1, 249.

d. Samuel set up such schools of prophecy, as indicated in 1 Samuel 19,20, where he was called the overseer of the choirs of prophets whom Saul encountered when searching for David in order to kill him.
e. Such prophet schools continued in the time of Elisha as reported in 2 Kings 3–4.
f. The music in these schools of prophecy did not include any frivolous dances or sensual tunes, even though such were surely to be found among the "large and depraved masses" of Israelites, just as, unfortunately, they are not lacking among those of the evangelical faith.
g. The schools of Christianity should bring in children of prophets as teachers. While in many places this is happening, there are also many false prophets and those who know nothing of the school of the Holy Spirit but draw only on the store of knowledge gathered through their natural abilities by book-learning (though even this is lacking in some).[37]

This brief proposal for educational reform in Lange's own day does not have enough details to know where musical instruction fits, but one can infer that it might resemble that which he describes of the Israelite schools. In other words, the rich tradition of Lutheran hymnody would be taught along with the encouragement to write new hymns as the Spirit moved them.

The story of David playing for Saul in 1 Samuel 16 is one of the most important passages where a biblical commentator reveals his view of music. When the evil spirit departed from Saul, was that through the natural power of music, through David's spiritual gift, through the words that were sung, or some combination? Different interpreters had offered such varying perspectives.[38] The quotation from Lange introduced in the opening paragraphs of this chapter comes from his commentary on this passage. We see there a recognition of both the natural power of music to move emotions and the divine origin of this power. Because Saul's problem was not an ordinary sickness of the spirit but rather an affliction of the devil, Lange says, the natural power of music was not sufficient. Thus, the curative effect cannot be ascribed solely to the music but to the special working of God. This happens, however, not through a direct divine intervention but through the prophetic gift that David had received through his anointing by Samuel. With the anointing (1 Sam 16,13), the spirit of the Lord, which Lange interprets as the Holy Spirit, came upon David; the Holy Spirit then gave him the ability to write psalms foretelling the messianic kingdom to come:

> As, then, David was from this time on a prophet of God and under the Cross, before he came into the government of the kingdom, he produced many psalms out of the fullness of the Spirit, and thereby he received the gift of θεοπνευστίας [inspiration] to write in the Psalms of the great mysteries of the kingdom of the Messiah.[39]

---

[37] Lange: Biblisch-Historisches Licht und Recht, Vol. 1, 276–277.
[38] See Irwin: Neither Voice nor Heart Alone, 30–32.
[39] Lange: Biblisch-Historisches Licht und Recht, Vol. 1, 303: "Wie denn David von dieser Zeit an ein Prophete Gottes war und unter dem Creutze, ehe er zur Verwaltung des Reichs kam,

In contrast to Saul's temporary gift of prophecy, David's was a lasting gift that remained with him even when obscured through his sins, enabling him to return to a state of grace through his penitential psalms. Nevertheless, the fact that Saul had previously experienced the spirit of God predisposed him to respond to this prophetic music to the extent that the evil spirit left him for a while.

For Lange, music has both natural and divine power, and the proper use of music is a combination of the two. Its natural ability to stir the emotions should be directed toward the praise of God.

> On a natural level it is noble and of great excellence, and in its harmony it is distinguished by a foundation that comes from God himself but is almost beyond scrutiny. Thus it can rightly be used for any awakening of the spirit that has the praise of God as its goal.[40]

This, says Lange, is how it was used in the schools of prophecy, in the Levitic temple services, and in the choirs described in Revelation. The improper use of music, on the other hand, is familiar from common experience, so much so that Lange considers it almost superfluous to mention. It is found above all in the great courts with their idle comedies and other theatrical performances and ear-pleasing music. What is noteworthy in Lange's discussion of this episode is that he never separates vocal and instrumental music, as if one were more sacred than another. Nor does he distinguish between the effect of the sung text and the appeal of the musical sound. Because David had the Holy Spirit within, and because Saul had a level of responsiveness based on experience, the music served a holy purpose. In the abstract, music is both natural and divine, and its use by a holy person for a holy purpose sanctifies it.

## 6  The Psalms

In the introduction to Lange's commentary on the Psalms, *Davidisch-Salomonisches Licht und Recht*, he describes David not only as the author of psalms but also as "ein vortreffliches Vorbild" ("an outstanding type") to Christ, foreshadowing the Messiah in his threefold office as high priest, king, and prophet. Though not descended from the tribe of Levi or the lineage of Aaron, he was anointed by God with God's Spirit and entrusted with the organization of Levitic worship. The book of Psalms was written through divine inspiration, which enabled David to

---

viele Psalmen aus der Fülle des Geistes gemachet, und dabey die Gabe der θεοπνευστίας empfangen hat, von hohen Geheimnissen des Reichs des Meßiä in den Psalmen zuschreiben."

[40] Lange: Biblisch-Historisches Licht und Recht, Vol. 1, 305: "Da sie auch natürlicher weise sehr edel und von recht grosser Vortreflichkeit ist, und in ihrer Harmonie sich ein von Gott selbst herrührender, ob wol fast unerforschlicher, Grund sich hervor thut; so solte sie billig zu einer solchen Erweckung des Gemüths gebrauchet werden, welche das Lob Gottes zum Zweck hat."

depict the reign of the Messiah in the new covenant as a spiritual kingdom and to foretell its spread throughout the earth, particularly in the final Sabbath period.[41]

David was not the only psalmist with a prophetic gift, however. The three Levites placed in charge of temple music—Asaph, Heman, and Jeduthun—were all said to have the gift of prophecy and to be led by the Holy Spirit, though only Asaph was credited with writing a significant number of psalms. When Jeduthun or the children of Korah are mentioned in psalm inscriptions, the meaning is usually that they are to sing or play the psalms written by David.

The importance of the Psalms rests not only in their accord with all of Mosaic and Jewish history but also as an indispensable link in the chain of divine revelation that reaches to the evangelists and apostles.[42] Not only do Christ and the apostles cite the Psalms in numerous passages, which Lange lists in detail, but the psalms themselves, in Lange's interpretation, contain frequent prophecies of Christ and of the end times. They combine law and gospel in a way that no other book of the Old Testament does. The knowledge and practice of inward worship expressed in the psalms exceeds that of the rest of the old dispensation to the extent that they are really suited for the new dispensation of the gospel.[43]

As for the music, Lange notes that the word "psalm" is derived from the Greek word meaning "to pluck" and therefore connotes the playing of a stringed instrument or singing while playing. Accordingly, in writing of the value of music, Lange specifically includes both vocal and instrumental music. His introduction to the book of Psalms has a general statement about music similar to but even more positive than that quoted above from his Chronicles commentary:

> Music, both vocal and instrumental, has a special θεῖον; that is, it has in itself that by which one can properly recognize and marvel at the wisdom and goodness of the Creator as the One who placed its [music's] foundation into human nature, arranging human understanding with keenness and reflection for harmonic inventions in song and sound, also arranging the tongue and voice in such a way that people become skilled in music through the astute art and practice of music; in string playing the fingers must also come into service very skillfully. According to its origin, which in this understanding is divine, and according to its natural excellence, music has the attribute of quite perceptibly and notably moving and delighting not only the hearing but also the mind with its harmonic charms. Indeed, depending on the manner in which the material and melody are organized and the instrument played, not only pleasant and cheerful but also gloomy and sad emotions can be evoked.[44]

---

[41] Joachim Lange: Davidisch-Salomonisches Licht und Recht. Oder Richtige und Erbauliche Erklärung Der geistreichen Psalmen Davids, Nach ihrem dogmatischen, moralischen und prophetischen Innhalt: Insonderheit von der Person, dem Mittleramte, auch dem Reiche Christi, Und von dem rechtschaffenen Wesen des Christenthums: Wie auch der lehrreichen Sprüche, auch des Predigers und Des Hohenliedes Salomons. Dazu kömmt Die Auslegung Des Propheten Daniels. Halle, Leipzig: [n.p.], 1737, 3–4.
[42] Lange: Davidisch-Salomonisches Licht und Recht, 5.
[43] Lange: Davidisch-Salomonisches Licht und Recht, 6–7.
[44] Lange: Davidisch-Salomonisches Licht und Recht, 9–10: "Die Music, so wol die Vocale, als Instrumentale, hat ein besonderes θεῖον, das ist, sie hat dasjenige in sich, woraus man die Weisheit und Güte des Schöpfers erkennen und billig zu bewundern hat: als der den Grund dazu in die Natur des Menschen geleget, und wie seinen Verstand mit Witz und Nachdencken, zur harmonischen Erfindung im Gesange und Klange, also auch seine Zunge und Stimme also eingerichtet hat, daß sie durch die sinnreiche Kunst und Uebung

In this context, Lange briefly traces the history of music, giving a slightly different account from the commentary on Genesis 4, where he seems to follow the tradition of crediting Jubal with the invention of musical instruments. Here he asserts that both instrumental and vocal music were practiced before the flood and that Jubal and the Canaanites cast aside the proper use of music in their decadent fiddling.[45] In Egypt, on the other hand, the Hebrew people made good use of music and passed it on to the "patriarchal church," as evidenced by the song of Moses and Miriam's playing of drums and other instruments with the Israelite women. Misuse also continued, however, as during the worship of the Golden Calf. With the schools for prophecy, as we saw in the time of Samuel, music was made a holy exercise. This practice reached its peak with David, who, as an outstanding musician inspired by God, arranged for the distribution of the 4,000 Levitic musicians throughout the year. Through their vocal and instrumental music they were a distinguished part of Levitic worship. On the basis of different Hebrew words, Lange explains that some psalms were sung without instruments, some with, and some may have involved an alternation of singing and playing. The exact nature of the instruments is unknown, but it is clear that some were blown, others plucked. Nor are the melodies or poetic patterns known, and one can only speculate about the meaning of the word *Selah* that appears so often.

Significantly, Lange does not make of Hebrew worship an allegory or symbol for internalized devotion in Christian worship but rather uses it to support a greater respect for music in worship in his own time: "Singing and making music, as long as it maintains its proper seriousness and a judicious simplicity, is a fitting part of public worship also in the time of the new covenant. It should, therefore, occur with appropriate faithful devotion and should not be neglected."[46] Echoing the many complaints of writers over the preceding century, Lange says that unfortunately many parishioners come only for the sermon (not even listening attentively to it), arriving too late for the music and leaving too soon.[47] While psalm singing can be appropriate and valuable, the church need not restrict itself to the poetic texts of the Bible. There is, Lange says, a rich treasure of hymns that shed light on evangelical beliefs and duties through pure and pleasant poetry. One should make use of these in both congregational and domestic worship, always keeping

---

zur Music geschickt sind, und bey den Säiten=Spielen ihnen auch die Finger geschicklichst zu Diensten stehen müssen. Nach ihrem Ursprunge, der in solchem Verstande göttlich ist, und nach ihrer natürlichen Vortreflichkeit hat die Music auch die Eigenschaft, daß sie mit ihrer harmonischen Anmuthigkeit nicht allein das Gehöre, sondern auch das Gemüth gar sinnlich und mercklich rühret und belustiget, ja, nach dem die Materie und die Melodie beschaffen ist, und das Instrument darnach geschlagen wird, nicht allein vergnügte und fröliche, sondern auch betrübte und traurige, Gemüths=Bewegungen erwecken kan."

[45] Lange: Davidisch-Salomonisches Licht und Recht, 10.
[46] Lange: Davidisch-Salomonisches Licht und Recht, 11: "Das Singen und Musiciren, wenn es nur bey der rechten Gravität und an sich sinnreichen Einfalt bleibet, ist billig auch zur Zeit des neuen Bundes ein Stück des öffentlichen Gottesdienstes, und soll daher billig wie mit gläubiger Andacht geschehen, also auch nicht versäumet werden."
[47] See, for instance, the criticisms of seventeenth-century Rostock theologians in Irwin: Neither Voice nor Heart Alone, 79–80.

in mind Apostle Paul's admonitions in Ephesians and Colossians for directing the singing to the right purpose.[48]

The "spiritual practice of music," then, does not indicate an internalization of music to the exclusion of audible music. While it is not entirely clear, Lange implies that actual music will be heard in the kingdom of glory when the new song is sung to Christ with harps and incense before the throne in Revelation 5,8. Neither is temple worship to be taken as a metaphor for a spiritualized worship in the age of the new covenant. David already had the awareness of the Messiah, but he felt a special presence of God in certain physical spaces. Commenting on Psalm 26,8 ("I love the house in which you dwell"), Lange notes that the temple had not yet been built but that the presence of God was experienced in the tent of meeting when the pillar of cloud rested over the tabernacle. While the church buildings of Lange's time were not comparable to the tent of meeting or to the temple but rather to Jewish synagogues, still they are places where, however imperfectly, the mysteries of God's kingdom are proclaimed and God is praised with music. Therefore, he urges, these places ought to be visited diligently for the hearing of the Word in faithful devotion, following the example of the Levites.[49]

Psalm 150 offers Lange an opportunity for a different perspective on the space of worship. He notes that the Hebrew word מָשִׁיעַ, which is usually translated as "firmament" in English, referred to the "immeasurably wide and high space of air" surrounding the earth's atmosphere and containing countless heavenly bodies in its incomprehensible extent. Lange is unsure how God might be praised in such a space and thus interprets it as referring figuratively to the heaven of glory. Accordingly, as the musical instruments named in this psalm are unfamiliar, it is useless to engage in speculation about them; rather, they should be taken in a spiritual sense as referring to the various gifts of grace by which the heart breaks forth in praise of God. Levitic music is thus a prefiguring of this variety of gifts. Whether metaphor or literal expectation, Lange wishes for himself and his readers to be among the "holy choirs of heavenly musicians and to join with them eternally in giving voice to the joyous and blessed Hallelujah."[50]

Ultimately, the music of the Levites has its counterpart in the new song of the harpists and choirs of the book of Revelation. Although David's songs were all new, comments Lange in relation to Psalm 33, the term "new song" applies to the Sabbath period of the new covenant as described above. Writing about "new song" in his commentary on Psalm 96, Lange says that the old song of praise was that of Moses in gratitude for physical deliverance. The "new song" is based on spiritual deliverance and release from the oppression of the Antichrist. It began with the song of the angels at the birth of the Messiah but only finds full expression during

---

[48] Lange: Davidisch-Salomonisches Licht und Recht, 11.
[49] Lange: Davidisch-Salomonisches Licht und Recht, 131.
[50] Lange: Davidisch-Salomonisches Licht und Recht, 673: "Mein inniger Wunsch zu Gott ist, daß auch ich mit allen meinen Lesern unter den heiligen Chören der himmlischen Musicanten möge erfunden werden, und auf ewig mit ihnen das fröliche und selige Hallelujah anstimmen."

the seventh trumpet when it will resound loudly in heaven and on earth. Lange then presents the relevant passages from Revelation (5,8–9; 14,3; 15,3; 19,1–8) as "a more complete antitype" to the deliverance from Egypt and includes also those other passages from the psalms and prophets that explicitly mention the "new song": Psalms 33,3; 98,1; 149,1; Isaiah 42,10. In keeping with his Pietist theology, Lange explains that the new song must be accompanied by a new heart, though unfortunately many sing songs of praise with an old heart that is dead to God.[51] Criticism of the unregenerate does not play a large part in Lange's treatment of this topic, however.

In his commentary on Psalm 149,1, Lange draws a connection to Revelation 19, describing the way in which the heavenly and earthly choirs are joined: "the triumph announced here is sung in such a way that the heavenly choirs from the new Jerusalem join in singing the triumph songs of the church on earth, or those on earth provide an echo, as it were, to those in heaven."[52] After citing several of the verses of Revelation 19, Lange then recalls the conclusion of the song of Moses with its prophecy of vengeance on God's enemies and mercy to the land of his people (Deut 32,43).

There are many other places in scripture, he recognizes, that have the same content, even if they do not explicitly mention "new song." One of these is Psalm 92, which has the inscription "a song for the Sabbath day." In interpreting this, Lange begins with the prefigurings: the first Sabbath as the seventh day of creation, the weekly Sabbaths of the Jews, the Sabbath year and the Jubilee year (after seven times seven years), and the conquest of Jericho on the seventh day with seven priests, seven trumpets, seven times around the city. There are prophecies of a Sabbath period of peace on earth, but the final Sabbath will be the thousand years of Christ's reign ushered in by the seventh angel blowing the seventh trumpet. All of this culminates in the singing of the new song with full choirs and instruments on heaven and earth joining in praise of God.[53] In doing so, people become like the angels, but they have even more reason to offer praise: the angels praise because of creation, but humans praise because of their redemption, sanctification and glorification (*Erlösung, Heiligung, Seligmachung*). In the act of praising they taste even higher delights of God's blessedness, making praise less a duty than a blessing.[54]

The contrast between merely being created and being given new birth is discussed in Psalm 149 as a basis for the joy of praising God with dancing, drums, and harps. The word *made* in verse 2 ("Let Israel rejoice in him that made him") signifies, according to Lange, not only the natural creation but also the supernatural rebirth, and it is the latter that awakens joy. Because of the assurance of fulfillment

---

[51] Lange: Davidisch-Salomonisches Licht und Recht, 425.
[52] Lange: Davidisch-Salomonisches Licht und Recht, 671: "als darinnen der alhier verkündigte Triumph also besungen wird, daß die himmlischen Chöre aus dem neuen Jerusalem zu den Triumph=Liedern der Kirche auf Erden mit einstimmen, oder die auf Erden zu denen im Himmel gleichsam ein Echo geben."
[53] Lange: Davidisch-Salomonisches Licht und Recht, 407.
[54] Lange: Davidisch-Salomonisches Licht und Recht, 408.

of prophecy, the children of Israel can sing a song of triumph, and the church on earth can sound forth a joyous echo of the joyous sound in heavenly Jerusalem as described in Revelation.[55] Non-human creatures are not excluded from the joy of redemption. In Psalm 148, we see sun, moon, stars, earth, animals, trees, and birds being called on to praise the Lord. Lange explains that when the Sabbath period arrives, the curse that came upon all creatures because of human sin will be lifted and the lost blessing will be reinstated. This is in accordance with Romans 8,21, where it is projected that creation itself will be set free from service to that which is perishable. When the blessed condition is restored, writes Lange, everything in the kingdom of nature will serve the converted and sanctified people to the praise and glory of God.[56]

## 7   The Gospels

Music, as is well known, does not play a significant role in the gospel accounts, but there are two passages that lend themselves to commentary on the topic. The first is found in Luke's account of Jesus' birth with the angels singing to the shepherds. This becomes for Lange an occasion to write about praise as the highest form of service to God and also about angels as models for humans.

As told by Luke, a single angel appeared first, announcing the birth of the Savior, and was then joined by a multitude of angels singing "Glory to God in the highest." While Luke leaves the number unspecified, Lange draws on Daniel 7,10 and Revelation 5,11 to conclude that it was a massive number like thousands of thousands. Lest we imagine some overwhelming chaos of sound, Lange reminds us that God is a God of order, and this applies above all to angels. They would have been divided into legions or regiments, like an army, under the authority of an archangel and under the ultimate authority of Christ as Prince. Their task is to praise God, who alone is worthy of praise both in himself and in his works, especially in offering his son for the sake of the human race. It is cause for a manifold and unending Hallelujah to arise from the human race, and the angels take part in this joy through their song of thanks and praise. It reminds Lange of the angels' song in Isaiah 6, "Holy, holy, holy is the Lord of hosts," though neither here nor in his Isaiah commentary does he comment further on any musical significance of Isaiah's vision.

The lesson to be learned here is that, in order for believers to become like angels in the life to come, they should devote themselves to the praise of God in this life. Unlike prayer, where one is also concerned with oneself, praise is directed exclusively to glorifying God. Material for offering praise has been provided most of all in the Psalms. Lange quotes extensively here from Psalms 103 and 144–150. Psalm 150 leads Lange to remark on the temple music of both

---

[55] Lange: Davidisch-Salomonisches Licht und Recht, 672.
[56] Lange: Davidisch-Salomonisches Licht und Recht, 670.

voices and instruments, noting that David was a master of instrumental music from the time of his youth. Without any specific comment on instrumental music in his own time, Lange more generally urges readers to join David in applying all the strength of grace received to say, "Praise the Lord, O my soul, and all that is within me, praise his holy name."[57]

The other reference to music in the gospels is the short report in Matthew 26,30 and Mark 14,26: "When they had sung the hymn, they went out to the Mount of Olives." Significantly, Lange does not read this as referring to just any hymn of their choosing, as is done today, but to the Jewish Passover tradition of singing the Hallel. Jesus and his disciples would probably have sung Psalms 113 and 114 before the Passover meal and Psalms 115 through 118 after the meal and the institution of Holy Communion. As a conclusion, Psalm 136 with its 26-fold repetition of "for his mercy endures forever" would have marked the end of the observance, and Lange speculates that this may be the specific hymn to which the verse refers. Through his example, Lange concludes, Jesus demonstrated that no meal is to be carried out without prayer and thanksgiving.[58]

## 8  The Epistles

Two passages from the Pauline epistles have been normative for Christian musical practice, though the various interpretations of the passages have emphasized different elements. On the one hand, Paul specifically instructs the faith communities of Ephesus and Colossae to sing but also to do so "filled with the Spirit" (Eph 5,19) and "with gratitude in your hearts" (Col 3,16).[59] Lange's commentary is well balanced with attention to both the musical and devotional aspects.

As explanation for the specific connotation of "psalms, hymns, and spiritual songs" or, in German, "Psalmen, Lobgesänge und Lieder," Lange notes that these terms have more to do with the manner in which they are composed and performed than with the content. The subject matter may be the same, but they may differ in whether they are written in poetic meter or not, whether they are accompanied by instruments or not, and whether they are sung by one choir or more.[60] More specifically, Lange identifies the terms as follows:

---

[57]  Joachim Lange: Evangelisches Licht und Recht, Oder Richtige und Erbauliche Erklärung der heiligen Vier Evangelisten, und der Apostel=Geschichte. Vol. 2. 2nd ed. Halle, Leipzig: [n.p.], 1736, 54.

[58]  Lange: Evangelisches Licht und Recht, Vol. 2, 337.

[59]  In saying that Paul gives these instructions, I am reflecting Lange's understanding of the authorship of these letters. Modern scholarship places these two letters in the category of "disputed" writings of Paul, though the issue continues to be analyzed and debated. See Paul and Pseudepigraphy. Ed. by Stanley E. Porter and Gregory P. Fewster. Leiden, Boston: Brill, 2013, esp. 173–195.

[60]  Joachim Lange: Apostolisches Licht und Recht, Das ist Richtige und erbauliche Erklärung Der sämtlichen Apostolischen Briefe, Pauli, Jacobi, Petri, Johannis und Judä. Halle: Waisenhaus, 1729, 661.

1. *Psalmen* are songs accompanied by a musical instrument, as was known of the psalms of David and practiced in public worship.
2. *Lobgesänge* are those songs, of which there are many in the Old Testament, in which God is praised for his being, his will, his works, and his beneficences.
3. *Lieder* are all other songs dealing with spiritual matters, whether in the form of instruction, exhortation, or consolation, which may also include the praise of God. Both *Lieder* and *Lobgesänge* may at the same time also be psalms when accompanied by musical instruments.

In the Luther Bible, *Lieder* is modified by *geistlich* in Ephesians and by *geistlich, lieblich* in Colossians. Lange also defines these terms:

4. Those songs are *geistlich* that deal with spiritual matters. If in their composition they "flowed out of a good treasure of the heart and full of spirit and power," then they can also be called *geistreich*. [This was a word frequently used in connection with hymns at the time, most notably in the title of Freylinghausen's hymnal, *Geistreiches Gesangbuch*. While the modern meaning of *geistreich* is "witty" or "brilliant," the relevant 18th century meaning was that of a more intense level of "spiritual."[61]]
5. *Lieblich* is similar to *geistreich* in this context and connotes that the song is pleasing to God because it is not just lovely to hear but is sung "out of the fullness of a heart sanctified by the grace of God."[62]

Lange's further discussion of these two passages expresses a high level of appreciation of music. As in his statements in Chronicles and Psalms, he calls both vocal and instrumental music a "very noble science and practice, and certainly a true gift of God in nature, which is sanctified through the material and devotion of those who sing and play."[63] This is a significant statement that bridges the view of music as an element of nature with that of music as sacred. Lange uses music as an example of how natural arts and sciences can be made holy through the grace of God and used to praise him. The ability to write a good verse, set it well to a certain form and melody, and then sing it skillfully with pleasing instrumental accompaniment is a "very lovely science and gift of nature." When it then penetrates the senses and sets the soul in motion, the heart is filled with the Holy Spirit, and music is sanctified.

The corollary to the sacred use of music is that it can also be misused, which can happen in various ways. The most obvious is in the singing of worldly songs, especially drinking songs. More subtle is when one pays attention only to the sound

---

[61] Grimm and Grimm: Deutsches Wörterbuch, Vol. 5, col. 2791. URL: https://www.woerterbuchnetz.de/DWB?lemid=G05877 (accessed August 2, 2023).
[62] Lange: Apostolisches Licht und Recht, 808.
[63] Lange: Apostolisches Licht und Recht, 661: "eine sehr edle Wissenschaft und Ubung, und gewiß eine rechte Gabe Gottes in der Natur, welche durch die Materie und Andacht der singenden und spielenden geheiliget wird." All the remaining material in this section comes from either pages 661–662 (Ephesians commentary) or 807–809 (Colossians commentary) of *Apostolisches Licht und Recht*.

of the music without any devotion; then one is nothing more than "a noisy gong or a clanging cymbal" (1 Cor 13,1). A performer can also misuse music, observes Lange, by falling in love with his own artistry and skill, listening to himself with pleasure rather than singing to the Lord. A "simple heart" is needed for singing to the Lord.

Lange offers pastoral understanding to those who have good intentions of singing and praying with devotion but find their minds easily distracted. Not that this is to be taken lightly, for the Apostle Paul instructs us to keep alert in singing and praying (Eph 6,18), but a distinction is to be made between the fantasies of the mind and the will of the heart. Devotion, says Lange, depends on the heart or will being directed toward God in holy desire: "But the heart can be and remain directed to God even when the power of imagination in one's head is taken over by extraneous images and thoughts."[64] One should try to ward off such distractions but not to become anxious or fearful that one's prayers will not be heard.

Remarkably, in stressing again his disapproval of those who come to worship too late for the music, Lange goes so far as to call singing the main element of the service. If what is to happen is service to God ("Gottesdienst"), then singing fits that criterion in a way that a sermon does not. Through a sermon God serves us with his Word, whereas singing is a means of serving and honoring God.

While singing is a way of giving honor to God, it is also for edification, or, in the words of Colossians, for teaching and admonishing one another. These two factors belong together, Lange explains, as teaching is directed toward the understanding and admonishing toward the will. Yet this is not left to the teachers alone; because the listeners belong to the spiritual priesthood, there is a collective or reciprocal responsibility. Accordingly, this does not take place solely in public worship but also in a house church within the family or a gathering of Christian friends. Believers offer encouragement to one another and give witness to their living hope of eternal life. The clergy do have a responsibility to instruct the congregation in the correct meaning of the hymns, as many are not understood or sung properly. Lange recommends that preachers take the first part of their sermons for this instruction as fits the liturgical year. Especially for those listeners who cannot read the Bible and learn by hearing, the hymns are more familiar than Bible verses. When people are ill, they are better served when the pastor quotes hymns they know rather than Bible verses they do not know. Hymn singing is also worthwhile for those who have leisure when traveling, and workers can sing hymns while they work, as long as it is not done merely out of habit and is not accompanied by idle conversation.

Germans can be particularly grateful for the rich supply of "geistreiche Gesänge," Lange declares. He is pleased with the numerous different hymnals published in various places that, collectively, contain so many hymns they "can scarcely be counted." German poetry has been brought to a "high degree of

---

[64] Lange: Apostolisches Licht und Recht, 809: "Es kan aber das Herz zu Gott gerichtet seyn und bleiben, wenn auch schon die im Haupte befindliche Einbildungs=Kraft mit fremden Bildern und Gedancken eingenommen wird."

perfection," and the best and holiest application of this art is in hymnody. Clearly, Lange is a defender of new hymns as well as old, and he is convinced that early Christians also created new hymns out of the "fullness of the Spirit" and out of the freedom of public worship. In addition, as hymns are important for refuting scriptural errors, particularly those of the papacy, Lange also takes pride in the success of the evangelical church for making the Bible available, particularly the Canstein Bible Institute for publishing hundreds of thousands of Bibles in various editions.

An aspect of music's value that we might expect to see discussed in this commentary is less apparent than expected, i.e., its power to affect the emotions. This can be explained by the ambivalence of Pietists toward emotions.[65] Lange does use the word "Affect" twice in these passages. In the commentary on Col 3,16 of how hymns are to be used for teaching, Lange explains that, as humans are made of both body and soul, both must work together. It depends most of all, he says, on the affect of the heart, for singing with the mouth is of no use if the heart is not in accord. Singing is a kind of prayer, and the same devotion is required of both. This explanation is not about how music creates the proper affect but about how the proper affect is essential for the hymn singing to be of value. In commenting on Eph 5,20 ("giving thanks to God the Father at all times"), Lange again uses the word "Affect" as a disposition of the heart. Noteworthy is that he calls for it to be "beständig" ("constant"); in other words, it is no changeable emotion but a permanent orientation of the soul.

Lange's discussion of the phrase "Let the word of Christ dwell in you richly" elucidates this point. The "word of Christ" should be rightly understood as the person of Christ with his Word dwelling in the heart. The Word is not a guest who might then go away; rather, to use a different metaphor, the Word is like a perennial plant in the heart, where it spreads and is digested through faith, becoming daily nourishment for the soul. Lange had used the Luther translation when citing Col 3,16 ("Lasset das Wort Christi reichlich unter euch wohnen"), but in his commentary he pointed out that the Greek ἐν ὑμῖν that Luther had translated as "unter euch" ("among you") was really "in euch" ("in you"). Christ is thus not just among Christians but is in them, dwelling within, rooted within. This concept is explored in greater depth in the fourth volume of Lange's *Die richtige Mittel=Straße*, subtitled *Christus in uns*.[66] The *Mittel=Straße* series follows the order of salvation from "Christ for us" in justification through rebirth with illumination to sanctification with Christ dwelling within. This level of communion with Christ is clearly aspirational rather than an every-Sunday worship experience.

---

[65] Cf. Irwin: Neither Voice nor Heart Alone, 139, and discussion in previous chapter on Francke's view of joy.
[66] Joachim Lange: Der richtigen Mittel=Straße Zwischen den Irrthümern und Abwegen Vierter und letzter Theil / In der Lehre Christus in uns zur Heiligung. Halle: Renger, 1714.

## 9 Music in the Book of Revelation

The importance for Lange of the Book of Revelation should be apparent from the numerous references already cited. Throughout his commentaries on other books of the Bible, Lange refers to John's Apocalypse as the culmination of biblical prophecy. The Bible forms a unified whole, and a passage of the Old Testament can shed light on a New Testament passage or vice versa. It is worth noting that, even though I have organized this chapter according to the customary biblical order, Lange's commentary on Revelation was the second volume to be published in his "Licht und Recht" series, following the *Apostolisches Licht und Recht* (1729) on New Testament epistles. In the preface to his *Apocalyptisches Licht und Recht* (1730), he reports that he would have been prepared to include it with the epistles commentary, but as that was already quite long (824 pages), the combined volume would have been too large for the binder. Issuing the Revelation commentary separately has the advantage that he can add a thorough explanation and analysis of Vitringa's system of exegesis, thus aiding the reader's understanding of the book.

Lange recognizes that the Book of Revelation is difficult to comprehend, and even when one believes one has arrived at the Holy Spirit's meaning, not all readers agree. No religious community, he points out, has a formal statement on apocalyptic matters in its confession, making it all the more difficult for exegetes to come to a common interpretation. That should not prevent anyone from a diligent pursuit of the correct understanding of the book's meaning, however. The groundwork has been laid not only by Vitringa but also by Spener in his writings on the hope of better times. Lange reviews in his preface the points he had made in previous works to defend Spener's position. Contrary to the interpretation of many, the binding of the Antichrist has not yet occurred, and the thousand-year reign has not begun. Yet the promise of the blessed times to come is a matter for joy, and Lange feels impelled to explain how the prophecies will be fulfilled.[67]

Living as we now are in the kingdom of grace, John's apocalyptic vision reveals the kingdom of glory that is to come. This is particularly vivid in the depiction of the twenty-four elders singing a new song while holding harps and golden vessels (Rev 5,8–9). Admittedly, the music is not of primary importance in this vision, for the musical images are signifiers of the Levites as harp-players and the priests as the trumpeters, and together these stand for the elect, who are spiritual priests. Furthermore, in an unusual realistic observation, Lange remarks that John could hardly have heard any harp playing because both hands of the elders were full, and they could not have played the harp while also carrying bowls of incense.[68]

Yet even if these are symbols of spiritual matters, John could well have imagined that he heard music. Thus the music is in fact significant, and Lange is moved to describe here, as he would do in his Old Testament commentaries, how excellent the music of David's time was and how well organized and skilled the

---

[67] This paragraph is a condensation of Lange's preface to his *Apocalyptisches Licht und Recht*.
[68] Lange: Apocalyptisches Licht und Recht, 62.

Levites and priests were in their singing and instrument playing. Recalling the glorious music that attended the dedication of the first temple, Lange calls it "an excellent foreshadowing of the glorious praise of God that shall and will resound in the kingdom of God in the kingdom of grace and of glory."[69] For illustrating the kingdom of grace, he recalls Paul's words in Ephesians 5,18–20 and Colossians 3,16, and for the kingdom of glory he references not just the immediate context of Revelation 5 but also passages of chapters 14 and 19. There is no implication here that Hebrew temple music is merely a metaphor for a spiritual meaning that would be realized at a later stage. Lange praises music in words similar to those we encountered in his other commentaries: "One must recognize here the excellence of vocal and instrumental music. Certainly there rests within it, in accordance with its depth and harmony, a certain ϑεῖον, which rightly leads one back with wonder to its Designer, God."[70]

The proper use of music, however, is found only among believers. The abuse of music among "children of this world" is great, and even among believers few truly know how to use it well. If someone has a musical gift, he should use it to the correct purpose. The music that one has learned as a youth should continue to serve to awaken the praise of God. In such a way believing Christians become like angels already here on earth.[71]

For those who use music improperly, the words of Revelation 18,21–22 apply: when Babylon is destroyed, the sound of harpists, minstrels, flutists, and trumpeters will be heard no more. The Luther Bible did not translate this verse with particularly pejorative terms for those who made music ("Stimme der Sänger und Saitenspieler, Pfeifer und Posauner"), so Lange turns to the Vulgate Latin to elaborate on the word translated as "singers." *Citharoedus*, according to Lange, means "those who sing artificially along with their instruments" ("welche zu den Instrumenten künstlich singen").[72] For the meaning of *Saitenspieler* he turns to the Greek *mousikon*, which then is translated as the German *Musikant*, a term generally applied pejoratively to street musicians or, as in the NRSV translation above, minstrels. Why he says they sing "mit blosser Stimme" ("with naked voice"? "with voice alone"?) is unclear, but he applies this as a negative judgment on Italian singing, "in which the Italians, and especially the Romans, excel above other nations, and they also have a special kind of abused people."[73] Lange seems to have some sympathy for what castrati have suffered, but their mode of singing is itself an abuse of music.

---

[69] Lange: Apocalyptisches Licht und Recht, 62: "daß solches alles ein vortrefliches **Fürbild** gewesen von dem herrlichen Lobe Gottes, welches im Reiche Gottes, in dem Reiche der Gnaden und der Herrlichkeit, erschallen sollte und würde."

[70] Lange: Apocalyptisches Licht und Recht, 62: "Man hat hierbey die **Vortreflichkeit** der Vocal- und Instrumental- Music zu erkennen. Gewiß es lieget in derselben an sich selbst, nach ihren Tiefen und nach ihrer Harmonie, ein solches ϑεῖον, welches einen billig auf den Urheber, Gott, mit Verwunderung zurück führet."

[71] Lange: Apocalyptisches Licht und Recht, 63.

[72] Lange: Apocalyptisches Licht und Recht, 158.

[73] Lange: Apocalyptisches Licht und Recht, 158: "darinnen die **Italiäner**, und sonderlich die Römer, vor andern Nationen excelliren, dazu auch eine besondere Art gemißbrauchter Leute haben."

The proper mode of praising God cannot be learned by imitating the song of God's children but only by inner conversion. The new person can then sing the new song. While Lange looks for symbolic rather than literal meaning in the numbers that appear in these chapters, the prophecy of Rev 14,3 that only 144,000 could sing the new song signifies a limitation: no one will succeed to the church triumphant whose soul has not been sanctified.[74] The number 24 in reference to the elders around the throne (Rev 4,4), on the other hand, is a more expansive symbol: it refers to the whole body of Christ that is already in the church triumphant as well as to those who will arrive there when their spiritual victory is complete.[75] Interestingly, the term *Musicanten* loses its pejorative connotation when applied to heavenly musicians, who also include the angels.[76] As for the number of angels, calculated depending on the translation of Rev 5,11 as many thousands of thousands or a hundred thousand times ten thousand, Lange is satisfied to call it an incalculable number. The resulting sound of these countless angels singing with loud voice to God and the Lamb, joined by the four beasts and twenty-four elders is "indescribably glorious" even before the voices of all other creatures are added (Rev 5,13).

In an encouraging word to his readers that seems to imply both the reality of the heavenly music and the spiritual preparation required, Lange writes, "Blessed is the one who in the future will be able to join in the singing" ("Wohl dem, der künftig wird mit einstimmen können!").[77] Reflecting on the joy that surrounds the marriage of the Lamb (Rev 19,7), Lange observes that the German has two words that seem to mean the same, *freuen* and *frölich sein*. This is partly for emphasis, he says, but there is also a difference: *Freude* rests deep in the heart, whereas *Frölichkeit* flows out from the heart to give expression to that joy in words, gestures, and works. Both belong together, he believes, and are distinct from earthly and sinful joy because they are directed toward the glory of God, not one's own honor or desires.[78]

The repeated shouts of "Hallelujah" in this heavenly song of joy recall the Hallel psalms (113–118) that were sung by the Hebrews during their festivals. We encountered them in the commentary on Jesus' Passover meal, but here Lange mentions the Feast of Tabernacles. This triumphal song in Revelation 19 is a song of praise to glorify God for completing the process of salvation that he had begun. The 24 elders represent the church militant on earth that is progressing toward

---

[74] Lange: Apocalyptisches Licht und Recht, 134. This should not be confused with the Reformed concept of limited atonement, by which God determined who would receive saving grace. Lange adhered to the Lutheran position that grace was offered to all but that not all would respond. In an appendage to his *Prophetisches Licht und Recht* entitled "Biblischer Anhang Von der Evangelischen Hauptlehre, Der Allgemeinen Gnade Gottes," Lange explains that God's grace is general, not particular, but that free will allows humans to receive or reject that grace. His defense of free will was central to his criticism of Christian Wolff and other philosophers that he accused of turning humans into mental machines.
[75] Lange: Apocalyptisches Licht und Recht, 53.
[76] Lange: Apocalyptisches Licht und Recht, 134.
[77] Lange: Apocalyptisches Licht und Recht, 66.
[78] Lange: Apocalyptisches Licht und Recht, 161.

triumph; joining in song with the church triumphant in heaven indicates that both are governed by the same Spirit and share in the same benefits. When they sing "Amen, Hallelujah," Lange takes this as a reference to Psalm 106,48 as well as the preceding verse (47) in which the Jewish people pray to be redeemed and to be gathered from among the nations in order to praise God's name.[79]

This theme of praise is predominant in Lange's comment on passages about music. His faith is not an internalized or reclusive spirituality but one that celebrates the work of God in history. The prophecies of the Old Testament are tied to the book of Revelation, where their fulfillment can be explained as a historical progression, divided into seven periods. These periods are connected in Lange's commentaries through frequent cross references pointing out types and antitypes and the fulfillment of Old Testament prophecy. The psalms play a large role in connecting prophecy to fulfillment, largely because Lange regards David as holding the threefold Messianic role of prophet, priest, and king. However, his musical skill also validates music's special divine power to move hearts toward the praise of God.

## 10 Excursus on Music and Morality

There is little in the preceding discussion of biblical commentary on music that would identify Lange as a Pietist. His view on the unity of scripture might connect him to Francke, but his prophetic framework connects him more to the Netherlandic Cocceian/Vitringian School. We have seen little of the conflict or ambivalence that Francke expressed in struggling between a metaphorical or literal application of biblical accounts of music. To be sure, the type/antitype approach to biblical interpretation has inherent elements of metaphor, but Lange consistently affirmed both vocal and instrumental music rather than turning the latter into metaphor.

Where Lange's Pietist identity comes to the fore is in the moral theology of music. This is explored not in his biblical commentaries but in his polemical works written in opposition to the Orthodox. Here he addresses the doctrine of adiaphora, known in German as *Mitteldinge* and in English as "indifferent matters." Whereas Lange was open to differing perspectives on the prophetic theology that he derived from Dutch Reformed thinkers, the one issue on which Lange would not compromise was on *Mitteldinge*. This is, as he sees it, such a fundamental error of the orthodox Lutherans that it perverts all other teachings. Of the many places in his writings where he makes this point, one of the most extensively developed is in Part 4 of his *Die richtige Mittel=Straße*. As the title indicates, he is attempting to take a middle path between the spiritualistic fanatics and those who, in his view, falsely claim their orthodoxy. The teaching of orthodox Lutherans on "middle matters," or things that are neither good nor bad in themselves, had, according to Lange, been based on Aristotelian, not Christian, ethics.

---

[79] Lange: Apocalyptisches Licht und Recht, 160.

## 10 Excursus on Music and Morality

In explaining his ethical system, Lange discusses the human situation from a threefold standpoint: the law of nature, of civil society, and of the spiritual community. Crucial to Lange's denial of indifferent actions is his view that all three of these sources of law are in harmony. The law of nature was given by God, and indeed the whole moral law was originally given to humans as images of God. With the Fall, this likeness was mostly extinguished, but there remained sufficient knowledge and power of the will to lead a rational and virtuous life in this world. Civil society, if it is of the right sort, will also be based on this natural law. What is lacking for both natural law and civil law is the knowledge of revealed law that leads to eternal life. The revealed law is not only, as some might think, the Ten Commandments but also the height and depth, length and breadth of these commandments as revealed through the prophets, through Jesus and his disciples; thus, broadly understood, it includes the gospel as well, extending to all voluntary human actions.[80]

Breaking down a moral action into its components, Lange examines the source or agent, the purpose, the manner, and the object. Stated most succinctly in his Latin exposition, Lange writes, "The law of God requires that the agent be spiritual, free of sin and perfectly good."[81] Because there is no such person, damnation can only be avoided through the grace of the gospel, which simultaneously absolves guilt and grants a new spiritual inclination to do good. This capacity increases gradually and enables one to follow the law, if not perfectly, at least truly and sincerely. Lange finds numerous terms for this in Latin, such as *regeneratio, nova creatio, spiritualis circumcisio*, and more, while in German he writes of "Christus in uns." The purpose of every moral action should be to honor God and glorify his name, following the exhortation of Paul to the Corinthians, "Whether you eat or drink or whatever you do, do everything to the honor of God" (1 Cor 10,31).[82] If the person and the purpose are in accordance with Christian faith, then the form of the action will also be proper. Taking Romans 14,23 as his scriptural lead for this point ("whatever does not proceed from faith is sin"), Lange regards self-denial as a necessary corollary, for our own will and desires are not those of Christ.

The object of the action, however, does not factor into the morality of the act. The object itself belongs to the class of natural things rather than moral acts, and we can only label it good or bad in relation to its use or context. Some examples he gives are that wine in itself is good though it can be moral or immoral depending on the use. Cards for playing games are useless things, but as physical objects, they are of good material and therefore become part of a moral act only when used. It is clear from many other passages of Lange's writing that card-playing is always bad, but in his example he manages to find a way in which cards could be part of a good act, i.e., when a faithful and wise father snatches them from his naughty

---

[80] Lange: Mittel=Straße, Vol. 4, 16–17.
[81] Joachim Lange: Antibarbarus Orthodoxiæ Dogmatico-Hermeneuticus, Sive Systema Dogmaum Evangelicorum. Halle: Meyer, 1711, 72: "Lex reqvirit, ut agens sit spiritualis, peccati expers & perfecte bonus."
[82] Lange: Mittel=Straße, Vol. 4, 19.

son and throws them into the fire. Even poison can be part of a good act when it is used to kill noxious insects for the well-being of the household.[83]

In summary, then, there is not even the slightest action of the will that does not have moral value, and there can therefore be no indifferent actions. This extends even to internal thoughts, desires, and affects, for the circumcision of the heart or the indwelling Christ reorients the feelings and thoughts as well as the outward actions.

> For everything that we do or omit to do, we do or omit either outwardly with gestures, words, and deeds or inwardly with thoughts, deliberations, and desires or affects [...]. Therefore it is incontrovertible that for humans nothing is indifferent; rather, all one's actions, be they ever so small and imperceptible, fall within moral teachings or are connected thereto and are thus to be declared legitimate or illegitimate.[84]

Music, however, was generally classified with ceremonial adiaphora, not moral acts. Is there such a category for Lange? He recognizes that "so-called ecclesiastical adiaphora [...] are certain church customs and ceremonies that God in his Word neither commanded nor forbade and that therefore it is a matter of Christian freedom to accept them or not."[85] Like the objects of one's moral actions, however, ecclesiastical adiaphora occur in a context that gives them a moral value, either for good or for ill. The decision to employ a certain rite entails an intention regarding its purpose. As the guideline for all actions is to do everything to the honor of God and in the fear of God, ritual actions must also have this intention. A particular ritual act may be either good or bad, depending on the personal agent and his motivation.

Lange takes church music, and particularly instrumental music, as his example for this category of adiaphora. In itself, such music was neither commanded nor forbidden as a necessary part of public worship at the time of the New Testament. Furthermore, music itself is a praiseworthy area of knowledge, and therefore, objectively speaking, Christian freedom allows for it to be introduced or not. Once it was introduced, however, it took on moral qualities; it became either good or bad depending on the source and intention of the persons who introduced it. Thus, while it remains an ecclesiastical adiaphoron that is not necessary for public worship, it is, when included, either good because it is done appropriately in the fear of God or sinful when it is performed out of mere custom combined with much vanity.

---

[83] Lange: Mittel=Straße, Vol. 4, 21–22.
[84] Lange: Mittel=Straße, Vol. 4, 24–25: "Denn alles / was wir nur thun / oder auch unterlassen / thun oder unterlassen wir entweder euserlich mit Geberden / Worten und Wercken / oder innerlich / mit Gedancken / Rathschlägen und Begierden oder Affecten. [...] Daher es denn unwiedersprechlich ist / daß es dem Menschen keine indifferenz lasse / sondern all sein Beginnen / es möge auch so klein und so subtil seyn / als es immer wolle / unter die Moralitæt setze / oder unter seine Verbindung ziehe / und daher es für rechtmäßig / oder unrechtmäßig / erkläre."
[85] Lange: Mittel=Straße, Vol. 4, 26–27: "Die wahre Art der Natur der so genannten adiaphororum ecclesiasticorum [...] sind gewisse kirchliche Gebräuche und Ceremonien / welche Gott in seinem Worte weder geboten / noch verboten hat / und daher ists in Christlicher Freiheit gestanden / sie anzunehmen / oder nicht."

In consideration of the fact that in itself it was neither directly nor indirectly commanded as a necessary part of public worship at the time of the New Testament, nor was it forbidden as a matter conflicting with it—for in itself it is a praiseworthy discipline—, it has been, objectively speaking and in accordance with Christian freedom, a matter of indifference whether to approve and introduce it or not. But for those who first decided to introduce it in different places and actually carried this out, their action did not remain indifferent; rather, their efforts had moral value and were thus good or evil in accordance with the principles and rationales of those persons who introduced it. And this holds true also thereafter for all musical practices. And although the instrumental music being considered remains an *adiaphorum ecclesiasticum* in public worship, considering that one can well leave it out, still the musical activities are not indifferent but rather either good, if they happen properly in the fear of God, or evil and sinful, if, instead of the fear of God and all that it demands, they only take place as a mere custom accompanied by much vanity. From this it is easy to recognize how the acceptance and retention of ecclesiastical adiaphora in all their forms and categories are to be judged according to true moral principles.[86]

Other activities involving music in secular contexts are also treated by Lange, not as ceremonial adiaphora but among the activities that had been categorized by some as moral adiaphora. Interesting is that Lange not only labels these activities as sinful or useless but "unvernünftig"; whether this should be translated as *unreasonable* or *irrational*, it seems to reflect an 18th century view of rationality and practicality. Here and in many other passages throughout his works, dancing is the subject that most stirs his ire. Whether artful or popular, dance in all the forms known in the society of his time was to him both sinful and irrational.[87] Next came theatrical performances such as comedies and operas. Music appeared in this section only as an appendix, as it is in itself good, but it can be and has been abused. Used properly by those who fear God, music serves to cheer the spirit and sanctify the name of God ("zur Ermunterung des Gemuths / also auch zur Heiligung des Namens Gottes"). As a component of comedies and operas, however, music has been greatly abused. To expound on this point, Lange introduces

---

[86] Lange: Mittel-Straße, Vol. 4, 27–28: "In Ansehung dessen / daß sie an sich selbst weder directe, noch indirecte, als ein nothwendiges Stück des öffentlichen Gottesdiensts zur Zeit des N. Testaments gebothen / noch auch / als eine demselben entgegen stehende Sache / verbothen worden / da sie an sich selbst eine löbliche Wissenschaft ist; so ist der Christlichen Freiheit objective indifferent gewesen / sie zu belieben und einzuführen / oder nicht. Aber diejenigen / so hier und da zu erst diesen Schluß der Einführung gefasset / auch würcklich volzogen / haben / deren Handlung ist nicht mehr indifferent geblieben / sondern hat seine Moralitæt gehabt / und ist also gut / oder böse gewesen / nachdem die einführende Personen nach den principiis und caussis solches ihres Fürnehmens beschaffen gewesen sind. Und dieses gilt denn auch hernach von allen Musicalischen Ubungen. Und ob wol gedachte Instrumental-Music in öffentlichen Versammlungen / in Ansehung dessen / daß man derselben wol entberen kan / ein adiaphorum ecclesiasticum bleibt; so sind doch die Handlungen der Music nicht indifferent, sondern entweder gut / wenn sie in der Furcht Gottes auf gehörige Art geschehen; oder böse und sündlich wenn / an statt der Furcht Gottes und dessen / was diese erfodert / sich nur eine mit vieler vanitæt verknüpfte bloße Gewohnheit bey derselben befindet. Wie aber nach den principiis der wahren Moralitæt die Annehmung und Beybehaltung der adiaphororum ecclesiasticorum, und deren werth oder unwerth selbst / in allen ihren Gattungen und Arten zu beurtheilen sey / ist hieraus leichtlich zu erkennen."

[87] For more on Pietist objections to dance, see my article, Joyce Irwin: Dancing in Bach's Time: Sin or Permissible Pleasure? In: Bach Perspectives 12, 2018, 17–35.

a lengthy quotation from Gottfried Vockerodt, who wrote many lengthy works opposing the orthodox teaching on adiaphora.[88] This passage, in which Vockerodt harshly chastises musicians for their worldly ambition, is much more negative than anything Lange wrote about music in his own words.[89]

Yet the issue of wrongly interpreted adiaphora is no less central for Lange than for Vockerodt. After describing the sinfulness of other behaviors that some had designated as indifferent, such as card and board games, feasts, jocularity, and excess accumulation of wealth, Lange explains how the defense of such activities undermines the whole of Christian teaching. If the Christian ethical principle is "Whatever you do, do it to the honor of Christ," there can be no indifferent actions.

> The alleged doctrine of adiaphora, or fleshly indifferentism, is truly and in multiple ways a major and fundamental error and yeast that sours and spoils the whole evangelical teaching; it falsifies, distorts, and destroys the whole counsel of God or the whole order of salvation.[90]

This statement is the twelfth in a series of assertions that the teaching of indifferentism perverts or destroys essentially all the teachings of Christian faith that have any bearing on an individual's relationship to God. This refers to Christian teachings on sin, law, gospel, grace, repentance and rebirth, justification and union with Christ, peace with God and joy in the Holy Spirit, the workings of the Holy Spirit, discipleship, spiritual strength, the cross of Christians, and Christian freedom.[91]

The negative comments relating to music, however, are not about music in the abstract, much less church music. They concern the behavior of people who use music without devotion, without a holy intention. To be sure, this position was offensive to those who wanted music to be judged according to the quality of the music or the performance rather than by the moral character of the performer. This was a major point of contention, though the Orthodox would all agree that music had been used in irreverent ways and that sacred music should be carried out with heartfelt devotion as well as with musical skill. If the term "subjective" is used to identify Pietist approaches to music, it needs to be understood as a matter of moral principle, that is, that the subjective status of the individual determines the value of the act.

---

[88] The quotation on pp. 66–69 is from Vockerodt's *Mißbrauch der freyen Künste / insonderheit der Music*; Lange lists this and Vockerodt's four other major works on p. 99. On Vockerodt's views on adiaphora, see Irmgard Scheitler: Der Streit um die Mitteldinge. Menschenbild und Musikauffassung bei Gottfried Vockerodt und seinen Gegnern. In: Alter Adam, 513–530. See also Irwin: Neither Voice nor Heart Alone, 117–126.

[89] In his *Antibarbarus* Lange had traced the history of the "pseudadiaphoria" from Greek theater through early Christian writings against theater up to Gottfried Vockerodt's books against theater and the abuse of the music (Vol. 3, section 1, 4–62). Lange's lengthy quotations from Vockerodt at this and many other places reveal his reliance on Vockerodt and even a lack of original thinking about adiaphora.

[90] Lange: Mittel=Straße, Vol. 4, 96–97: "Die vorgegebene Mitteldings=Lehre / oder der fleischliche Indifferentismus ist ein rechter und vielfacher Haupt= und Grund=Irrthum / und ein Sauerteig / der die gantze Evangelische Lehre durchsäuert und verderbet / und den gantzen Rath Gottes / oder die gantze Heils=Ordnung / verfälschet / verkehret und vernichtet."

[91] Lange: Mittel=Straße, Vol. 4, 83–96.

Similarly, the term "individualistic" does not define Lange any more than it defines Francke. As non-separatist Lutherans, they held to the importance of remaining part of the church in spite of its faults. Lange opened the first volume of his *Die richtige Mittel=Straße* series with a lengthy explanation of why one should not separate from the church. Against the objection that church-going is for the weak and the beginners in the faith, not for the more advanced, Lange responds that not only can even the advanced learn from a sermon but, furthermore, public worship is not just about listening. It also involves singing and praying, and if others are doing this without devotion, a sincere worshipper can be a good influence.[92] God does not act through direct revelations, Lange contends in the second *Mittel-Straße* volume, but "through people with people."[93]

## 11  Summary

Joachim Lange held a high view of music as a gift from God and an important means of praising God. Through his view of the unity of scripture, he regarded Hebrew temple worship as a precursor to the music of the church and ultimately to the music of heaven. It was well organized and orderly, and it involved all the people, not just individuals. These factors should also characterize the music of the church. Although the Mosaic law was abrogated with the coming of Christ, and the Israelite people did not have full understanding of God's salvific work, many had prophetic gifts, and the music they created resulted from a prophetic spirit. David in particular was given supernatural understanding that enabled him to refer in his psalms to Christ's future redemptive acts. Old Testament worship, therefore, should not be seen as mere metaphor for a more spiritual form of worship but as a promise to be more fully realized in the future. Salvation history, in Lange's view, culminates in John's vision of the kingdom of glory in the book of Revelation, where the church triumphant praises God with joyful music.

This joyful music, to be sure, is performed only by the angels and the redeemed souls. Lange felt that only true believers could use music properly. When music was used to express worldly joy, it was an abuse of this good gift. In Lange's ethical system every action must be done to the glory of God, and there was no room for a neutral or secular use of music, especially not in operas, comedies, or dances. Other than the requirement that music have a moral purpose, Lange did not limit music to a particular style or form. He found traditional hymns valuable but also encouraged the writing of new hymns. Instrumental music was not differentiated from vocal music in his biblical interpretation, nor was it accorded merely symbolic significance. The differentiating criterion for Lange was the spiritual state and intention of those who were making music.

---

[92] Joachim Lange: Die richtige Mittel=Straße / zwischen den Abwegen der Absonderung von der euserlichen Gemeinschafft der Kirchen. Halle: Renger, 1712, 43.
[93] Joachim Lange: Der richtigen Mittel=Straße zwischen den Irrthümern und Abwegen Anderer Theil. Halle: Renger, 1712, 13.

Chapter Three

# A Heart Tuned for Praise: Johann Jakob Rambach (1693–1735) as Preacher, Professor, and Poet

Johann Jakob Rambach (1693–1735) was a younger colleague of Joachim Lange, having grown up in Halle, attended the Latina of the Franckesche Anstalten and then the University. He studied under August Hermann Francke and Joachim Lange, among others, and shared many of their theological perspectives. As noted in the chapter on Lange, Rambach was the person Lange had in mind to finish his biblical commentaries, were he not to live long enough himself. After studying in Halle, Rambach taught for four years at the university in Jena but returned to Halle in 1723, where he served as adjunct in the theological faculty and inspector of the orphanage, marrying Lange's daughter the following year. Upon the death of Francke in 1727, Rambach took up his professorate, teaching primarily homiletics and hermeneutics. After a conflict with Francke's son Gotthilf August, who succeeded his father as foundation director, over the requirement of documenting one's conversion process, Rambach accepted an offer to be professor and superintendent in Giessen.[1] Though he died after only four years there, many of his writings were published posthumously by students, primarily Ernst Friedrich Neubauer.

Scholars have disagreed about the historical placement of Rambach in relation to the movements of his time. Chi-Won Kang saw Rambach as very much a pupil of August Hermann Francke in the priorities of theological study and yet as going beyond his pietistic teachers in emphasizing philosophical study and a broad use of human reason in theology.[2] Walter Hug observed that, while there has been a consensus in seeing Rambach as a representative of Spenerian and Franckean Pietism, nevertheless there are influences of philosopher Christian Wolff in his methodology and other Enlightenment influences on his pedagogical thinking.[3] Helge Stadelmann, on the other hand, criticizes Hug and others for this characterization, regarding Rambach as having placed clear boundaries against the early Enlightenment; he prefers to place Rambach between rigid orthodoxy and

---

[1] Concerning this controversy, see August Tholuck: Geschichte des Rationalismus. Vol. 1: Geschichte des Pietismus und des ersten Stadiums der Aufklärung. Berlin: Wiegandt und Grieben, 1865, 28–31.
[2] Chi-Won Kang: Frömmigkeit und Gelehrsamkeit: Die Reform des Theologiestudiums im lutherischen Pietismus des 17. und frühen 18. Jahrhunderts. Giessen: Brunnen, 2001, 456.
[3] Walter Hug: Johann Jacob Rambach (1693–1735). Religionspädagoge zwischen den Zeiten. Stuttgart: Kohlhammer, 2003.

"so-called Pietism."[4] Frank Lüdke concludes that all these labels may be fruitless attempts to confine a multifaceted thinker within today's categories.[5]

Within the limits of this study of biblical interpretation in relation to music, it is not feasible to attempt an overall evaluation of Rambach's varied endeavors. As a theologian, he made his greatest contribution with his guide to hermeneutics, *Institutiones Hermeneuticae Sacrae*, followed by the German-language companion, *Erläuterung über seine eigene Institutiones Hermeneuticae Sacrae* edited by Neubauer. He was also an effective preacher, as evidenced in his published sermons and in his influential works on homiletics.[6] Of particular interest to us are his publications of hymn and cantata texts. His *Geistliche Poesien*, which contained seventy-two cantata texts and twenty hymns, as well as madrigals and sonnets, was first published in 1720 and followed by his *Poetische Fest-Gedancken* in 1723. Both were republished several times, and numerous composers set many of these texts to music.[7] Rambach also edited hymnals for use in churches and homes. At the request of Ernst Ludwig, the Landgrave of Hessen, Rambach prepared a hymnal for use in churches in 1733, dedicated to the Landgrave and entitled *Neu eingerichtetes Hessen-Darmstädtisches Kirchen-Gesang-Buch*. His expanded version for use in homes appeared in 1735 as *Geistreiches Haus=Gesang=Buch*.

In spite of his contributions to hymnody, Rambach wrote very little directly about music. He did not, like Lange, publish commentaries on all the books of the Bible or even of the book of Psalms. His *Collegium Historiae Ecclesiasticae* comes closest to being a commentary on the entire Old Testament, but it is organized according to historical periods and topics rather than biblical books and verses. A few other works by Rambach are commentaries on particular books of the Bible, such as Isaiah, Romans, and Colossians. To compile a collage of Rambach's picture of music, we need to draw from a variety of his writings, including sermons and meditations. The scattered mentions of music in these works do not comprise a systematic theology of music; they are enough, however, to lead to the conclusion that music was for him not in itself imbued with divine power. Nevertheless, when used in the right context and with the right motivation, it has glorious potential: "It should also not be the purpose to please others but rather the Lord; indeed, one

---

[4] Helge Stadelmann: Die Juden "hertzlich lieben": Johann Jacob Rambach und die Zukunft des jüdischen Volkes. In: Christen, Juden und die Zukunft Israels: Beiträge zur Israellehre aus Geschichte und Theologie. Ed. by Berthold Schwarz and Helge Stadelmann. Frankfurt/Main: Peter Lang, 2009, 218.

[5] Frank Lüdke: Johann Jakob Rambach in Halle und Gießen: Spätblüte des Pietismus an deutschen Theologischen Fakultäten. In: Johann Jakob Rambach (1693–1735): Praktischer Theologe und Schriftausleger. Ed. by Helge Stadelmann and Peter Zimmerling. Leipzig: Evangelische Verlagsanstalt, 2019, 11.

[6] Rambach's works are too numerous to list here. See his bibliography under Art. "Johann Jacob Rambach". In: Biographisch-bibliographisches Kirchenlexikon. Vol. 7. Ed. by Friedrich Wilhelm Bautz and Traugott Bautz. Herzberg: Traugott Bautz, 1994, 1299–1305.

[7] The publication history and known musical settings are thoroughly examined in Julian Heigel: "Vergnügen und Erbauung": Johann Jakob Rambachs Kantatentexte und ihre Vertonungen. Halle: Franckesche Stiftungen, 2014, esp. 165–191.

should sing to the Lord Jesus, to the Lord to whom all the hosts of heaven sing, and shout for joy to him whom all the angels of God adore."[8]

## 1 Old Testament Passages on Music

Regarding the first explicit mention of music in the Bible, Rambach notes that Jubal is not credited with inventing music as a whole. Recognizing that some have interpreted the two instruments mentioned in Genesis 4,21, *kinnor* and *ugabh*, as collectively referring to all musical instruments, Rambach believes that these are merely additional new instruments. He does credit Jubal with the necessary cleverness to invent musical instruments, but he is not convinced that this was done to the glory of God. As a descendant of Cain, Jubal belonged to a familial line accused of following their lustful self-interests. The suspicion for Rambach, then, is that Jubal used these musical instruments *ad carnis delectationem*, for delights of the flesh.[9]

The biblical episode that best reveals Rambach's view of music is the story of David and Saul. In contrast to Lange, Rambach does not believe that Saul ever received the Holy Spirit. He did come into the midst of the group of prophets, join in their prophetic singing and become a new person (1 Samuel 10); yet the new heart, according to Rambach, did not entail regeneration but rather the ability to carry out the duties of kingly governance, having previously been a common tender of goats and crops. Rambach believes Saul never received a sanctifying spirit, only a kingly spirit.[10] This gift of the spirit of royalty could be lost, whereas a gift of the Holy Spirit could not be lost. When, then, in 1 Samuel 16,14, it is reported that the good spirit departed from Saul, this refers to the kingly gifts, not a sanctifying spirit that he never had.[11]

David, by contrast, received the Holy Spirit in his anointing, which made him a brave leader in war, a prophet, and a "pleasing singer who served the whole church with his godly songs."[12] When Saul's doctors recommended music as a cure for his melancholy, David was called from his life as a shepherd because of his reputation for skilled harp-playing. Rambach does not treat this as a holy cure with music having divine power, however. Even though it was said that an

---

[8] Johann Jakob Rambach: Richtige und Erbauliche Erklärung der Ep. Pauli an die Colosser. Giessen: Krieger, 1740, 337 (on Col 3,16): "Es soll auch nicht der Zweck seyn, daß man andern gefalle; sondern dem **Herrn**, und zwar dem Herrn **Jesu** soll man singen, dem Herrn, dem alles Himmels=Heer singet, und jauchzet, und der von allen Engeln Gottes angebetet wird."
[9] Johann Jakob Rambach: Collegivm Historiae Ecclesiasticae Veteris Testamenti, Oder Ausführlicher und gründlicher Discurs über die Kirchen=Historie des alten Testaments. Vol. 1. Ed. by Ernst Friedrich Neubauer. Frankfurt/Main: Möller, 1737, 137.
[10] Rambach: Collegivm Historiae, Vol. 2, 195.
[11] Rambach: Collegivm Historiae, Vol. 2, 224.
[12] Rambach: Collegivm Historiae, Vol. 2, 224: "ja zu einem **Propheten** und lieblichen Sänger, der durch seine göttliche Lieder der gantzen Kirche gedienet hat."

evil spirit came upon Saul, this was more a gradual process of turning away from God and indulging his sinful desires, opening the door to Satan's power. The resulting melancholy sprang not from a personal disposition to despondency but rather from a bad conscience.

Rambach sees Saul's experience here as common among people of his own day, particularly theology students. When one hardens one's heart against the movements and convictions of the Holy Spirit, one can gradually come to a point of madness or delirium brought on by the stings of conscience. Those afflicted tend to ascribe it to a *malum melancholicum*, whereas in reality its source is a bad conscience because the soul is in a wrong place, namely outside communion with God.

Given the root cause, music could provide nothing more than palliation for Saul. To be sure, David sang lovely spiritual songs that mitigated Saul's melancholy affect and brought some space for clearer thinking when he was not so disturbed. The music, however, was just a temporary distraction: "What happened with Saul here was like when a child has body pains and becomes quiet when someone shakes a rattle or plays for them, but as soon as the child feels a new pang it begins to cry again."[13] Rambach then likens this to those who seek to escape their troubles by going out partying, getting drunk, and singing drinking and whoring songs, which only makes them more obstinate. There can only be intermittent relief if the root cause is not addressed. Only the power of Jesus' blood can heal a guilty conscience, and only after this has occurred does music have a spiritual effect: "When the conscience is healed, though, sacred music with the singing of spiritual and pleasant songs can then be used as a healing medicine against the spirit of sadness."[14]

In sum, while music can be efficacious for changing moods, it does not have a divine power to convert hearts. Though Rambach does not explore the nature or power of music explicitly, he discusses it here as a natural phenomenon, just as he discusses Saul's problem from a psychological perspective. Other interpretations of the story credited David's spiritual power, the words he sang, the intrinsic power of music, or a combination thereof for curing Saul of his madness. Rambach does not even see a cure as having occurred. Without a spiritual breakthrough, there is no meaningful change. Indeed, such an explanation is consistent with the later episode (1 Sam 18,10–11), in which David's music provoked Saul to throw his spear at David, an episode that is more difficult to explain if music has healing power.

How, then, does Rambach view David, and how does his view compare with that of Lange? In general, he shares the position of Francke and Lange that the Bible is a unified whole and that Christ is prefigured throughout the Old Testament. To elucidate this, Rambach gave lectures or meditations on the prophecies and

---

[13] Rambach: Collegivm Historiae, Vol. 2, 226: "Es ging dem Saul hier, wie einem Kind, das Leibes=Schmertzen hat und wol ein wenig stille wird, wenn man ihm was vorklappert und vorspielet, aber bald wenn ein neuer impulsus dolorum kommt, wieder zu schreyen anfängt."

[14] Rambach: Collegivm Historiae, Vol. 2, 226: "Wenn aber das Gewissen geheilet ist, so kan nachgehends Musica sacra, die Absingung geistlicher und lieblicher Lieder als ein heylsames Mittel gegen den Trauer=Geist gebraucht werden."

prefiguring of Christ in the Pentateuch, published in 1736 with the title *Christus in Mose*. In his 53rd meditation, he discussed whether David was a figure of Christ. First, he explained that the office of king in Israel prefigured Christ, and also that judges like Gideon and Samson were figures of Christ. Among the kings, David and Solomon were the foremost examples.

At the outset, Rambach states that it is undeniable that David belongs among the figures or types of Christ, pointing to various passages in the prophets where David and the Anointed One are used interchangeably. Rambach divides his analysis into the categories of person, office, suffering, and victorious deeds, all of which have parallels to Christ. Within the category of person, Rambach draws a parallel between David as skilled harp player and the gospel of Jesus, in which the new song of the Lamb is sung. Whenever the Bible refers to the "new song," Rambach takes it to mean Christ and the new dispensation.[15] Thus, its music is purely metaphorical: "the loveliness [of the gospel] is more pleasant than any playing of strings, and it can calm and silence the unrest of our spirit and our conscience in the most perfect way."[16]

The category of office includes the roles of shepherd, king, and prophet, in all of which David is a figure of Christ. The prophetic role, Rambach explains, is seen particularly in his psalms, "which are filled through and through with the suffering and glory of Jesus Christ."[17] For verification of David's inspiration, Rambach quotes the words attributed to David in 2 Samuel 23,2, "The spirit of the Lord spoke through me, and his speech occurred through my tongue." As a precursor of Christ, the great and true prophet, David sat at Christ's feet and found his highest pleasure in hearing the mouth of God speak.

In his suffering, David again prefigures Christ, showing in his life circumstances what Rambach calls an "astonishing similarity" with the suffering of Christ. David, Rambach says, knew through divine revelations that he should be a precursor of Christ in his suffering and persecution, and he alluded to this in his psalms, where he prophesied of the sufferings of Christ. Examples of this are references to enemies in Psalm 55 and particularly Psalm 41, to which Jesus' words, "the one who ate my bread," in John 13,18 refer. The rebellion of Absalom against David is a parallel to the plot against Jesus, with Psalm 2 ("Why do the nations conspire?") quoted in Acts 4,25.[18]

---

[15] Cf. Johann Jakob Rambach: Institvtiones Hermenevticae Sacrae. 2nd ed. Jena: Hartung, 1725, 169: "Vbi canticvm novvm ecclesiae canendum iniungitur, ibi de Christo, ac beneficiis nouae oeconomiae sermonem esse, intelligitur."

[16] Johann Jakob Rambach: Christus in Mose, oder Betrachtungen über die vornehmsten Weissagungen und Vorbilder in den fünf Büchern Mosis auf Christum. Ed. by Johann Philipp Fresenius. Frankfurt/Main, Leipzig: Spring, 1736, 622. Fresenius reports in the preface (§46) that these meditations were delivered in the orphanage during the "so-called singing hours" between January 15, 1724, and February 1, 1727.

[17] Rambach: Christus in Mose, 628: "Dieses sein prophetisches Amt leuchtet sonderlich aus seinen Psalmen hervor, welche von dem Leyden und von der Herrlichkeit Jesu Christi durch und durch angefüllet sind."

[18] Rambach: Christus in Mose, 629–632.

The fourth category in which David showed himself a precursor of Christ was in his glorious deeds and victories. In governing his kingdom, David accomplished great things, as in securing Mount Zion and making it his residence, a parallel to Christ's establishing his throne in spiritual Zion. The sacrifices David offered and distributed to the people prefigure Christ's sacrifice in his spiritual kingdom, where the gifts of the Holy Spirit are distributed. Interestingly, Rambach looks at David's accomplishments in the area of music as a skill of organization, saying nothing of the glory of the music or the importance placed in having so many musicians. Rather, the parallel to Christ is that God is a God of order and wants everything to proceed in good order, as directed in 1 Cor 14,40 and through the orderly distribution of tasks as found in Eph 4,11–12, with some being apostles and others prophets, evangelists, pastors or teachers.[19]

The importance of good order is the main point Rambach draws in his *Collegium Historiae* chapter on Levitic worship as instituted by David. While recognizing that Asaph, Heman, and Jeduthun (or Ethan, as Rambach names him here) excelled in sacred music and had the gift of prophecy, Rambach sees orderliness as the main lesson to be learned: David, by engaging God's prophets, provided quite carefully for well-regulated worship in the tabernacle, which could then be carried over to the first and second temples. Rambach was apparently quite disturbed by those he called "enemies of good order," of whom the majority were students, including students of theology, who felt that good order impinged on their academic freedom. From the clear organization of worship recorded in 1 Chronicles, these disorderly people "can easily conclude and learn that they are hated in the eyes of God because they do not have the divine characteristic, the love of good order."[20]

A meditation contained in another posthumously published collection of Rambach's essays, *Theologische Betrachtungen*, focuses more directly on the psalms as witnessing to Christ. In fact, Rambach lists here 51 psalm passages side by side with comparable passages from the New Testament.[21] Reminiscent of Francke's instructions to begin with the New Testament and use it as a tool to understand the Old Testament, Rambach says that this table provides a key to understanding the Psalms, because it was the same Spirit of Jesus Christ that spoke through David. Many New Testament passages refer directly to Moses, the Psalms, and the prophets, allowing the interpreter to see the connection clearly. Of the Old Testament writers who served as witnesses to the coming kingdom of Christ, David "shines as a star of first rank." Rambach's explanation of David's special place was, however, based as much on his historical lineage as on exceptional insight into the Messiah: "As this one had the special grace that the thread of promise

---

[19] Rambach: Christus in Mose, 634–635.
[20] Rambach: Collegivm Historiae, Vol. 2, 293.
[21] Johann Jakob Rambach: Die III. Betrachtung von dem Zeugnis der Psalmen von Jesu Christo. In: J. J. Rambach: Theologische Betrachtungen Uber einige Auserlesene und vortrefliche Materien der Dogmatischen, Polemischen, Moralischen u.s.f. Gottes=Gelahrtheit. Ed. by Adam Lebrecht Müller. Jena: Ritter, 1739, 55–57.

*1 Old Testament Passages on Music* 73

of the Messiah was tied to his family, so the foremost pursuit of his harp and the most noble content of his songs was to sing of this great king, who in his human nature would be his son but by divine nature his Lord (Ps 110,1)."[22] Other than to say that the Holy Spirit spoke through David, Rambach does not here clarify the mode or method of David's inspiration. Through a quote from Luther, however, he does emphasize that the importance of the psalms lies more in their content than in artistry of either words or music.

> And the loveliness of his psalms consists precisely in this, according to Luther's annotations (Jena ed. Vol. 8, fol. 140), namely: "to call something a beautiful text and beautiful music does not come only from the arts of language and music by which the words are set artfully and attractively and the song or melody sounds sweet and pleasant; rather it is from the theology and the spiritual understanding."[23]

As for David's music itself, the closest we have to a commentary by Rambach appeared in an appendix to the *Collegium Historiae*.[24] This appendix begins with an acknowledgement that Joachim Lange had treated the subject at length in his Old Testament history,[25] and for that reason Rambach would concentrate briefly on the most important matters. Actually, Rambach's and Lange's summaries are similar in both length and content; Lange's Psalm commentary, which would treat the subject at greater length, was at the press at the time the *Collegium* was being published, as Neubauer reported in a footnote.[26] Both summaries divide the subject into nine headings, not identical but similar, examining the authorship of the psalms, the titles, the numbering and organization, and the most important subjects. The music constitutes the sixth point in Rambach's study, the fifth in Lange's. These sections are relatively short, attempting to explain the meaning of the Hebrew terms and the types of instruments used, but admitting that little can be known about the actual sound of the music. Rambach, however, adds a pejorative comment on the music heard among Jews of his own day:

> If one wanted to measure the old Hebrew music according to the manner of singing that Jews use today in their synagogues, one would arrive at a very strange concept of it. For

---

[22] Rambach: Theologische Betrachtungen, 52: "Wie dieser die besondere Gnade hatte, daß der Faden der Verheissung von dem Meßia an seine Familie geknüpft wurde; Also war die vornehmste Beschäftigung seiner Harfe, und der edelste Inhalt seiner Lieder, diesen grossen König, der nach der menschlichen Natur sein Sohn, nach der göttlichen aber sein Herr seyn solte, Ps. 110, 1. zu besingen."
[23] Rambach: Theologische Betrachtungen, 54: "Und eben darinnen bestehet nach Lutheri Anmerckung (tom. 8 Jen. fol. 140) die Lieblichkeit seiner Psalmen, nemlich **nicht nur nach der Grammatica und Musica, daß die Wort zierlich und künstlich gestellet sind und der Gesang oder Thon süsse und lieblich lautet, das da heist schöner Text und schöne Noten; sondern vielmehr nach der Theologie und geistlichem Verstande.**"
[24] Neubauer, the compiler and editor of this work, announced that Rambach's meditations on the Psalms would be forthcoming, but I find no evidence that he completed this project. See footnotes in Rambach: Collegivm Historiae, Vol. 2, 295, 296, 312.
[25] Lange: Historia Ecclesiastica, 457–472.
[26] Rambach: Collegivm Historiae, Vol. 2, 312. In the same footnote, Neubauer also recommended Francke's introduction to the Psalms published in 1734.

today's singing by Jews is such a desolate and unpleasant clamor that it does not deserve the name of music.[27]

Not only is this negative comment different from Lange, but neither does Rambach include the positive lesson that Lange draws, i.e., that even though our knowledge of Hebrew psalmody is obscure, we can know that it is our duty to offer spiritual music, as commended by Paul in Eph 5,19 and Col 3,16.[28]

For the most part, Rambach and Lange share the same view of salvation history, influenced heavily by Vitringa though departing from him in some details. There are seven periods in history, and the last will be a Sabbath period, after the Antichrist is defeated, in which Jews and pagans will convert to the Christian faith and join in a universal church. On this basis, one can have hope of better times for the church. This topic of the future conversion of the Jews is more fully developed in Rambach's commentary on the book of Romans,[29] particularly chapters 9 to 11 where Paul himself wrote "All Israel will be saved" (Rom 11,26). Based on this commentary, Helge Stadelmann has portrayed Rambach as unusually pro-Jewish among the Lutherans of his time.[30]

The commentary on Isaiah gives a different impression of Rambach's attitude toward Jews. To be sure, Rambach regarded the Hebrew people from the time of Abraham as the adopted children of God whom God educated through wholesome laws and exalted in the flourishing times of David and Solomon. The book of Isaiah, however, was written when Israelites were perceived to have rebelled and acted faithlessly, when, as Rambach put it, "all malicious acts and sins were in vogue."[31] If Rambach had wanted to appeal to the Jews of his time, it seems curious that he would make a point of suggesting a more negative interpretation than Luther's of the Hebrew word פשע in Isaiah 1,2. Rambach finds in it the connotation not only of apostasy but also of opposition. Thus he quotes a translation found in a Worms Bible of 1527: "sind zu Schelmen an mir worden," that is, they have become knaves, rogues or scoundrels.[32] An indication of Rambach's attitude toward the Jews of his time is found in his commentary on Isaiah 61,5 ("Strangers shall stand and

---

[27] Rambach: Collegivm Historiae, Vol. 2, 305: "Wenn man die alte **hebräische Musick** abmessen wolte nach der heutigen Art zu singen, deren sich die Jüden in ihren Synagogen bedienen, so würde man sich einen wunderlichen Begrif davon machen. Denn das heutige Singen der Jüden ist ein solch wüstes und unangenehmes Geschrey, welches nicht nomen Musicae sacrae verdienet."
[28] Lange: Historia Ecclesiastica, 465: "Quandoquidem vero in tota re psaltica Hebræorum hodie pleraque nobis sunt, manentque obscura & incerta, eo magis noverimus, nostri esse officii, ut musicæ spirituali operam demus, commendatæ a Paulo Eph. V, 19. Col. III, 16."
[29] Johann Jakob Rambach: Ausführliche und gründliche Erklärung der Epistel Pauli an die Römer. Ed. by Ernst Friedrich Neubauer. Bremen: Sauerman, 1738.
[30] Stadelmann: Die Juden "hertzlich lieben", 213–234.
[31] Johann Jakob Rambach: Gründliche Erklärung des Propheten Esaiä, darin nach einer Einleitung, so wol in die Propheten überhaupt, als in den Esaiam insonderheit, alle Theile desselben ordentlich zergliedert und aus der Philologie und Hermeneutic erkläret. Ed. by Ernst Friedrich Neubauer. Züllichau: Frommann, 1741, 38.
[32] Rambach: Gründliche Erklärung, 40. Luther's translation had given only the charge of apostasy: "sie sind von mir abgefallen" ("they have fallen away from me").

*1 Old Testament Passages on Music* 75

feed your flocks"): "On the basis of this verse, today's Jews flatter themselves that we should all still become their servants and slaves who polish their shoes, chop wood, bring them water for tea and coffee and in sum should wait on and serve the holy people."[33] The book of Isaiah ends with the prophecy of doom to those who rebelled against God, and while Rambach recognizes that this will be the fate of any who rebel against God, he applies it specifically to the Jews of his time: "This is a clear description of the wicked Jews, who go around before our eyes like a monster."[34] While Rambach may have urged his listeners to treat Jews with love and refrain from attacks on their synagogues, I am not ready to agree with Stadelmann that Rambach's favorable exegesis of the Jews' future was matched by an equally favorable view of Jews in his own time.[35] As adamantly as he defended the assertion that Jews would ultimately be converted, he saw this as the final step in the fulfillment of Christ's mission more than an incremental process beginning in his own time, much less an acceptance of Judaism for its own sake.[36]

The element of this topic that is relevant to music in a broad sense is what Rambach said about Jews and worship. In several places, he noted that Levitic worship, as a component of the old dispensation, was abrogated with Christ, comparing it at one point to "an old worn-out piece of clothing that one finally puts aside."[37] Specific parts of the old dispensation to be rejected are found in Isaiah 66,1–4, where God condemns animal sacrifice and calls into question the building of houses of worship. To understand this, explains Rambach, "one must note that Isaiah was speaking in the name of God to the hypocritical Jews at a time when they were spending enormous amounts on the decoration of the temple. He addresses hypocrites who placed their highest worship in outward ceremonies."[38] Concerning sacrifices, Rambach had said in relation to Isaiah 1,11 that they did not please God because they were offered without penitence and faith, solely *ex opere operato*.[39] In a section directed against the Roman church, Rambach describes the

---

[33] Rambach: Gründliche Erklärung, 517: "Aus diesem Vers flattiren sich die heutigen Jüden, daß wir noch alle ihre Knechte und Sclaven werden sollen, die ihnen die Schuhe putzen, Holtz spalten, Wasser zu The und Caffe zutragen, und summa summarum dem heiligen Volck dienen und aufwarten sollen."

[34] Rambach: Gründliche Erklärung, 566: "Es ist diß eine deutliche Beschreibung der boßhaftigen Jüden, die vor unsern Augen als ein Scheusal herumgehen."

[35] Stadelmann: Die Juden "hertzlich lieben", 225.

[36] The fact that most of Rambach's works were edited and published posthumously by Neubauer complicates the assessment of Rambach's position. Rambach cannot be blamed for his editor's footnotes, but in reference to Isaiah 4:4, where Rambach had named the killing of the Messiah as among the crimes for which the Jews' hands were bloody (p. 83), Neubauer suggested for further reading the anti-Jewish book written by Johann Jacob Schudt: Judaeus Christicida gravissime peccans et vapulans. Frankfurt/Main: [n.p.], 1703.

[37] Rambach: Gründliche Erklärung, 436: "wie ein altes abgetragenes Kleid, das man endlich ableget."

[38] Rambach: Gründliche Erklärung, 555: "Diß zu verstehen, muß man mercken, daß Esaias im Namen Gottes mit den heuchlerischen Jüden rede, zu einer solchen Zeit, da sie die grössesten Unkosten auf den ornatum templi wendeten. Er redet an hypocritas, die ihren vornehmsten Gottesdienst in äusserlichen Cärimonien setzten."

[39] Rambach: Gründliche Erklärung, 45.

true worship of God as very simple, without laborious superstitions or expenditures, and without substituting thousands of mediators for one, adding regretfully, "people choose such things rather than the pure and simple worship of God."[40]

## 2  New Testament

For a more extensive discussion of worship under the new dispensation, we may turn to Rambach's treatment of one of the *loci classici* about music in the New Testament. His commentary on Colossians was edited from a handwritten manuscript by Conrad Caspar Griesbach and published in 1740. As we do not have a Rambach commentary on Ephesians, we may expect that both Col 3,16 and Eph 5,19 would be treated in much the same way.

In the previous chapter we observed Lange expanding on Luther's translation of the Greek ἐν ὑμῖν to include an individual indwelling of Christ as well as an interpersonal relationship. Similarly, Rambach takes the preposition to mean both *in* and *among*, saying that the Word of God is not just to be heard, read, and taken to heart, but that the heart should be so filled that it overflows and shares the Word with others. The Word dwelling in the heart gives it power to instruct and admonish others. Here Rambach chastises theology students who want to preach in their early years of study before the Word has taken deep root in their hearts. In such cases they are twisting God's order by speaking before they have the Word in their hearts, thus becoming noisy gongs and clanging cymbals. The concern for order should not, however, prevent non-ordained believers from teaching. It is, Rambach says, no incursion against those in the teaching office if believers instruct one another. To be sure, not everyone should teach from the pulpit or in large gatherings, but an ordinary Christian who is more advanced in faith than others should use that gift to serve the neighbor, and fathers and mothers should teach their children and their household.[41]

Even though the Colossians verse has music as the means of teaching and admonishing, Rambach treats the two activities as separate, not integrating this commentary on teaching with his discussion of singing. His explication of the terms *Psalmen*, *Lob=Gesänge*, and *Lieder* is brief and in part not very revealing. For instance, in defining "spiritual songs," he says they are identified by their content, i.e., about spiritual matters, by their purpose, which is to awaken and edify the spirit, and by their "Art und Einrichtung" ("style and arrangement"). Presumably, this concerns musical style, but no further explanation is given. While there is some mention of the effect of one's singing on others, it is very succinct: *Lob=Gesänge* are unaccompanied songs of praise in which one "lays bare the desires of one's heart to make the perfection of God known to others"; *Lieder* are all kinds of hymns "by which one encourages oneself or

---

[40] Rambach: Gründliche Erklärung, 483: "doch erwehlet der Mensch solche lieber as purum & simplicem Dei cultum."
[41] Rambach: Ep. Pauli an die Colosser, 334–335.

others to spiritual and holy affects."⁴² This latter category may include biblical texts such as the psalms, the songs of Moses, Deborah, Zachariah, Mary and Hannah, or they may be written by other enlightened ("erleuchtete") persons for the edification of the community. Surely, Rambach regards his own poems as fulfilling this purpose.

Rambach does recognize the appealing sound of music but not always as a positive good. Adding instruments to the singing, which is the defining characteristic of the term *Psalmen*, arouses the spirit ("Gemüth") and makes the praise of God more moving and pleasing. If the singing does not proceed from the heart, however, even the most pleasant songs are like noise to God, as in Amos 5,23. Many who have been given a pleasant and charming voice like to hear themselves sing or like to please others with their sound. In keeping with the following verse (Col 3,17), however, singing should only be done to the glory of God. It is a means of furthering one's growth in a spiritual and virtuous life and can be a blessing in times of need, as expressed in the line "Wenn ich in Nöthen bet und sing, so wird mein Hertz recht guter Ding," from the hymn *Ach Gott, wie manches Herzeleid*. Rambach was discouraged about the spiritual state of townspeople based on the kind of songs he was hearing: "If only one could hear more spiritual songs here than vulgar and obscene songs."⁴³

Better insight into Rambach's understanding of music in relation to the Christian life is found in a sermon on the Feast of the Visitation.⁴⁴ Entitled "On the True Praise of God," the three points of the sermon are: 1. the persons who are capable of true praise; 2. the matter with which it deals; 3. the manner in which it is to be carried out. The first point is crucial, as it is a distinguishing mark of the Pietist theology of music: the value of church music rests not primarily in the music itself but in the spiritual state of the person singing or playing.⁴⁵

In the original creation, Rambach explains, all persons had the duty of praising God and encouraging others through their own divine likeness. If they had remained in the state of innocence, the children of God on earth would have formed a great company with the children of God in heaven, that is, with the angels, and would have sung "Holy, holy, holy" antiphonally in unceasing praise of God. With the Fall this beautiful harmony was destroyed, and while the duty of praise remains, not everyone can fulfill the obligation:

> Satan put the instruments for praising God so out of tune that they give off a very raw, offensive, and unpleasant sound in God's ears. And although all people still have the obligation to glorify their Creator, they are not all in a position to observe and carry out this obligation in a manner that pleases God.⁴⁶

---

⁴² Rambach: Ep. Pauli an die Colosser, 336.
⁴³ Rambach: Ep. Pauli an die Colosser, 337: "O daß man nur mehr geistliche Lieder, als Schand= und Huren=Lieder, allhier hörete!"
⁴⁴ Johann Jakob Rambach: Evangelische Betrachtungen Uber die Sonn= und Fest=Tags=Evangelia Des gantzen Jahrs. Halle: Waysenhaus, 1730, 949–971, a sermon preached in the university church in 1727.
⁴⁵ Cf. Irwin: German Pietists and Church Music in the Baroque Age; also Heigel: "Vergnügen und Erbauung", 99–103.
⁴⁶ Rambach: Evangelische Betrachtungen, 950: "Der Satan hat die Instrumente des Lobes Gottes auf Erden dergestalt verstimmet, daß sie nun in den Ohren Gottes einen sehr

Taking as models Mary and Elizabeth, Rambach identifies as capable of praise those who love and fear God, no matter how lowly they may seem in the eyes of the world. The faithful and upright are "the living instruments from which the praise of God resounds."[47]

Becoming a faithful person, of course, is not a result of one's own will or motivation but of the Holy Spirit working in the heart. Continuing the musical metaphors, Rambach writes, "This Spirit of God must also tune the harp of one's heart if it is to play a pleasant song of praise."[48] In this context he cites Ephesians 5,18, explaining that, in order to be filled with the Spirit, this Spirit of God's glory must transfigure ("verklären") the glory of God in one's heart, from which then the praise will issue forth. One's natural pride must be broken through humility and repentance so that one can receive the grace of God and rejoice in God's mercy. This is not a transitory but a transformative experience through which the Spirit takes up residence in the heart. Only such a person is capable of praising God.

Given the infinite perfection of the divine being, there is no lack of subject matter for praise. The wondrous works of God may be found in the realms of nature, grace, and glory. Even God's judgment and punishment of the proud and haughty can be praised, as Mary does in her song. Rambach shows special receptivity to the wonders of nature, embarking on an elegy to tiny flowers and to the earthly globe resting on air, to the spring season in which nature is renewed, to the clouds that hover above to provide protection from the sun and water for the ground, and to the stars that astonish in their shining orderliness. All this, however, cannot compare to God's works in the realm of grace: the depth of his love, his justice, holiness, truth, omnipotence, and the great work of salvation. God's blessings to us and to others are a matter for praise, and here also Mary provides an example in singing of his fulfillment of promises to the people of Israel and to the whole human race. In sum, there is so much material for praise "that you will have to save the largest part of your sacrifice of praise until blessed eternity."[49]

From Rambach's third point, the manner in which praise is to be offered, we might expect some practical advice, but for the most part this section continues to focus on devotion, not musical practice. The "Art und Weise" of praise is through heart, mouth, and deed. Again, Rambach states that any praise offering that does not issue from the presence of God in the heart is hypocrisy and not pleasing to God. An unbeliever has very little understanding of the greatness and wisdom of God; only when a person allows the Spirit of Glory into the soul can he acquire a

---

rauhen, widrigen und unangenehmen Ton von sich geben. Und ob gleich noch auf allen Menschen die Schuldigkeit haftet, ihren Schöpfer zu verherrlichen; so sind sie doch nicht alle in dem Stande, diese Schuldigkeit auf eine Gott wohlgefällige Art zu beobachten und zu entrichten."

[47] Rambach: Evangelische Betrachtungen, 951.
[48] Rambach: Evangelische Betrachtungen, 952: "Eben dieser Geist Gottes muß auch die Harfe deines Hertzens stimmen, wenn auf derselben ein angenehmes Lob=Lied gespielet werden soll."
[49] Rambach: Evangelische Betrachtungen, 960: "du wirst so viel finden, daß du den grösten Theil deiner Lob=Opfer bis in die selige Ewigleit wirst versparen müssen."

concept of the majesty of God. "Thus the heart must first recognize, esteem, honor, and marvel at the sublime majesty of God that shines forth from his attributes, words, works, mercy and judgment."[50] Here in essence we see the Pietist belief that an intellectual grasp of the Bible or theology is not possible without the inner working of the Holy Spirit. Understanding of God comes not through any natural capability but through inner transformation.

These inner sensations of the heart must then be expressed in words, so that the knowledge of divine wonders can spread and reproduce. Mary, for instance, did not remain dumbstruck on hearing the news announced, but she expressed the movements of her heart in a lovely song of praise "which the Spirit of God caused to be written down as an unforgettable remembrance."[51] David also expresses in Psalm 145 how he must tell of God's goodness and glorious deeds. Rambach then suggests three ways of using the tongue to glorify God—by speaking with others about God, by speaking with God in prayers that include praise, and by singing songs of praise, as recommended in Col 3,16. Predictably, Rambach stresses the phrase, "sing and play to the Lord in your hearts." The emphasis on the heart does not mean that the song is to remain in the heart, for this is the section on praising with the mouth. Nor are there any restrictions of instrumentation; Psalm 150 is evidence that instruments may be used to increase devotion, and it applies in New Testament times.[52] None of it is of any value, however, if it does not proceed from faith:

> For if devotion of the heart does not give life to the singing, it cannot be pleasing to the Highest, even if all the rules of the art are observed and all the delights not only of the human voice but also of all musical instruments are joined to it. If the singing is to succeed in glorifying God, it must flow from faith (Ps 106,12), occur with comprehension and consideration of the content (Ps 47,[7]), and it must be carried out with a well-prepared mind (Ps 57,[7]), with earnestness and zeal (Ps 108,[1]), with a joyful spirit (Ps 68,[3–4], Ps 92,[4], James 5,13), and with agreement of mouth and heart so that one may sing with David, "My lips and my soul sing praise to you" (Ps 71,23).[53]

---

[50] Rambach: Evangelische Betrachtungen, 962: "So muß also zuvorderst das **Hertz** die erhabene Majestät Gottes, die aus seinen Eigenschaften, Worten, Wercken, Wohlthaten und Gerichten hervorstrahlet, erkennen, hochschätzen, ehren und bewundern."
[51] Rambach: Evangelische Betrachtungen, 962: "welchen der Geist Gottes zum unvergeßlichen Andencken hat niederschreiben lassen."
[52] Rambach: Evangelische Betrachtungen, 963: "Daß aber bey dem Singen zur mehrern Ermunterung der Andacht auch Instrumente gebrauchet werden können, das mag der 150 Psalm, der in die Zeiten des neuen Testaments hineinsiehet, einen ieden lehren."
[53] Rambach: Evangelische Betrachtungen, 963: "Denn wenn die Andacht des Hertzens nicht das Singen belebet, so kan dasselbe dem Höchsten nicht wohlgefallen, wenn auch alle Regeln der Kunst dabey beobachtet, und alle Annehmlichkeiten nicht nur der menschlichen Stimme, sondern auch aller musicalischen Instrumente damit verknüpfet würden. Soll das Singen zur Verherrlichung Gottes gereichen, so muß es aus dem Glauben fliessen, Ps. 106, 12. es muß mit Verstande und Erwegung des Inhalts geschehen, Ps. 47, 8. es muß mit einem wohlzubereiteten Gemüthe Ps. 57, 8. mit Ernst und Eifer, Ps. 108, 2. mit Freudigkeit des Geistes, Ps. 68, 4.5. Ps. 92, 5. Jac. 5, 13. und mit einer Ubereinstimmung des Mundes und Hertzens verrichtet werden, so daß" man mit David sagen könne: **Meine Lippen und meine Seele lobsingen dir**, Ps. 71, 23." (Numbers in brackets in translation were adjusted to English numeration.)

Rambach regrets that music is so often used for wantonness, and he wishes that poetry would be freed from the yoke of servitude to vanity so that it could sing of the perfections and great works of both nature and grace. It is clear both from his attention to poetry and from the mention in the previous quote of "understanding and consideration of the content" that the text of a song is crucial, perhaps indispensable.

The third way in which God is to be praised is through action, which entails a renunciation of any pursuits that do not serve his glory, especially all self-glorification. Even suffering can be to God's glory if it is from giving over one's will to him. Rambach's description at first is a metaphorical use of musical imagery: "No harmony is sweeter, more lovely, and more pleasing to his ears than this, when our will is in accord with his will, when we do what he has commanded and endure what he has decided." But then he returns to praise of the mouth with Job as an example of praise in the midst of suffering, concluding with an image that seems to affirm actual music while placing it in a heavenly context: "When God reaches for his rod, and his children at the same time reach for a harp in order to play for him a song of praise and sing of his unchangeable love and faithfulness, that is a music that comes close to that of the angels, or may even exceed it."[54] At the very end of the sermon, Rambach returns to heavenly imagery. This time he utters a vision of eternity in which any imperfections of the praise that is offered on earth will be purified: "You will receive new and purely tuned harps in order to play an eternal song of praise to God and to the Lamb that was slain and to the seven spirits before his throne."[55]

Heavenly music comes into play again in a sermon on the Feast of St. Michael, delivered in the academic church in 1729. While music is only one of the many angelic activities discussed by Rambach, it is one of the ways in which humans may join in community with the angels and connect earth to heaven. Believers "unite with the angels in the praise of God and let, as it were, a holy echo resound to the Hallelujah and the 'Holy, Holy, Holy is the Lord of Hosts' that is sung in heaven by the cherubim and seraphim."[56] Those who are united with Christ, or "transferred into the heavenly Being," are already able to overcome the separation from these angelic beings by joining in their songs of praise and duties of devotion:

---

[54] Rambach: Evangelische Betrachtungen, 965: "Keine Harmonie ist süsser, lieblicher und angenehmer in seinen Ohren, als diese, wenn unser Wille mit seinem Willen übereinstimmet; wenn wir thun, was er befohlen, und leiden, was er beschlossen. [...] Wenn Gott zur Ruthe greifet, und seine Kinder zu gleicher Zeit zur Harfe greifen, ihm ein Lob=Lied zu spielen, und seine unveränderliche Liebe und Treue zu besingen; das ist eine Music, die der Englischen gleich kommt, wo nicht gar dieselbe übersteiget."

[55] Rambach: Evangelische Betrachtungen, 970: "und da ihr neue und rein gestimmte Harfen empfangen werdet, Gott und dem Lamme, das erwürget ist, und den sieben Geistern, die vor seinem Throne sind, ein ewiges Lob=Lied zu spielen."

[56] Rambach: Evangelische Betrachtungen, 1433: "Sie vereinigen sich mit den Engeln im Lobe Gottes, und lassen gleichsam auf Erden ein heiliges Echo wiederschallen auf das **Halleluja** und auf das **heilig, heilig, heilig ist der Herr Zebaoth**, welches im Himmel von den Cherubinen und Seraphinen gesungen wird."

Mix yourselves into their choirs in the spirit of faith, sing along in their songs of praise that they sing to the Lamb that was slain; practice carrying out the will of God, and occupy yourselves, in the midst of the business of this life, with the holy efforts that they carry out before the throne of God.[57]

There is no indication that Rambach thinks of heavenly music as merely metaphorical; he mentions such details as that, like the angels, the blessed will not eat, drink, or marry, but he does not say that they will have no mouths. While he does not speculate on how either angels or the redeemed in heaven can make music without physical bodies, the implication is that the music is real.

## 3  On the Value of Hymns

The preceding sections have depicted an either/or moral status of music: for the unregenerate, music has no value; for the regenerate, it serves for the praise of God and strengthening in faith. While there has been some recognition of its use in encouraging others and communicating one's faith to others, little has been said about the power of music to change affects. To be sure, in the example of Saul and David, music did ameliorate Saul's distress, but it worked on a purely natural level. It did not, as Luther had said, drive away the devil. Music would seem, for Rambach, to serve as an expression of internal spiritual movements rather than as a means of eliciting such movement.

The picture is somewhat more complex, however. As Julian Heigel demonstrated, Rambach thought of his preaching audience not as divided simply into unconverted and converted but as fitting into different stages of conversion. While Heigel finds one sermon that identifies six different categories of belief and unbelief, a threefold division is most common, with those who are ready for repentance constituting the middle group.[58] For such persons, music can play a role in the process of conversion.

Rambach's sermon for the 3rd Sunday of Advent, 1725, on "good emotions" explains the role of the affective power of music and sermons. At the outset he notes that people talk of being moved, sometimes to tears, by a sermon, by scripture or another edifying book. These feelings, he says, are "effects of prevenient grace when God, through his Word and other means, to a certain extent allows some light to penetrate a person's understanding and also to some degree inclines the will toward the good in order to prepare the way for his conversion."[59]

---

[57] Rambach: Evangelische Betrachtungen, 1441: "Mischet euch öfters im Geist des Glaubens in ihre Chöre, stimmet mit ein in ihre Lob=Lieder, die sie dem erwürgten Lamme singen, übet euch in der Vollbringung des Willens Gottes, und beschäftiget euch, mitten in den Geschäften dieses Lebens, mit den heiligen Bemühungen, die sie vor dem Thron Gottes verrichten." A similar appeal for joining in song with the angels is in Rambach's 1728 sermon on the birth of Jesus, Rambach: Evangelische Betrachtungen, 62.

[58] Heigel: "Vergnügen und Erbauung", 129.

[59] Johann Jakob Rambach: Erkenntniß der Wahrheit zur Gottseligkeit, oder Predigten über verschiedene Evangelische Texte. Halle: Waisenhaus, 1727, 51–52: "Wirckungen der

Recognizing that those who have the indwelling Spirit as a constant guide to their will also experience fluctuations of intensity in their spiritual affections, Rambach sets them aside here to focus on those who are not yet converted. These movements of prevenient grace in the unconverted are as if Christ is knocking on the door of a heart that has not yet opened. There are three functions of this kind of grace: to remove any obstructions that lie in the way of repentance, to provide opportunities for conversion, and to awaken movement in the heart of a dead sinner. The ordinary means through which this grace works is through the Word of God, both law and gospel, sometimes working through the natural conscience and reason, sometimes through the heart and the will. Of the latter sort are the feeling of humility in realizing the depth of God's love, the feeling of unrest in confronting Jesus' suffering and crucifixion, and the feeling of joy in imagining eternal life. In this context, hymns have a special power to evoke these feelings: "Lovely spiritual hymns in particular have a secret power to affect the mind and to fill it with good impulses."[60]

As a lively preacher, Rambach provided stories with illustrations of the power of hymns. In one sermon he told of a woman who had secretly killed a child. As she was passing by a house, she heard the singing of the hymn "O Ewigkeit, du Donner=Wort!" It put her in such a state of anxiety that she herself went and reported her crime, giving as a reason that her soul could still be saved.[61] Another woman was overtaken with shame while singing *Jesu meine Freude* with the realization that she could not sing it honestly.[62] Music at a funeral can often evoke an emotional response: "Sensitive and tender-hearted persons can easily be moved to tears by the mournful melody of a funeral hymn, by sad music, by looking at a corpse, etc."[63] In another book narrating children's conversion stories, Rambach tells of a girl who was "very awakened" by the singing of spiritual songs and went around the house singing hymns she learned in school; the end of her short life was also accompanied by the singing of a hymn. In her case, hymns were a means by which she deepened a faith that was already present at a young age. In another story, a hymn served to prepare a child for the penitential struggle that

---

zuvorkommenden Gnade, da Gott durch sein Wort und andere Hülfs=Mittel theils in den Verstand des Menschen einiges Licht eindringen lässet, theils seinen Willen zum Guten neiget, um ihm dadurch den Weg zu seiner Bekehrung zu bahnen."

[60] Rambach: Erkenntniß der Wahrheit, 62: "Insonderheit haben geistliche liebliche Lieder eine geheime Kraft, das Gemüth zu afficiren, und es mit guten Regungen zu erfüllen."

[61] Rambach: Erkenntniß der Wahrheit, 59: "Eine Weibes=Person, die heimlich ein Kind umgebracht hatte, hörte, da sie bey einem Hause vorbey ging, das Lied singen: **O Ewigkeit, du Donner=Wort**! etc. und ward dadurch in eine solche Bangigkeit gesetzet, daß sie selbst hinging, ihr Verbrechen anzeigte, und als Anlaß gab, daß ihre Seele noch gerettet werden konte."

[62] Rambach: Erkenntniß der Wahrheit, 68–69: "So ward eine Person von einer empfindlichen Schaam überfallen, als sie in der Kirche das Lied mitsung: **Jesu, meine Freude**! und von ihrem Gewissen bestrafet wurde, daß sie es nicht mit Wahrheit singe."

[63] Rambach: Erkenntniß der Wahrheit, 82: "Wohllüstige und weichhertzige Personen können leicht durch die klägliche Melodey eines Sterbe=Liedes, durch eine traurige Music, durch den Anblick eines Todten, u.s.w. zu Thränen bewogen werden."

led to regeneration, though Rambach carefully attributes the causation to God, not the hymn, saying that God prepared her through the hymn.[64]

Interestingly, in the sermon on good emotions, while Rambach also gives Augustine as an example of being moved by grace, he does not mention Augustine's discussion of the singing of hymns, which was a *locus classicus* for examining the role of music in the church. Rambach's analysis centers on Ambrose's rhetorical skill as the tool through which grace worked: "[Augustine] had no higher intention when listening to Ambrose's sermons than to let his ears be tickled by the elegant words. Along with the words, however, God also poured into his mind, unnoticed, the material that this eloquent teacher presented."[65]

Because Rambach taught homiletics, it may be understandable that he focused on Ambrose's preaching rather than the hymns that also moved Augustine. Music was for Rambach only one of the means God used for knocking on the sinner's heart. Many other examples that do not mention music are included in this sermon. The important point of the sermon is that such emotional responses are still within the realm of nature, though grace may be at work in them. One should not deceive oneself into thinking that these feelings are sufficient. The true work of repentance and change of heart must go much deeper than these transitory emotions. If one continues to listen to the voice of the natural conscience, however, God will offer more grace to lead the sinner to sincere repentance and true conversion.[66]

As a tool for eliciting emotions that may draw the listener in the direction of an experience of faith, then, hymns and other external factors have value, but they themselves do not have spiritual power. Only God's grace working in the heart has power to lead a person to repentance and conversion. Without that, singing or performing the holiest music would still be a sinful activity, for "the best outgrowths of corrupt nature are rotten fruits of a rotten tree."[67]

## 4  Affections

Pietists are generally regarded as placing a high value on subjective religious feelings. Poetry of this period that appeals to emotions is often labeled as Pietist or influenced by Pietism. The preceding section should have shown the fallacy of such simplistic labels. The Baroque age in general saw widespread interest in the "doctrine of the affections." The popularity of operas showed the attraction of musical drama as a means of engaging an audience by eliciting emotions.

---

[64] Johann Jakob Rambach: Christliches und Biblisches Exempel-Büchlein für Kinder, Pt. 2. 3rd ed. Leipzig: Friderici, 1742, 1–19.
[65] Rambach: Erkenntniß der Wahrheit, 56: "Er hatte bey Anhörung der Predigten Ambrosi keine höhere Absicht, als an den zierlichen Worten desselben seine Ohren zu kützeln: Gott aber flößte ihm mit den Worten auch zugleich die Sachen, welche dieser beredte Lehrer vortrug, unvermerckt in sein Gemüth."
[66] Rambach: Erkenntniß der Wahrheit, 84.
[67] Rambach: Erkenntniß der Wahrheit, 83: "Die besten Wirckungen der verderbten Natur sind faule Früchte eines faulen Baumes."

Religious cantatas were introduced to use the same musical means as opera to elicit emotions from religious subject matter. Gottfried Ephraim Scheibel defended such a carryover by saying that the emotion was the same, no matter whether the subject was secular or sacred.[68] While Pietists notoriously opposed operas and church cantatas, they did not necessarily disagree that the emotions were the same. The question was not about the feelings themselves; it was about the person who felt them.

Rambach followed in the line from Johann Conrad Dannhauer through Spener and Francke of theologians who discussed affections in the context of biblical hermeneutics. For a full understanding of a scripture passage, these authors believed, it is valuable to know not just the written words but also the affect of the writer. Against those who thought this undermined scriptural authority or raised doubts about the legitimacy of inspiration, Rambach responds that the Holy Spirit did not put affects to sleep during inspiration but, instead, stimulated and sanctified the affects. The writers did not cease to have affects, and they often wrote of them. Paul certainly retained his natural temperament even after his conversion. The Holy Spirit accommodates to the characteristics of the writers, and those who give expression to their affects write in a livelier and more palatable manner.[69]

Nevertheless, Rambach insists on a distinction between natural and spiritual affects and claims that the affects of the regenerate do not emerge from the same sources as those of the natural or unredeemed person. The affects of a natural man come from the senses or the understanding; the affects of a spiritual and regenerate person come from a soul that has been enlightened by the spirit of God and made holy.[70] The unregenerate may well relate to some of the emotions found in scripture, for example, the envy of Joseph's brothers, but they do not understand the difference between natural and spiritual affections. This understanding is only possible through *aisthesis*, or spiritual sensation. This Greek word appears in Philippians 1 in the phrase ἐν ἐπιγνώσει καὶ πάσῃ αἰσθήσει, which Luther had translated as "in allerlei Erkenntnis und Erfahrung," which conveys the sense of experience that is lacking in English translations such as NRSV's "with knowledge and full insight." This verse had been thoroughly explicated by Lange as the basis for talking about spiritual experience, and Francke had used the concept to explain how a reborn person can understand the affects of the writers of scripture.[71] While

---

[68] Gottfried Ephraim Scheibel: Zufällige Gedancken Von der Kirchen-Music. Wie Sie heutiges Tages beschaffen ist. Frankfurt/Main, 1721; trans. by Joyce Irwin, in: G. E. Scheibel: Random Thoughts about Church Music in our Day (1721). In: Bach's Changing World: Voices in the Community. Ed. by Carol K. Baron. Rochester, NY: University of Rochester Press, 2006, 227–249.

[69] Johann Jakob Rambach: Ausführliche und gründliche Erläuterung über seine eigene Institvtiones Hermenevticae Sacrae. Ed. by Ernst Friedrich Neubauer. Giessen: Krieger, 1738, 377–379.

[70] Rambach: Erläuterung über seine eigene Institvtiones Hermenevticae Sacrae, 381–389.

[71] Joachim Lange: Disputatio Exegetico-Dogmatica De Experientia Spirituali. Quam ex Epist. ad Philipp. c. 1. v. 9, 10. Demonstratam. Halle: Henckel, 1710. On Francke, see Simon Grote: The Emergence of Modern Aesthetic Theory: Religion and Morality in Enlightenment Germany and Scotland. Cambridge, UK: Cambridge University Press, 2017, 74–82.

the concept of aesthetics would emerge as a branch of philosophy with Alexander Gottlieb Baumgarten, who studied under Francke and later taught for a few years in Halle, the term did not yet have its later connotation of the philosophy of art or beauty. Still, it is possible to show the influence of Baumgarten's Pietist education on his later aesthetics, as Simon Grote has done.[72]

The application of Rambach's understanding of affects to worship can be found in his advice to preachers. In attempting to communicate to the congregation, the preacher should know the difference between affect and affectation. One should strive to have the same affect as the writer of scripture but should not try, for instance, to go with Paul in rapture to the third heaven. To engage in histrionics through vocal affectations is for comedians, not preachers.[73] As with music, the authenticity of the worship leader is of primary importance. The same concern for authenticity motivates Rambach's critique of poetry, as we will see in the next section.

## 5 Poetry and Style

As noted at the outset, Rambach published a considerable number of hymn and cantata texts in addition to editing several hymnals. We have seen how, in discussing music, his stress is more on the text than the musical sound. One might hope to find in his essay on "The Abuse and Proper Use of Poetry" some reflection on poetry as an art form.[74] This hope fades quickly, however. After a first clause calling poetry "a noble gift of the Most High," Rambach finishes the sentence by observing that, like other divine gifts, it has been subjected to "miserable abuse."[75] The abuse comes of using this tool in the service of one of the three most prominent vices—sensuality, ambition, and avarice. For nine of his eleven sections, Rambach elaborates, often in quite colorful and entertaining manner, on the ways in which these vices are manifested by poets, turning only in the last two sections to the proper use of poetry, namely to serve God, one's neighbor, and the improvement of one's own disposition. By dealing so harshly with other poets, Rambach feeds the stereotype of an art-hating Pietist.

He turns his attention first to ancient poets such as Ovid and Catullus for their lascivious poems but almost excuses them as being part of a pagan society with gods who were themselves unchaste. Less understandable in his view is such poetry from poets who pretend to be worshippers of a God who is the enemy of impurity. Some wedding poems, for instance, cannot be read without embarrass-

---

[72] Simon Grote: Pietistische 'Aisthesis' und moralische Erziehung bei Alexander Gottlieb Baumgarten. In: Aufklärung 20, 2008, 175–198.
[73] Rambach: Erläuterung über seine eigene Institvtiones Hermenevticae Sacrae, 392.
[74] Johann Jakob Rambach: "Von dem Mißbrauch und rechtem Gebrauch der Poesie," published as preface to his *Poetische Fest=Gedancken Von den höchsten Wohlthaten Gottes* (2nd ed: Jena: Ritter, 1727) and as Meditation 14 of his *Theologische Betrachtungen*, 259–278. My citations will be from the latter because of the more convenient pagination.
[75] Rambach: Theologische Betrachtungen, 259.

ment, and some student albums contain shameful verses that should be burned. Other writers are more subtle and hide their poison under ambiguous allusions issuing from their impure imaginations. All such poets will meet the judgment that awaits those who cause a stumbling block to others (Matt 18,7), "even if their skillfulness is admired by the whole world and their gallant poems are esteemed as utterly unsurpassable masterpieces."[76]

A particular grievance to Rambach is the practice of mixing sacred devotional poetry with gallant arias and facetious jests in a single volume, thus joining Christ with Belial. It is evident that such poets express themselves better when writing of forbidden things, as that is the direction of their minds: "For here [in spiritual matters] they have to swim with their pens against the stream and force their vain minds to think about God and divine things; whereas in unchaste matters they are swept away by the stream of infectious passion and find themselves right in their own element."[77]

If some respond that their poetry is an innocent amusement, appealing to Titus 1,15 to claim that to the pure all things are pure, Rambach's rejoinder is to point to the rest of the verse: "to the impure and unbelievers, nothing is pure, as their minds and consciences are both impure." What they put forth as love poetry is, according to Rambach, nothing other than impure, disordered passion that should be snuffed out before it bursts into flames and consumes body and soul.[78]

Turning to the second vice, ambition, Rambach compares those who seek to be admired for their masterpieces to Nebuchadnezzar, who demanded that all his subjects bow down and worship his golden statue (Daniel 3,5–6). Their time would be better spent preparing for eternity than trying to ingratiate themselves with powerful people by exaggerating their deeds. The poets falsify the truth by turning dwarfs into giants and common actions into unprecedented wonders. A common affect of the ambitious is anger and desire for revenge, and these writers may turn to satire under the false pretext of moral guidance. It is rare that anyone is aided by having minor faults subjected to ridicule, and it is irresponsible for these poets to compare themselves to preachers, much less to Christ. When Jesus proclaimed judgment in Matthew 23, it flowed from compassionate sorrow, which is completely lacking among the satirists.[79]

Finally, the greedy abuse poetry by writing for profit, especially by composing glowing eulogies about people who were known to have lived an evil life. They turn "a hideous drunkard into a model of moderation, depict an arrogant chap as the natural image of humility, make a miser into a benefactor, and put forward a

---

[76] Rambach: Theologische Betrachtungen, 263–264: "wenn auch ihre Geschicklichkeit von aller Welt bewundert, und ihre galante Gedichte für lauter unverbesserliche Meister=Stücke geachtet würden."
[77] Rambach: Theologische Betrachtungen, 265: "Denn hier [in geistlichen Materien] müssen sie mit der Feder wider den Strom schwimmen, und ihr eitles Gemüth zwingen, an Gott und göttliche Dinge zu gedencken; da sie hingegen bey unkeuschen Sachen von den Strom der Lust=Seuche fortgerisse[n] werden, und sich in ihrem rechten Element befinden."
[78] Rambach: Theologische Betrachtungen, 269.
[79] Rambach: Theologische Betrachtungen, 269–273.

half-educated bloke as a marvel of the scholarly world, as long as they get their fee for it."[80]

To summarize, Rambach's critique of poetry lies in the area of morality, not literary style. Nor does it touch on inspiration, as the secular subject matter of the poetry being discussed would not qualify it for consideration as inspired. The writers, though they may consider themselves Christian, are living immoral lives and are influencing others in immoral ways. In addition to the moral vices that provide the main outline of the essay, the poets transgress against the moral law. In one passage Rambach accuses the ambitious of disobeying the first, second and eighth commandments, that is, of worshipping false gods, misusing God's name, and bearing false witness. The proper aim of poetry, Rambach finally explains in the last two sections, is to honor God and encourage moral improvement in others. Even wedding, funerary, and tribute poems can serve the goal of moral improvement and are therefore not inappropriate for Christians to write.[81] Not the form but the content is the criterion for evaluation.

Julian Heigel offers the interesting speculation that Rambach's motivation in writing this preface to his book of poems was to create distance between his creative efforts and those of others in order to protect himself from criticism. Rambach was making use of madrigal and cantata forms that were associated with secular love poetry, while he wanted to legitimate these forms for sacred content.[82] In the preface to his first volume of cantata texts, published in 1720, Rambach had tried to deflect some responsibility for choosing a cantata form by reporting that he had been asked by Johann Gotthilf Ziegler to write a text for the concerted music in the Ulrichskirche.[83] He had also given credit to Menantes (Christian Friedrich Hunold) as his poetry instructor, yet, prior to arriving in Halle, Hunold had been forced out of Hamburg for writing a scandalous satirical novel. This first volume of Rambach's poetry was praised, though with some suggestions for improvement, by Gottfried Ephraim Scheibel in his 1721 work advocating the transfer of operatic forms into church music.[84] Whether Rambach's second preface was designed to distance himself from such an affirmation of secular style and from Hunold's irreligious reputation can only be surmised.[85]

This adoption of innovative forms is one of the factors that complicate the historical classification of Rambach, as mentioned at the beginning. Pietists were

---

[80] Rambach: Theologische Betrachtungen, 274: "einen häßlichen Trunckenbold als ein Muster der Mäßigkeit vorstellen; einen Hochmüthigen als ein natürliches Ebenbild der Demuth abschildern, einen Geitzigen zu einem Mildthätigen machen; einen halb-Gelehrten als ein Wunder der gelehrten Welt aufstellen, wenn sie nur ihre Gebühr dafür bekommen."
[81] Rambach: Theologische Betrachtungen, 277.
[82] Heigel: "Vergnügen und Erbauung", 82.
[83] Johann Jakob Rambach: Geistliche Poesien. Halle: Neue Buchhandlung, 1720, fol. 7b.
[84] See Scheibel: Zufällige Gedancken. Details of Scheibel's critique of Rambach were omitted from my translation.
[85] During the years in Halle when Rambach would have known him, Hunold also wrote congratulatory poems that J. S. Bach used for cantatas in praise of Prince Leopold of Anhalt-Cöthen. These also would seem to fit within Rambach's description of misuse of poetry.

known for criticizing elaborate church music, and this blurring of lines between sacred and secular styles would seem to go against everything they stood for. Yet the opposition to introducing the cantata style into churches was not solely, or even primarily, led by Pietists.[86] Heigel describes the various factors at issue in the cantata debates and concludes that style was not determinative in deciding the appropriateness of music: "The question whether music is edifying or offensive is determined not according to its stylistic formation but rather according to the inner mindset of the individual, who, in accordance with his state of grace, is capable of producing spiritual affects both as a musician and as a listener."[87] In discussing the performance of Rambach's cantata texts as set by Ziegler for the Ulrichskirche in Halle, Heigel also deduces Francke's approval of the cantata style: "The fact that cultivation of church music at St. Ulrich's was intensified under Francke can serve as further evidence that the Halle Pietists were open to figural music in the church if it served the purpose of 'edification.'"[88]

Rambach's position on style in preaching may shed light also on his views on style in poetry. In the preface to his collections of sermons in *Evangelische Betrachtungen*, he says that the style of expression in preaching should be clear, pure, and simple. Clarity demands that one avoid both archaisms and neologisms, overly long sentences and too many parenthetical remarks. Words should flow naturally and be understood by both the learned and unlearned. Purity requires avoidance of foreign and scholastic terms but also vulgar popular sayings. Simplicity applies to all "high poetic phrases, florid epithets, callous puns, oratorical circumlocutions, pretentious mystical or otherwise paradoxical and foreign-sounding expressions, along with such formulations as smack of court and chancellery style or even of novels or the theater."[89] The desired simplicity will be in accordance with biblical style and phraseology.

---

[86] See my chapter "The Cantata Debate" in Irwin: Neither Voice nor Heart Alone, 127–139, and Jürgen Heidrich: Der Meier-Mattheson Disput. Eine Polemik zur deutschen protestantischen Kirchenkantate in der ersten Hälfte des 18. Jahrhunderts. Göttingen: Vandenhoeck & Ruprecht, 1995.

[87] Julian Heigel: Die Legitimation der Kantate mithilfe des hallesch-pietistischen Affektkonzepts. In: Die Kantate als Katalysator: Zur Karriere eines musikalisch-literarischen Strukturtypus um und nach 1700. Ed. by Wolfgang Hirschmann and Dirk Rose. Berlin: De Gruyter, 2018, 212: "Die Frage, ob Musik erbauend oder anstößig ist, richtet sich nun nicht nach ihrer stilistischen Ausformung, sondern nach der inneren Haltung des Einzelnen, der gemäß seinem Gnadenstand dazu befähigt ist, die geistlichen Affekte sowohl als Musiker wie als Zuhörer zu produzieren."

[88] Heigel: "Vergnügen und Erbauung", 166: "Die Tatsache, dass die Pflege der Kirchenmusik an St. Ulrich unter Francke intensiviert wird, kann als ein weiterer Beleg dafür gelten, dass die Halleschen Pietisten offen sind für die Figuralmusik in der Kirche, wenn diese dem Zweck der 'Erbauung' dient."

[89] Rambach: Evangelische Betrachtungen, 26: "hohe poetische Redens=Arten, schwülstige epitheta oder Bey=Worte, kaltsinnige Wort=Spiele, oratorische Umschreibungen, hochgetriebne mystische, oder sonst paradox und fremdklingende Ausdrücke aus, samt solchen Formeln, die nach dem Hof= und Cantzeley=Stilo, oder gar nach Romänen und nach dem Theatro schmecken."

Rambach hopes that his sermons conform to these guidelines and is willing to make corrections if they do not. He admits the possibility that some poetic manners of speech may have inadvertently crept in, but he also thinks that some people mistake lively and emphatic expression for poetic speech. When the metaphors flow from the fullness of a sanctified affect, they should not be criticized as poetic but appreciated as effective communication: "If the tropes and figures usher forth from a sanctified affect and remain within the bounds of modesty, then they do not belong to the mistakes but rather to the adornments of speech and bring to it an incisive emphasis and a pleasant liveliness."[90] Again the criterion for judging an art, in this case the art of oratory, is primarily whether it proceeds from a holy affect.

In addition to new poetic forms, Rambach also shows receptivity toward a new direction in theology, i.e. physicotheology, by which the natural world gained enhanced appreciation as evidence of God's creativity. Rambach makes direct reference to poet Barthold Heinrich Brockes' *Irdisches Vergnügen in Gott* as providing glorious specimens of giving honor to God for his marvelous works in the realm of nature.[91] This pleasure in creation is defended in Rambach's book on ethics under the topic of loving God alone. Rightly or wrongly, Pietists had been charged with rejecting any love of creatures as sinful and in conflict with the command to love only God.[92] Rambach explains that one may love things that are effects of God's goodness and that may evoke praise and gratitude toward him. Examples include the taste of a delicious meal, the smell of a beautiful flower, the singing of a bird, or the sound of a musical instrument. To be sure, the pleasure enjoyed in these things is not an end in itself but leads back to God: "This little brook of pleasure leads into the unfathomable sea of his love and mercy." He criticizes Augustine as having gone too far in declaring pleasures of the senses to be sinful. Why, he asks, would God have placed so much sweetness and attractiveness in creatures if they were not to be enjoyed?[93] It is not solely pleasure that the natural world provides, however, but also a sense of awe. That sense of awe is a component of the experience of the sublime, which is emerging as an important theme in the Age of Empfindsamkeit. Rambach shows some awareness of this theme when he refers to the prophets' "sublime manner of writing" and the "holy shudder" that attends reflection on God's majesty.[94]

It would be a mistake, however, to take these comments out of the context of Rambach's Pietist theology. In the matter that Lange saw as crucial, that is, whether

---

[90] Rambach: Evangelische Betrachtungen, 27: "Wenn die tropi und figurae aus einem geheiligten Affect herrühren, und in den Schrancken der Bescheidenheit bleiben, so gehören sie nicht unter die Fehler, sondern unter die Zierden der Rede, und bringen derselben einen durchdringenden Nachdruck und eine angenehme Lebhaftigkeit zuwege."

[91] Rambach: Theologische Betrachtungen, 276.

[92] Valentin Ernst Löscher: The Complete Timotheus Verinus. Trans. by James L. Langebartels. Milwaukee, WI: Northwestern, 1998, 150–155.

[93] Johann Jakob Rambach: Moral=Theologie oder Christliche Sitten=Lehre. Frankfurt/Main: von Sand, 1738, 797.

[94] Rambach: Theologische Betrachtungen, 275. This would be a subject worthy of further study in Rambach's works.

there can be any indifferent moral actions, Rambach takes the same position as Lange: within civil law there may be indifferent actions, but within the moral law, an action is either directed toward good or toward evil, depending on the intention and form. Rambach is most offended by the same activities that disturbed Lange: dancing, card-playing, and comedies.[95] Like Lange, he distinguished between indifferent things, where one has a certain freedom of choice, and indifferent actions, which is an inadmissible category.

Despite a certain openness to new trends in poetry and to physicotheology, Rambach's music-theological stance is directly in line with that of Francke and Lange. To say this is not to disagree with the thesis of Julian Heigel, who chose by entitling his study *Vergnügen und Erbauung* to put more emphasis on the literary context. This short chapter has only attempted to derive a theology of music from Rambach's writings, while Heigel in his conclusion named the variety of perspectives from which he had assessed Rambach's work: "gallant poetry, pietistic hermeneutic of the affections, pietistic homiletics, early Enlightenment theory of knowledge, early Enlightenment-pietistic rhetoric and various musical aesthetics."[96] Even these do not exhaust all the approaches to Rambach, such as, for example, Richard Muller's view of him as a scholastic theologian within Pietism.[97] Nevertheless, based on the sources relating to music and the Bible, I am inclined to agree with Ernest Stoeffler's characterization that Rambach's works "may be considered the fullest systematic expression of the original Hallensian understanding of Protestantism."[98]

## 6  Selected Themes in Rambach's *Geistliche Poesien*

A comprehensive study of Rambach's poetic writings is beyond the scope of this chapter. Even Heigel's book-length study was limited to his cantatas with a focus as much on form and musical settings as on content. An article by Daniela Wissemann-Garbe in the recent collection of essays on Rambach edited by Stadelmann and Zimmerling provides a valuable systematic overview of Rambach's hymnological work with a structural outline of his hymnals and a list of melodies indicated[99]; in the same collection, Uwe Swarat examined the theology of Rambach's baptismal hymn.[100] In an earlier article in *Pietismus und Neuzeit*, Martin

---

[95] Rambach: Moral=Theologie, 854. See also pp. 534–535.
[96] Heigel: "Vergnügen und Erbauung", 218.
[97] Richard A. Muller: J. J. Rambach and the Dogmatics of Scholastic Pietism. In: Consensus 16, 1990, Issue 2, 7–27.
[98] F. Ernest Stoeffler: German Pietism During the Eighteenth Century. Leiden: Brill, 1973, 44.
[99] Daniela Wissemann-Garbe: Johann Jakob Rambach in hymnologischer Sicht. In: Johann Jakob Rambach, 173–201.
[100] Uwe Swarat: Der Bund eines guten Gewissens mit Gott: Die Theologie des Chorals "Ich bin getauft auf deinen Namen" von Johann Jakob Rambach. In: Johann Jakob Rambach, 203–227.

## 6  Rambach's Geistliche Poesien

Zeim looked more broadly at Rambach's perspective on poetry in the context of the Galant style of his time.[101] None of this valuable scholarship constitutes a thorough study of Rambach's poetic work, nor can I here offer more than a sampling of themes in his cantatas and other poems that are related to topics explored in the first part of this chapter.

Rambach classified his poetic works under the categories cantata, sonnet, madrigal, and hymn ("Geistliche Lieder"), but the subject matter is always scripturally or morally based. Of the two objectives that Rambach offered his readers in the preface to *Geistliche Poesien* and that served as the title for Heigel's study, pleasure and edification (*Vergnügen und Erbauung*), the second is definitely more prominent. The madrigals almost all cite a scriptural text as their basis. Those that are not explicitly based on a scripture passage are on a religious or moral theme. Readers who have a preconception that madrigals are mostly secular love songs may be surprised to find such titles as "On the hardness of the human heart" and "On the suffering of the faithful." There is nothing secular in Rambach's madrigals, which are classified as such based on poetic form, not content.

Because he wrote a year's cycle of cantata texts and published a cycle of sermons as well (*Evangelische Betrachtungen Uber die Sonn= und Fest=Tags=Evangelia des Gantzen Jahrs*), it is tempting to think that these could be correlated, but a few spot checks make this unrealistic. The sermons, of course, are much longer and touch on a number of themes in the course of 20–30 pages. They were also preached a few years later than the publication of the cantatas; most are dated between 1725 and 1729. The dedication of the 1720 poetry collection indicates that most were written in Pöltzig, where he had spent the summer of 1719 recuperating from health problems. As there is no intrinsic connection between the cantatas and any sermons preached by Rambach, I will simply choose some texts that illustrate points made earlier in the chapter.

### 6.1  The Joy of Heartfelt Praise

The sermon on the Feast of the Visitation discussed at length above had the theme of praise of God. The cantata for the same day begins with an interesting juxtaposition of the hymn "Lobet den Herren" ("Praise to the Lord, the Almighty") with the opening line of the Magnificat, "Meine Seele erhebt den Herren."

> Lobet den Herren, den mächtigen König der Ehren,
> meine geliebete Seele! das ist mein Begehren.
> Meine Seele erhebt den Herren.
> Kommet zu hauf!
> Psalter und Harfe, wach auf,
> Lasset die Musicam hören.
> Und mein Geist freuet sich Gottes meines Heylandes.[102]

---

[101]  Martin Zeim: Die pietistische Lyrik Johann Jacob Rambachs. In: Pietismus und Neuzeit 18, 1992, 95–117.

[102]  This and succeeding quotations in this section are from Rambach: Am Tage der Heimsu-

No other lines from the song of Mary are included in the cantata. Next comes a recitative declaring that the most blessed activity is to take pleasure in God and dedicate one's strength to his praise and glory:

> Diß ist das seligste Geschäffte
> In Gott vergnügt zu seyn
> Und seine Kräffte
> Zu dessen Ruhm und Lobe weyhn.

Those who live on earth but have their minds already in heaven do not grow tired of speaking of God's acts and thus rise on the wings of faith to heaven. In that holy sanctuary, they hear the praise of the Lamb and experience heaven on earth:

> In jenem Heiligthum
> Erschallet stets des Lammes Ruhm
> Die hier nun nicht darinnen müde werden,
> Die haben schon den Himmel auf der Erden.

Next, the lowliness of the earthly being is expressed in an aria professing Jesus as the sole object of praise:

> Lobt, ihr Thoren, Koth und Erden.
> Jesus soll mein Lob=Lied seyn.
>     Er allein
> Soll von mir gerühmet werden.[103]

There follows a single strophe from a chorale by Johann Christian Lange, "Mein Hertzens=Jesu, meine Lust." Lange had been part of Francke's circle in Leipzig, then worked under mystical Pietist Johann Wilhelm Petersen in Lüneburg before eventually becoming philosophy professor in Giessen. The writer of the 1883 article on Lange in the *Allgemeine Deutsche Biographie* stated that most of his hymns were written during his time in Lüneburg and that Petersen's effusive style is reflected in Lange's poems.[104] Indeed, the rapturous image of addressing Jesus sweetly while lying with one's heart on Jesus' breast is not typical of Rambach's style.[105]

---

chung Mariä. In: Rambach: Geistliche Poesien, 186–188. See also discussion of this and other Marian cantatas by Lutherans of the time in Mark A. Peters: Marian Theology in Printed Cantata Librettos for the German Lutheran Church, 1704–1754. In: Yale Journal of Music & Religion 3, 2017, Issue 1, 93–118, esp. 111. DOI: https://doi.org/10.17132/2377-231X.1062 (accessed July 18, 2023).

[103] Interestingly, this aria is placed in the section on thoughts of death in the collection of compositions by Johannes Schmidlin: Singendes und Spielendes Vergnügen Reiner Andacht, Oder Geistreiche Gesänge, Nach der Wahl des Besten gesammlet. Zürich: Bürgklisch, 1752, 567.
[104] Art. "Lange, Johann Christian". In: Allgemeine Deutsche Biographie 17, 1883, 640–641.
[105] Martin Zeim does point out instances of erotic imagery applied to the loving relationship between a believer and Jesus, but these images, according to Zeim, are integrated into a biblically based, dogmatically sound message: "Um so klarer aber ist daraus ersichtlich, daß Rambach erst nach sehr gründlicher, dogmatisch-biblischer Vorbereitung solch ein Bild bringt, nämlich erst dann, wenn die Phantasie durch Vorhergehendes in die spezielle religiöse Thematik hineingeführt ist. Es werden also auch hier literarische Mittel ganz in den Dienst der Verkündigung gestellt." Zeim: Die pietistische Lyrik, 111.

> Mein Hertzens=Jesu, meine Lust
> An dem ich mich vergnüge
> Der ich an deiner Liebes=Brust
> Mit meinem Hertzen liege.
> Mein Mund hat dir ein Lob bereit,
> weil ich von deiner Freundlichkeit
> so grosses Labsal kriege.

The recitative that follows returns to third person mode, using words of emotion and sensation but without a rhapsodic first-person formulation. To praise Jesus is to feel true joy as if in the most pleasant pasture; worldly desire, on the other hand, brings sadness and bitterness of heart. The dictum then summarizes this recitative with the verse of Nehemiah 8,10, "May the joy of the Lord be your strength." The closing aria alludes to the idea encountered in the sermon that the faithful become living instruments for the praise of God:

> Willst du wahre Freude fühlen,
> So muß Jesus in dir spielen.

The themes and mood of this cantata correspond to the sermon for the same feast day and may be summarized by saying that praise of God that comes from a heart filled with the Spirit is pleasing to God and brings joy to the believer.

## 6.2 The Struggle between Good and Evil

The themes and mood of the cantata for the Feast of St. Michael, by contrast, are different from those of the sermon cited earlier in this chapter. Of course, there is far more in the sermon than the passages I selected, but the cantata has none of the vision of heavenly community with the angels. Rather the focus is on the threat posed by Satan and the protection provided by Jesus as the hero and by Michael as the leader of the angels defeating the dragon. The closing aria describes the protection provided by the angels, and the chorale is a verse of "Ein feste Burg" with the battle imagery of God fighting for powerless humans.[106]

Imagery of conflict and battle is in fact prevalent throughout Rambach's poetry. The cantata for Easter Day begins with an aria depicting the victory of Christ over his enemies:

> Der Sieges=Fürst kommet! erzittert, ihr Feinde.
> Er schwinget die Fahne: verstummet und schweigt!
>   Er stehet, er sieget;
>     Ihr fallet, ihr lieget,
> Entwaffnet, verwundet, in Fesseln gebeugt.

---

[106] Rambach: Am Fest Michaelis. In: Rambach: Geistliche Poesien, 189–190.

Paul's use of battle imagery in 1 Corinthians 15,54–55 provides the scriptural basis for this approach, which is not an unusual Easter theme in Christian history, but it is striking that musical references in the cantata bring to mind martial music with trumpets and drums: "Laß zu des Siegers Ehren | Die Paucken und Posaunen hören."[107]

Granted, the cantata for the second day of Easter brings the theme of sadness at Jesus' death turning to joy that he is alive; furthermore, choruses of Hallelujahs are sung. The final aria, however, returns to the triumph of victory with the enemies sinking into a hellish swamp:

> Ich sehe die Feinde zun Füssen schon liegen.
> Sie sincken zusammen in höllischen Sumpf.
> Ich singe Triumph![108]

While the battle theme may not be unusual for Easter, it is more surprising to find it in the Christmas cantatas. The final aria for Christmas Day, together with the closing chorale "Schweig, arger Feind," leaves the listener with the satisfaction of victory over the enemy, whose arrows break apart against Immanuel's defenses:

> Rüstet euch, erboste Feinde!
>    Stürmet! Und gebet doch eilend die Flucht.
> Will Immanuel mich schützen,
>    So erzittern
>    Und zersplittern
> Eure Pfeil, und eure Blitzen,
>    Und mich nährt die Friedens=Frucht.

One might have expected the cantata to end with the more joyous aria that comes in the middle, alluding to the song of the angels at Jesus' birth and celebrating the union of heaven and earth:

> Willkommen, willkommen, Erlöser der Erden!
>    Dir jauchzet entgegen die sehnende Welt.
> Die Lüffte durchdringet ein Freuden=Gethöne
> Es schallen die Lieder der himmlischen Söhne,
>    Da Gott sich zu sterblichen Menschen gesellt,
> Da Himmel und Erde vereiniget werden.[109]

## 6.3    The Word Incarnate and the Troubled Soul

The cantata for the third day of Christmas takes up a different theme, that of Incarnation, playing on the ambiguity of the term *Word*. A human word is invisible, but the Word that sustains the world has, through a masterpiece of love, become visible and touchable.

---

[107] Rambach: Am ersten Oster=Tage. In: Rambach: Geistliche Poesien, 71–74.
[108] Rambach: Am andern Oster=Tage. In: Rambach: Geistliche Poesien, 74–76.
[109] Rambach: Am 1. Weynacht=Feyertage. In: Rambach: Geistliche Poesien, 12–14.

> Wenn ist dergleichen je geschehn,
> Daß man ein Wort kan sehn,
> Ja fühlen und mit Händen fassen?
> Ein menschlich Wort
> Geht durch die Lufft unsichtbar fort,
> Und hat sich nie betasten lassen.
> Das Wort, das alles stützt und hält,
> Das diesen Bau der Erden
> Aus nichts hat sichtbar dargesgtellt,
> Will nunmehr selbst auf Erden sichtbar werden.

The message is that the Lord who created the earth has become a creature of earth in order to bring the earthly children back to God. Even though Rambach highlights the physicality of the birth with reference to the senses of vision and touch, there is no sentimental sweetness of the child in the manger. There is a sober sense of gratitude at the exchange that has lowered Jesus in order to elevate humans, this time expressed in a first-person aria:

> Jesus wird ein Menschen=Kind,
> Daß ich Gottes Kind soll werden,
> Seht! Er trägt mein Jammer=Kleid;
> Schenket seine Herrlichkeit
> Einer armen Hand voll Erden.[110]

The emotion-laden expression of either a troubled or an enraptured soul that may be stereotypical of Pietism is rare in Rambach, though not entirely absent. The cantata for the second Sunday after Epiphany is set as a dialogue between Jesus and a soul overcome with suffering and tears. After the soul's first plea, Jesus responds that his hour has not yet come. After the second plea, his response is from his answer to Martha after Lazarus' death, explaining his delay in coming: "Have I not said this so that you would believe, that you should see the glory of God?" The soul then understands that she must quiet her own thoughts and give herself over to hope. When stubborn self-will is released, Jesus invites her to rest in his lap like an innocent child:

> Nun aber, da du dich von Trotz und Unmuth loß
> In meinen Liebes=Schooß
> Als ein unschuldig Kind geleget,
> So wird mein Mutter=Hertz erreget.
> Nun soll dein Wunsch geschehn,
> Nun solst du meine Hülfe sehn![111]

The duet that follows brings to mind the arias of Bach's "Wachet auf" cantata 140, in which the two singers speak to one another with similar yet different lyrics:

---

[110] Rambach: Am 3. Weynacht=Feyertage. In: Rambach: Geistliche Poesien, 17–20.
[111] Rambach: Am 2. Sonntage nach der Erscheinung Christi. In: Rambach: Geistliche Poesien, 35.

| Soul | Jesus |
|---|---|
| Nimm mein Hertz, o Jesu hin! | Nimm den Trost, o Seele hin! |
| Ich verleugne meinen willen, | Ich erfülle deinen Willen, |
| Ich betäube meinen Sinn. | Ich erfreue deinen Sinn |
| Du kanst meinen Kummer stillen. | Ich will deinen Kummer stillen. |
| Nimm mein Hertz, o Jesu hin! | Nimm den Trost, o Seele hin! |

The troubled soul also finds expression in some hymns in his *Poetische Fest=Gedancken*, such as one bemoaning the inability to feel the joy of Jesus' victory over death, "Klagen einer betrübten Seele an dem Freuden=Fest ihres Erlösers." In ten strophes the soul bemoans its inability to find release from the pangs of conscience. Aware of the joy possible with Jesus, this soul has not been able to attain it:

> Ich höre wohl von Sieg und Wonne singen;
> Doch scheint ein banger Trauer=Thon
> Bey dem Triumph in meinem Ohr zu klingen,
> Und spricht der neuen Freude Hohn.
> Ich fühle nichts von jener Lust
> Die deiner treuen Diener Brust
> Zu dieser frohen Zeit erfüllet,
> Und ihres Hertzens Kummer stillet.[112]

Another hymn, entitled "Oster=Thränen" ("Easter Tears"), expresses the struggle to be assured that the tears come from the right source and that the whole self is truly given over to God:

> Du bists, mein Heyl, so viel ich weiß,
> Nach dem ich mich mit Thränen sehne
> [...]
> Siehst du noch was in meiner Brust,
> Das dich nicht sucht, das dich nicht meynet
> Das nicht um dich, mein Schaz, und seine Sünden weinet:
> So handle nur damit nach deines Herzens Lust.[113]

Tears, Rambach makes clear, are not in themselves an indication of spiritual struggle. One can be deceived and confuse "Scherz" ("joke") with "Schmertz" ("pain"), as warned in his madrigal "On the False Tears of the World" ("Uber die falschen Thränen der Welt").

> Verstellte Welt!
> Wer deinen Thränen trauet,
> Der hat aufs Meer ein Haus gebauet,
> Das in einander fällt.
> Dein Weinen gehet nicht von Hertzen.[114]

In the sonnet "On the Power of Earnest Prayer" ("Uber die Krafft des ernstlichen Gebets"), he expresses the confidence that a sincere, sighing prayer that comes from faith will be heard:

---

[112] Rambach: Poetische Fest=Gedancken, 89–90.
[113] Rambach: Poetische Fest=Gedancken, 97.
[114] Rambach: Geistliche Poesien, 206–207.

> Kein Seufzer ist umsonst, der in der Angst gebohren,
> Kein stummes Sehnen ist bey unserm Gott verlohren.
>    Ist nur der Glaube da, so ist alles gut.[115]

The emotional state of the believer may change according to circumstance, but the love that binds the believer to Jesus is the constant in the relationship:

> Ein Hertz, das Jesum liebt, ist durch ein festes Band
> In Sturm und Sonnen=Schein mit ihm genau verbunden.
> [...]
> Den Heyland laß ich nicht: wenn Wind und Welle kämpft,
> Der Heyland läßt mich nicht; weil er das Wüten dämpft.[116]

In all the poems about doubt, struggle, faith, and love, the seriousness of the Christian life comes through, but one hymn, "On the Seriousness and Tranquility of the Lord Jesus" ("Über die Ernsthafftigkeit und Stille des Herren Jesu"), addresses this theme directly. Holding up Jesus as a model of seriousness, Rambach makes his point that there are no adiaphora: Jesus, it seems, neither made nor laughed at jokes, nor did he engage in any frivolous activity:

> Spiel, Tantzen, Schertz, und was die freche Welt
> Für Zeit=Vertreib und Mittel=Dinge hält,
> War allzumal ein Eckel deiner Sinnen;
> Du nanntest es ein thörigtes Beginnen.
>
> Es sprach dein Hertz zum Lachen: du bist toll!
> Zur eitlen Lust: du bist von Rasen voll!
> Du weintest offt aus Wemuth=vollen Hertzen,
> Wer aber hat dich sehen üppig schertzen?[117]

## 6.4  The Majesty of God

The majority of Rambach's poems, whether hymns, madrigals, or cantatas, address themes of the Christian life, as distinct from the nature of God. This may seem inconsistent with his claim, noted earlier in the chapter, that the Christian would never exhaust all the available material for praising God. We do find some hymns labeled "On the majesty and holiness of God," "On the omnipresence and omniscience of God," "On the omnipotence of God," and "On the perfect wisdom of God."[118] These are meant as hymns of praise and are couched in the second

---

[115] Rambach: Geistliche Poesien, 233.
[116] Rambach: Uber die Verbindung des Hertzens mit dem Herrn Jesu. In: Rambach: Geistliche Poesien, 231–232.
[117] Rambach: Geistliche Poesien, 282–283. A footnote provides the reference to Ecclesiastes 2: 2 for the first two lines of the second of these strophes.
[118] "Über die Majestät und Heiligkeit Gottes," "Über die Allgegenwart und Allwissenheit Gottes," "Über die Allmacht Gottes," "Über die vollkommne Weisheit Gottes." Rambach: Geistliche Poesien, 267–278.

person, addressing God. The first begins in that mode with the accompanying sense of unworthiness at addressing such a majestic being:

> O Grosser Geist! o Ursprung aller Dinge!
> O Majestät voll Pracht und Licht!
> Wer ist, der dir ein würdig Lob=Lied singe:
> Welch sterblich Hertz erzittert nicht?
>     Stellt sich der Seraphinen Schaar
>     Vor deinem thron verhüllet dar,
> Wie solte nicht ich Hand voll Erden
> Vor dir voll Furcht und Schauer werden!

The next strophe places the singer with Isaiah, asking for lips to be touched by the burning coal from the altar, falling to knees at the sound of the "Holy, holy, holy." The poem closes with the plea to receive a holy heart until such time as "Holy" can be sung eternally:

> Schenck uns ein Hertz, das heilig ist,
> Weil du, der Vater, heilig bist.
> Bis du uns an den Ort wirst bringen.
> Da wir ein ewig **Heilig!** singen.[119]

Many portions of the other hymns on God's attributes, however, seem more like theological instruction for the congregation than actual praise of God. One strophe in the hymn on God's omnipotence, for example, addresses freedom of the will as God's self-limitation of his power:

> Zwar pflegst du nicht im Gnaden=Reich
> Nach unumschränckter Macht zu handeln.
>     Da gehet alles recht und gleich
> Ein jeder kan in Freyheit wandeln.
>     Du öffnest da das Tod= und Lebens=Thor,
>     Legst Wohl und Weh der freyen Seele vor.

Another strophe explains that, while God has established order in nature, he has sometimes overridden that order through miracles.

> Du hast die Ordnung zwar gesetzt,
> Nach welcher die Natur muß wircken.
>     Doch hast du selbst sie offt verletzt
> Und läßt dich nicht von ihr umzircken.
>     Die grosse Zahl so vieler Wunder zeugt,
>     Daß deine Macht weit über alles steigt.[120]

This selective look at Rambach's poems and cantatas does not pretend to be comprehensive but is perhaps sufficient to make the point that his poetry is primarily sermonic. He was, after all, a preacher and professor of theology, and in that context it was his goal to instruct his congregation or his students to listen to God's

---

[119] Rambach: Geistliche Poesien, 267–270.
[120] Rambach: Uber die Allmacht Gottes. In: Rambach: Geistliche Poesien, 272–275.

Word and apply it to their lives. Through rhetorical skills, whether in sermon or poetry, he intended to engage not only the mind but also the will and the heart. These three were not to be separated. Seldom does the emotional thrust of one of his poems even come close to being characterized as sentimental. Emotion must always be subject to the test of sincerity, and both depend on right knowledge of scripture. Rambach never lost himself in indulgent aestheticism but was always the teacher and theologian seeking to guide others toward a truly committed life of devotion to God.[121]

# 7    Summary

The variety of Rambach's writings in different genres allows scholars to view him from different perspectives and identify him according to different categories. While he absorbed elements of literary style and perspective from the wider world, he remained firmly within the Pietist camp. For him, the Bible was a unified whole with the Old Testament prefiguring the New. He criticized the outward ceremonies of Hebrew worship but appreciated the orderliness of temple music, emphasizing that God is a God of order. Music itself has no curative power but can only heal when the Holy Spirit is working through the conscience. When the heart is filled with the Spirit, it overflows in song to the praise of God. Believers need not be ordained clergy to share the Word with others or to write songs for others' edification, but only those who are spirit-filled are capable of praising God.

Rambach drew clear lines between the regenerate and the unregenerate and between sacred and secular poetry. He strongly criticized the poetry of those who wrote for fame or worldly reward. Music and poetry should be written only for the glory of God and the edification of others. The distinction was not so much a matter of style as of content and motivation. While advising that worship should be simple and poetic imagery appropriate, Rambach offered no clear guidelines on the form of music to be used in worship. The only true criterion, as the distinguishing feature of Pietist theology, is that it emerge from a regenerate heart and be carried out in faith.

---

[121] Martin Zeim, in his analysis of the galant elements in Rambach's poetry, concludes that Rambach valued the poetic style of his time but subordinated it to his stated purpose of poetry, namely the glory of God and the service of neighbor: "Er unterstellt die Dichtung aller Lebensgebiete dem Zweck der Ehrung Gottes und Besserung des Nächsten. [...] Sein Hauptanliegen ist dabei, daß der Inhalt religiös-pietistischer Tendenz diene." (Zeim: Die pietistische Lyrik, 116–117).

Chapter Four

# Old and New Wine Blended: A Period of Transition

## 1  Siegmund Jakob Baumgarten (1706–1757)

The generation of Halle theologians who followed Lange and Rambach brought dramatically different approaches to the study of the Bible. Siegmund Jakob Baumgarten, who had been educated at the Glaucha Pädagogium, joined the Halle university faculty in 1732 and became professor in 1734. (His younger brother Alexander, mentioned in the previous chapter, joined the philosophy faculty a few years later.) Early in Baumgarten's tenure, tensions developed between him and other Halle theologians such as Joachim Lange and Gotthilf August Francke, who believed him to be straying too close to the thought of Christian Wolff, the philosopher ousted from Halle in 1723 in a movement led by Lange. This time, rather than accommodating Lange, the Prussian court appointed a commission, which decided in favor of Baumgarten, allowing him to remain on the Halle faculty. In a university marked by rivalry between Pietists and Enlightenment thinkers, David Sorkin sees Baumgarten as overcoming the divisions among those parties as well as the Orthodox: "By reconstruing key Pietist notions, he managed to reconcile a transcendent, orthodox Lutheranism grounded in the mysteries of grace and revelation with Enlightenment thought in the form of Wolff's mathematical method."[1]

In the effort to denote distinct theological periods, German historians have written of this period around 1740 as the time of *Übergangstheologie* ("transitional theology"), leading the way to what may be called "New Protestantism" or "Neology." Emanuel Hirsch described transitional theologians such as Johann Franz Buddeus, Christoph Matthäus Pfaff, and Siegmund Jakob Baumgarten as taking an eclectic approach that was indebted to both Orthodoxy and Pietism but sought to avoid divisive controversies while also engaging with the latest intellectual currents in natural law and philosophy. Of these figures, Hirsch found Baumgarten the most difficult to classify because of his influence on students who would later take diametrically opposed positions.[2] Paul Knothe, summarizing Baumgarten's theology, described him as maintaining a conservative connection

---

[1]  David Sorkin: Reclaiming Theology for the Enlightenment. The Case of Siegmund Jakob Baumgarten, 1706–1757. In: Central European History 36, 2003, Issue 4, 509.
[2]  Emanuel Hirsch: Geschichte der neuern evangelischen Theologie im Zusammenhang mit den allgemeinen Bewegungen des europäischen Denkens. Vol. 2. Gütersloh: Bertelsmann, 1951, 318–319, 370.

with Orthodoxy and Pietism but also seeking to link up both methodically and substantively with modern ways of thinking.³ Martin Schloemann, while recognizing the importance of other transitional theologians, identified Baumgarten as occupying a key position in the turning point to actual Enlightenment theology.⁴ Alessandro Nannini, writing about the role of affects in Pietist theology, identifies the 1740s as a transitional decade with Baumgarten as a key figure in moving from a supernatural to a natural view of affects. With this move, influenced by Wolffian philosophy, pursuits in the areas of sacred hermeneutics, spiritual poetry, and homiletics no longer needed to be legitimated on grounds of divine inspiration.⁵ While Nannini discusses other representatives of this shift in thinking, there is no more important figure to represent the transition away from the core period of Pietism in Halle than Siegmund Jakob Baumgarten.

In the early years of his teaching, Baumgarten relied on previous works from the Halle faculty, using Rambach's *Institutiones hermeneuticae sacrae* for his hermeneutics lectures and turning to Freylinghausen's *Grundlegung der Theologie* and Lange's *Oeconomia Salutis Evangelica* for doctrinal theology. In the preface to his *Unterricht von Auslegung der heiligen Schrift*, Baumgarten named as the best and most useful guides for biblical interpretation the works of Lange, Rambach, Francke and other authors commonly used by Lutheran interpreters.⁶ One name that is noticeably absent, however, is Campegius Vitringa. Instead of reading the Bible as a unified prophetic scheme, Baumgarten took a more historical approach. Each passage needed to be understood within its context of time and place and with a view to the orientation, personality, and ability of the writer.

This in itself was in accord with the Halle method of exegesis, but to understand the historical origins of the text meant for Baumgarten also the possibility of errors or faulty memories on the part of the writers. Divine inspiration did not mean verbal transmission. To study the Bible with the use of all the tools of textual interpretation is not, according to Baumgarten, fundamentally different from studying any other text. Nor is a converted person necessarily better equipped to understand the meaning than an unregenerate interpreter. While granting a role to divine grace in the proper understanding of scripture, Baumgarten nevertheless contradicted a central claim of previous Halle Pietists:

---

[3] Paul Knothe: Siegmund Jakob Baumgarten und seine Stellung in der Aufklärungstheologie. In: Zeitschrift für Kirchengeschichte 46, 1928, Issue 9, 536.

[4] Martin Schloemann: Siegmund Jakob Baumgarten. System und Geschichte in der Theologie des Übergangs zum Neuprotestantismus. Göttingen: Vandenhoeck & Ruprecht, 1974, 19.

[5] Alessandro Nannini: The Language of Affects. From 'Pathologia Sacra' to 'Pathologica Aesthetica'. In: Gefühl und Norm. Religion und Gefühlskulturen im 18. Jahrhundert. Beiträge zum V. Internationalen Kongress für Pietismusforschung 2018. Ed. by Daniel Cyranka et al. Halle: Franckesche Stiftungen, 2021, 177–190.

[6] Siegmund Jakob Baumgarten: Unterricht von Auslegung der heiligen Schrift. Halle: Bauer, 1742, 3. See also Marianne Schröter: Siegmund Jacob Baumgarten. *Unterricht von Auslegung der heiligen Schrift* (1742). In: Handbuch der Bibelhermeneutiken. Von Origenes bis zur Gegenwart. Ed. by Oda Wischmeyer. Berlin: De Gruyter, 2016, 639–649.

Therefore, an unconverted as well as a converted person can perceive the correct understanding of Holy Scripture, because the influence of divine truths occurs also in the effects of prevenient and preparatory grace; likewise, by contrast, a converted as well as an unconverted person can err in the exegesis of Holy Scripture.[7]

This is not to make biblical exegesis into a purely cognitive exercise, for experiential understanding adds depth. The preceding quotation is somewhat modified by the sentence that follows: "Yet the insight into passages that deal with divine changes of mind and workings of grace must be far clearer and more intuitive through actual experience of them than is possible without the experience."[8]

Baumgarten speaks more often of a change of attitude ("Gemütsfassung") than of conversion, and in defining conversion he gives the following elements: 1) a transition from a status of natural corruption into a status of union with God; 2) a change of the whole "Gemütsfassung" toward God, and 3) turning away from sin and toward God through Christ.[9] This turning to God must proceed from belief or faith, which has three components: a living recognition ("Erkenntnis") of God as our highest good, the reconciliation ("Versönung") made possible through Christ, and the beneficial fruits and divine promises that result. The understanding must be convinced of the correctness and reliability of these promises to the degree that all doubts are overcome. In sum, "Glaube", which can be translated as either belief or faith, has both cognitive and volitional or affective elements, which can be defined separately but are all part of a necessary process:

> The essential parts of faith can rightly be divided such that there must first be a convicting knowledge that includes assent; second, a desire and longing for a share in these promised goods, which is called in scripture a hunger and thirst for God and his grace (Ps 42.3, Matt 5,6); and third, trust in the certain fulfillment thereof through patient expectation and on this basis a confident joyfulness.[10]

In good orthodox manner, Baumgarten explains that the conversion process is the work of God through the established means, namely the Word of God in both law and gospel. The law provides awareness of sin and awakens the conscience,

---

[7] Baumgarten: Auslegung der heiligen Schrift, 18: "Folglich kan ein unbekehrter sowol als ein bekehrter den richtigen Verstand der heiligen Schrift einsehen, zumal da der Einflus götlicher Warheiten in den Willen der Menschen auch bey den Wirckungen der zuvorkommenden und bearbeitenden Gnade Gottes stat findet: so wie im Gegentheil ein bekehrter sowol als ein unbekehrter in Auslegung der heiligen Schrift irren kann."

[8] Baumgarten: Auslegung der heiligen Schrift, 18: "Obgleich die Einsicht solcher Stellen, die von götlichen Veränderungen des Gemüts und Gnadenwirckungen handeln, durch die eigene Erfahrung derselben weit klärer und anschauender werden mus, als ohne dieselbe möglich ist."

[9] Siegmund Jakob Baumgarten: Unterricht vom rechtmässigen Verhalten eines Christen, oder Theologische Moral. Halle: Bauer, 1738, 115–116.

[10] Baumgarten: Unterricht vom rechtmässigen Verhalten, 125–126: "**Die wesentliche Stücke des Glaubens** können auch füglich so eingetheilet werden, daß **einmal** überzeugende Erkentniß dahin gehöre, so den Beyfal mit in sich fasset, **zweytens** Verlangen und Sehnsucht nach einem Antheil an diesen verheissenen Gütern; so in der Schrift ein Hunger und Durst nach Gott und seiner Gnade genant wird **Ps.** 42, 3. **Matth** 5, 6. und **drittens** Zuversicht, durch ruhige Erwartung der unausbleiblichen Erfüllung davon, und getrosten Freudigkeit darüber."

and the gospel makes known the path toward overcoming sin. If one does not resist the call of grace, God works his changes in the person, sometimes through personal experiences, such as deliverance from danger or suffering felt to be punishment for sin.

The significant departure from some, though not all, Pietist conceptions of conversion[11] is that Baumgarten does not expect that this change of mentality ("Sinnesänderung") will take place in an instant or at an identifiable point but gradually. In some cases it may be quick, but it may go through many stages. For some it is easy, for some difficult; some are certain of their conversion, others not, but in all cases it is constantly in need of renewal: "The whole life of a Christian may fairly be called a continual repentance or turning away from sin and turning toward God."[12] Accordingly, Baumgarten does not divide readers of the Bible into two distinct categories, as if only the converted had the necessary illumination for understanding it. He does require of an exegete, in addition to his extensive list of academic and intellectual abilities, certain attitudinal characteristics: zealous desire for truth, indefatigability, modesty, fairness, and submissiveness to God, both in the respectful handling of God's Word as well as the careful exercise and observance of its truths.[13] These could all be classified within the realm of nature, not grace, and are quite different from the illumination that is thought by Lange to accompany regeneration.

Another core hermeneutical principle of other Halle theologians was that Christ is the kernel of scripture. One has to look hard to find this in Baumgarten; it does appear in his *Glaubenslehre*, part 3, toward the end of his chapters on scripture. He explains here that to say that Christ is the kernel and main content of Holy Scripture is to say that Christ in his person and work is the primary new and revealed truth that is most essential in the formation of the whole divine revelation. It not only comprises a very important part of scripture but also ties all the other revealed truths together, such that without knowledge of this basic truth the others cannot be usefully or properly applied. It does not mean, however, that the immediate content and literal meaning of each scripture passage is to be interpreted as dealing with Christ.[14]

With the weakening of the concept of Christ as the kernel of scripture comes the absence of the belief in the unity of scripture. Baumgarten does believe that the whole content of scripture was arranged by God to contain no more or less than was necessary for its purpose, which is the union of God and people. He also occasionally finds types and antitypes that connect the Old and New Testaments,

---

[11] On the variety of Pietist positions on conversion, see Strom: German Pietism and the Problem of Conversion.
[12] Baumgarten: Unterricht vom rechtmässigen Verhalten, 135: "Das gantze Leben eines Christen wird billig eine beständige Busse, oder Abkehr von Sünden und Zukehr zu Gott genant."
[13] Baumgarten: Auslegung der heiligen Schrift, 203.
[14] Siegmund Jakob Baumgarten: Evangelische Glaubenslehre. Vol. 3. Ed. by Johann Salomon Semler. Halle: Gebauer, 1766, 171–172.

but he is much less inclined to make specific claims about prophecy than were his predecessors. Concerning the prophetic parts of scripture, he writes:

> Most of the events or the history of Holy Scripture, and thus also its narratives, are so arranged according to the highest wisdom of God that they may be regarded and used in accordance with their secret, remote, indirect meaning and at the same time as prophecies of future events and spiritual truths, because the whole condition of the Israelite people and the context of their fortunes and experiences must yield anticipations of the spiritual people of God in the New Testament.[15]

In discussing the difference between the Old and New Testaments, Baumgarten explains that the Old was a preparation for the New and, being less perfect and complete, was destined to give way to it.[16] The Israelites also had only a mediated revelation through Moses, whereas the people of the New Covenant knew the Son of God directly through his incarnation. Furthermore, the Old Testament applies only to the Israelites and their descendants, while the New Testament is so general that it extends to all people on earth. The nature of the order of salvation also differs:

> The performance of actions belonging to the order of salvation in the Old Testament consisted of feeble, corporeal, figurative, and constantly repeated exercises of worship; in the New Testament, by contrast, the inward fellowship and union with God, the spiritual and reasonable service of God in spirit and truth is prescribed and instituted.[17]

Not all of this, to be sure, differs from the position of Francke or Lange, as they also regarded Israelite religion as external and Christian faith as inward and spiritual. The difference is in the reduced interest in reading the Old Testament as a prefiguring of the New and in looking for specific applications of typology.

An example of the difference may be seen in Baumgarten's commentary on Psalm 47. While he does state that the psalm can be understood as referring to Jesus' ascension, he does not make a direct connection between the psalm and the New Testament accounts of the ascension. The main point of the psalm for Baumgarten is that God's glory is over the whole earth and that the faithful should seek to spread that message. Too often, he observes, people are ashamed to share the good news. All the injunctions in this psalm to sing praises, to clap hands, and to rejoice with a glad sound are encouragements, as well as commands, to

---

[15] Baumgarten: Evangelische Glaubenslehre, Vol. 3, 75: "Die meisten Begebenheiten oder Geschichte der heiligen Schrift, und also auch die Erzälungen derselben, sind nach der höchsten Weisheit Gottes so eingerichtet, daß sie ihrer geheimen, entfernten, mittelbaren Bedeutung nach zugleich als Weissagungen künftiger Begebenheiten und geistlicher Warheiten angesehen und gebraucht werden können; weil die ganze Verfassung des israelitischen Volks und der Zusammenhang ihrer Schicksale und Begebenheiten Vorbilder des geistlichen Volks Gottes im neuen Testament abgeben müssen."

[16] Baumgarten: Evangelische Glaubenslehre, Vol. 3, 247.

[17] Baumgarten: Evangelische Glaubenslehre, Vol. 3, 249: "Hat die Verrichtung der zur Heilsordnung gehörigen Handlungen im alten Testament in dürftigen, leiblichen, vorbildlichen und beständig zu wiederholenden Uebungen des Gottesdienstes bestanden; da im Gegentheil im neuen Testament die innere Gemeinschaft und Vereinigung mit Gott, der geistliche, vernünftige Dienst Gottes im Geist und in der Warheit, verordnet und eingesetzet worden."

express gratitude for all God's mercies. To be sure, God does not need our praise, and sometimes we may not feel the direct effects of God's mercy, but we need to cultivate an attitude of praise for his work in extending his kingdom throughout the world.

The musical references in Psalm 47, accordingly, are less about any actual historical use of instruments or singing than about the intended meaning. The sound of the trumpets indicates that the message is not a secret but is known throughout the world. The clapping of hands is a sign of penetrating joy even in times of sadness. The only explicit mention of actual music is in explanation of the loud songs of joy: Christians often sing songs and even rejoice, but the important qualification is the intention of directing the praise to God and the attention of the mind to this purpose.

> In Christendom it has surely come about that many hymns are sung in honor of Christ, and one often shouts with joy, but the apposition that appears here makes the actual difference. It reads: "to God we should," that is, shout with joy in his honor so that our mind is directed to him; we should shout for joy and rejoice "with a joyous sound." In this way a mind that is gathered, directed to God, lifted up, and free of all distractions is required, so that this is not carried out to please others or ourselves, or out of mere custom. Rather, one is to shout with a joyful sound to the honor of God, who tests the hearts and minds, who sees into the hidden depths and recognizes the most secret motions that occur there.[18]

Elsewhere Baumgarten describes the kind of worship that is displeasing to God. Just as the criterion for proper praise was the subjective orientation and intention of the worshipper, so improper praise is judged according to the subjective status of the individual. Baumgarten does not use terms such as unregenerate or unconverted, but he does require that there be a readiness to repent and to receive grace:

> Thus it is not enough to raise up the hands; they must also be pure and holy. That is to say, if our prayer is to be pleasing to God, it must occur from a repentant heart that is assured of God's pardon or at least desirous thereof, standing within the workings of grace of the Spirit of God. The praise of God must therefore be an inward activity, and it must flow out of and be brought to God from a mind governed by love of the good and hatred of evil.[19]

---

[18] Siegmund Jacob Baumgarten: Erbauliche Erklärung der Psalmen. 2 Vols. Ed. by Johann Salomon Semler. Halle: Gebauer, 1759, Vol. 1, 853–854: "In der Christenheit ist es wol dahin gekommen, daß man Christo zu Ehren viele Lieder singet, es wird oft gejauchzet; aber der Beisatz, der hier stehet, machet den eigentlichen Unterschied aus. Es heist: **wir sollen Gott**, das ist, ihm zu Ehren jauchzen, so daß unser Gemüt auf ihn gerichtet sey; wir sollen jauchzen und uns freuen **mit frölichen Schalle.** Also wird ein gesamletes, zu Gott gerichtetes, erhabenes und von allen Zerstreuungen freies Gemüt hierzu erfordert, daß wir nicht etwa nur Menschen oder uns selbst zu gefallen, noch aus blosser Gewonheit, die einmal eingefüret worden; sondern Gott zu Ehren, der Herzen und Nieren prüfet, der ins Verborgene siehet und die geheimsten Bewegungen so dabey vorgehen, erkennet, jauchzen mit frohem Schalle."

[19] Baumgarten: Psalmen, Vol. 1, 552 (commentary on Psalm 29): "Also ists nicht genug, die Hände aufzuheben, sie müssen auch rein und heilig seyn, das ist, unser Gebet mus aus einem busfertigen und der Begnadigung Gottes versicherten, oder doch darnach begierigen und unter der Gnadenarbeit des Geistes Gottes stehenden Herzen geschehen, wenn es Gott wohlgefallen sol. Es mus also das Lob Gottes eine innere Beschäftigung seyn, und es mus aus einem Gemüte herfliessen, mit einem solchen Gemüte Gott gebracht werden, das eine herschende Liebe zum Guten, und einen herschenden Has gegen das Böse hat."

When faced with explicit mention of musical instruments in the psalms, Baumgarten turns them into figures of speech. This is not to say that he regards them as allegories or prefigurings of New Testament truths. Rather, he finds the spiritual meaning behind the outward ceremonies of the Israelites. To give thanks to God on the zither or praise him with the 10-stringed psaltery means,

> Make it known in the best and most glorious way that you can imagine, in every manner possible for you: [...] These are indeed just manners of speech that derive from the public worship of the Israelites in those times, but in fact they indicate that one should not be ashamed of God but rather gather all one's capabilities together to pursue the praise, veneration, adoration, and glorification of God among other people just as we would do in other important circumstances in the world.[20]

To say that Baumgarten's focus is on the inward disposition of the individual, does not, then, mean that it stops there. Throughout his psalm commentary, he emphasizes that one should go public with one's praise. Yet his purview is of the whole world and the universal church; the practical details of congregational worship are not foremost in his mind. Perhaps the institutional church is a given for him, and his concern is to broaden the thinking of church people. Whatever the reason, the repeated message in his psalm commentary is that the name of the Lord is to be known throughout the earth. Psalm 8 is particularly useful in this regard, teaching us "that the knowledge of God is not bound to a certain place, a people, or one or another person."[21]

In his *Glaubenslehre*, Baumgarten describes the church as a unity and a union with Christ as the head; the body is constituted of members joined together in faith and love through their bond to Christ. As in the quotation from the Psalm 8 commentary, he writes in the *Glaubenslehre* that the *ecclesia catholica* is not limited by race, ethnicity, age, time, place, or any other external factor. In this respect, it differs from the church of the Old Testament that was restricted to a particular people. It is true that there is no salvation outside the church, but this does not refer to any specific religious party, whether Catholic or Protestant. Only the invisible church can claim universality. Whether a church organization is part of the true church depends on conformity to apostolic teachings, to preaching the Word and administering the sacraments. Lest this seem like a modern ecumenical position, it should be pointed out that Baumgarten labeled as enemies of the church those who caused disorder in worship or church discipline, those who created

---

[20] Baumgarten: Psalmen, Vol. 1, 617 (commentary on Psalm 33): "Macht aufs allerbeste und herlichste, so gut als ihr auf eine ersinliche Weise könnet, auf alle euch nur mögliche Art, bekant: [...] Dieses sind zwar lauter Redensarten, die von dem öffentlichen Gottesdienste der **Israeliten** der damaligen Zeit hergenommen worden, die aber doch in der That so viel anzeigen: man dürfe sich Gottes nicht schämen, man müsse vielmehr alle seine Fähigkeiten zusammen nemen, und das Lob, die Verehrung, Anbetung und Anpreisung Gottes bey andern Menschen so weit treiben, als wir bey andern wichtigen Angelegenheiten in der Welt thun würden."

[21] Baumgarten: Psalmen, Vol. 1, 141 (commentary on Psalm 8): "daß die Erkenntnis Gottes nicht an einen gewissen Ort, an ein Volk, an einen und den andern Menschen gebunden sey."

division or schisms in the church, and syncretists who exhibited indifference to truth. Christian community, therefore, should maintain right teaching and worship and aid its members in coming to changes of heart and thus to full union with the invisible church of Christ and the faithful. The outward church community is to be used for the inner improvement of oneself and others, and for this reason it must be protected against decline and, furthermore, made stronger to spread its purpose.[22]

Clearly, Baumgarten did not reject organized worship or congregational singing, but these were a means to a higher end. Commenting on Psalm 50, he credits Asaph with this insight despite his leading role in Levitic ceremony. One would have thought, suggests Baumgarten, that Asaph would have placed great importance in the outward observances, but we see the opposite in this psalm, "how, after divine insight and inspiration, he agitated quite zealously against the abuse of fleshly trust in the mere outward cultivation [of worship]."[23] In the psalm, God asks for a sacrifice of thanksgiving rather than a sacrifice of bulls or goats. Applied to worship of Baumgarten's day, the lesson is

> that God is not served by mere outward exercises of worship, by mere church services and other kinds of liturgical acts, by singing, praying, Bible reading, giving of alms or whatever name it may have—all of which are in themselves good, praiseworthy, necessary and indispensable things—if our heart is not in them, if we do not do them out of a willing spirit, for the sake of God, and also out of love, trust, and reverence toward God, and if we do not thereby serve God in spirit and in truth.[24]

When Baumgarten moves from a literal to a metaphorical understanding of musical instruments, then, it should not be taken as a rejection of audible music or of instruments in congregational worship but rather as lifting worship to a higher level. In discussing Psalm 150, he names the instruments and mentions their characteristics and the role they played in Israelite worship or festivities. Without stating a preference for any specific instrument or making reference to use of instruments in his own time, he concludes that they are all useful as long as they are used to the glory of God. In the process, he gives an approving nod to human creativity as well as to the pleasures of the senses:

> Thus this sixfold indication of the various aids for praising God means, taken together, that whatever human ingenuity can devise for musical sound must be sacred to the Lord. And so different kinds of sensual pleasure are named as a sign that whatever other kinds

---

[22] Baumgarten: Evangelische Glaubenslehre, Vol. 3, 596–609.
[23] Baumgarten: Psalmen, Vol. 1, 900: "wie er nach götlicher Einsicht und Eingeben wider den Misbrauch des fleischlichen Vertrauens auf die blos äussere Abwartung desselben, gar ernstlich geeifert."
[24] Baumgarten: Psalmen, Vol. 1, 909: "Daß Gott mit blossen äussern gottesdienstlichen Uebungen, mit dem blossen Kirchendienst und andern Arten gottesdienstlicher Handlungen, mit Singen, Beten, Bibellesen, Almosengeben und wie es auch Namen haben mag, welches alles an sich gute, löbliche, notwendige und unentberliche Dinge sind, dennoch allein nicht gedienet sey, wenn unser ganzes Herz nicht dabey ist, wenn wir es nicht aus einem freiwilligen Geiste, um Gottes willen, auch aus Liebe, Vertrauen und Ehrfurcht gegen Gott thun, wenn wir nicht dabey Gott im Geist und in der Warheit dienen."

## 1  Siegmund Jakob Baumgarten

can also be devised must all be used to the service, honor, and worship of God with the employment of the senses.[25]

The call in Psalm 81 to use a variety of instruments to praise God indicates that Asaph wanted to make the communal worship of God as attractive as possible. "Here Asaph wants to call upon the whole church and the believers of that time to arrange and conduct this adoration, worship and veneration in community, publicly, and as pleasingly as possible."[26] The passage becomes an occasion for Baumgarten to compare the Pauline instructions concerning music in worship. This interpretation of Ephesians 5:19 is a succinct recognition of the power of music to stir hearts:

> There Paul reports in a New Testament manner what the music of the Old Testament was meant to depict and represent, namely the gratifying, delightful inner movement of the heart, the surging, harmonizing movement of the soul toward praise and glory of God that is so pleasing to oneself as well as to others.[27]

Contained in this sentence are several important points. First, the music of the Old Testament serves to model or preview the music of the New Testament. This is not to say that Christians are to try to replicate the sound or use equivalent instruments, but it does indicate that Baumgarten sees no dichotomy or disjunction between the two testamental periods. Second, Baumgarten recognizes the emotional power of music and its ability to move the soul. He expresses no suspicion of music as a merely sensual enjoyment. Third, it has an effect on others as well as oneself. The sense is that music unifies the powers of the soul, and perhaps brings souls together, toward the praise of God.

Further insight into Baumgarten's meaning may be gained from his exegesis of the passage in his book on the Pauline letters. His approach in this volume is to provide a philological analysis of specific words or phrases rather than a cohesive interpretation, but his explication of λαλοῦντες ἑαυτοῖς, the opening words of Ephesians 5:19, gives an interesting perspective on spiritual joy. As these words follow the instruction not to be drunk with wine, Baumgarten sees Paul as comparing the effects of the Spirit to the effects of wine: "as drunkards, people filled

---

[25] Baumgarten: Psalmen, Vol. 2, 1131: "Folglich wil diese sechsfache Anzeige der verschiedenen Hülfsmittel des Lobes Gottes überhaupt so viel sagen: was menschlicher Witz von Wohlklang erdenken kan, das müsse dem Herrn heilig seyn. Und da werden denn nur ein und andere Arten genant, vom sinlichen Vergnügen, zum Zeichen, daß, was dergleichen von anderer Art auch erdacht werden kan, das alles müsse zum Dienst, zur Ehre und Anbetung Gottes mit Anwendung der Sinnen gebraucht werden."

[26] Baumgarten: Psalmen, Vol. 2, 154: "Hier wil Assaph die ganze Kirche und alle Gläubigen der damaligen Zeit auffordern, diese Verwunderung, Anbetung und Verehrung Gottes gemeinschaftlich, öffentlich und aufs lieblichste, so gut es nur möglich sey, anzustellen und einzurichten."

[27] Baumgarten: Psalmen, Vol. 2, 154: "Da meldet Paulus auf eine neutestamentische Weise, was die Musik des alten Testaments habe abbilden und vorstellen sollen, nemlich, die erfreuliche, liebliche, innere Rürung des Herzens, die aufwallende, übereinstimmige und dem Menschen selbst so wol als auch andern recht angeneme Bewegung der Seele zum Lobe und Preise Gottes."

with wine are inclined to chattering, happy singing, and other evidence of their joy and overactive blood flow, so you are free, indeed obliged, to let similar effects of this spiritual joy be seen." Then the question remains whether the overflowing joy of the heart is to be expressed just to oneself or with others, and he decides in favor of sharing not indiscriminately but with other believers who share the same experiences and effects.[28]

His explanation of the difference among the musical forms mentioned in Ephesians 5:19 (ψαλμοῖς, ὕμνοις, ᾠδαῖς) does not focus on whether there is instrumental accompaniment, as had most interpreters in his tradition. The term *psalms* he takes to refer to those that are in fact in the biblical books of Psalms. "Hymns" refers to the remaining songs that are in other books of the Bible. The third term he considers as referring to those that are "self-made." Another way of distinguishing is according to the content, that is, whether they are instructive songs, songs of praise, and prayer songs; it is unclear whether he understands the Greek terms to correlate directly with these three types. At any rate, the modifier πνευματικαῖς, which he takes apply to all three, separates them from sinful, fleshly songs, as they are all either inspired by God or deal with divine matters.

Another benefit of a mixture of songs and forms is for variation in congregational use. In explicating Colossians 3,16, Baumgarten writes of bringing out a variety of sound for retaining the attention as well as the enjoyment of the congregation. The congregational use of songs should occur in the most pleasant way possible, utilizing the aid of the senses. The phrase ἐν χάριτι means for Baumgarten both "through grace," that is, out of a living knowledge of the experience of divine grace, and "with delight" ("mit Wohlgefallen"), for the pleasure of yourselves and others. To this latter end, music should be arranged freely ("ungezwungen"), in a pleasurable but also orderly manner. That it should also be done ἐν ταῖς καρδίαις, means that the singing is not to come merely from the lips but from the heart, with devotion and fervor, so that the thoughts and desires agree with the words. It also means that even when the outward practice of music is either interrupted or impossible, the singing of the heart can continue.[29]

The interpretation of this Colossians verse in Baumgarten's commentary on Psalm 81 focuses more on this latter idea. It seems that public gatherings do have value but are a minimum starting point. This is a somewhat different attitude from that of those Pietists whose criticism of church gatherings focused on the sinfulness of preachers or congregants. Without condemning others, Baumgarten conveys the sense that his own time alone with God is at a higher level than group gatherings. The individualism that is often given as a defining Pietist characteristic is, I suggest, expressed more clearly here than it was by Francke or Lange.

---

[28] Siegmund Jacob Baumgarten: Auslegung der Briefe Pauli an die Galater, Epheser, Philipper, Colosser, Philemon und Thessalonicher. Ed. by Johann Salomon Semler. Halle: Gebauer, 1767, 319–320: "wie betrunkene, mit Wein erfüllte Leute zum Geschwätz, fröhlichen singen und allerley Bezeugung ihrer Freude und wallenden Bewegungen des Geblüts geneigt sind; so stehts euch frey, ja liegt euch ob, gleiche Wirkungen dieser geistlichen Freude blicken zu lassen."

[29] Baumgarten: Auslegung der Briefe Pauli, 691.

Therefore, we must not limit this exhortation merely to congregational worship of God, although that can also be connected with taking pleasure in God and should be used for that purpose. Everyone can satisfy this exhortation and encouragement of the Holy Spirit if one only sings in the heart to God in seclusion, applying to this intent all the inward movements and desires that arise so that they are directed to God in a pleasing manner and remain directed to him.[30]

The mention of the music of psaltery and harp in Psalm 92 provides another occasion for Baumgarten to reflect on the best understanding of Paul's instructions. To "sing and play in your hearts to the Lord" could mean, he speculates, that both outward movements of the spirit ("Gemütsbewegungen") and inward movements of the heart should be involved, because any outward praise, even if it happens in the most pleasant manner, is displeasing to God without devotion and the movement of the soul. Baumgarten prefers a second interpretation, however, that makes the outward music non-essential: "Even if no such external occasion could take place in a sensory manner, it can still happen inwardly, in spirit and truth, for we can bring to God in a concordant, harmonizing way such worship and such praise as is more pleasing to him than all music."[31]

If the musical message of both Israelite worship and the early church is a metaphor for a higher spiritual devotion, it should not surprise us that eschatological passages are read metaphorically. When encountering the phrase "Sing a new song" in the psalms, Baumgarten makes the obvious connection to the use of the same term in John's Revelation. In commenting on the phrase in Psalm 33, he points to its appearance in both Isaiah (42,10) and Revelation (5,9 and 14,3). David, through his gift of prophecy, was able to envision how God would pour out new mercies and, in particular, bring salvation through the sending of the Messiah. The term "new song," then, is a contrast to Levitic ceremonies and the old "shadow work" of past times. While Baumgarten takes the Isaiah passage to refer to the grace of the new covenant, he does not make the Revelation passages into a prophecy of the kingdom of glory or eternal blessedness. The closest he comes to a vision of heaven is in saying that the new song is "a song such as has not yet been heard in all the time the earth has stood and that no one would have been able to imagine if God himself in his wisdom had not invented a means of restoring our well-being and put it into effect."[32] Although this is similar to the language sometimes used

---

[30] Baumgarten: Psalmen, Vol. 2, 154–155: "Also dürfen wir diese Aufforderung nicht blos auf die gemeinschaftliche Verehrung Gottes einschränken, obgleich solche auch mit einem Vergnügen über Gott verbunden seyn und dazu gebrauchet werden sol. Es kan ein jeder dieser Aufforderung und Ermunterung des heiligen Geistes nachkommen, wenn er auch nur im Verborgenen, in seinem Herzen Gott singet, wenn er durch den Geist Gottes sein Herz recht zubereitet, und alle innere Bewegungen und aufsteigende Begierden dazu anwendet, daß sie auf eine liebliche Art auf Gott gerichtet werden, und auf ihn gerichtet bleiben."
[31] Baumgarten: Psalmen, Vol. 2, 315: "wenn auch keine dergleichen äussere Gelegenheit auf eine sinliche Art statfinden könte, so sol es doch innerlich, im Geist und in der Warheit geschehen, da wir Gott auf eine übereinstimmige, wohl harmonirende Weise, eine solche Verehrung, ein solches Lob, das ihm besser gefält, als alle Musik, bringen können."
[32] Baumgarten: Psalmen, Vol. 1, 618: "ein solches Lied, das noch nicht erhöret worden, seit dem der Erdboden gestanden, das auch kein Mensch hätte erdenken können, wenn Gott

to refer to the auditory sensations to be expected in the life to come, Baumgarten's comment itself applies to the means of salvation available in this life rather than the ultimate fulfillment in the life to come.

The term "new song" appears again in Psalms 96, 98, and 149. In each instance, Baumgarten refers to Revelation, quoting extensively from chapters 5, 14, and 15 in his commentary on Psalm 96. Here the message is that in the fullness of time God will show his favors through the Redeemer to all people, who should then respond by giving honor and singing praise to God.[33] For Psalm 98, Baumgarten goes beyond the universal message to personalize it: the new song requires a new sensibility or a new heart, a new "Gemütsfassung". Without this, no one is in a position to satisfy God's requirements.[34] This point is then expanded in his commentary on Psalm 149, where he first recognizes the knowledge of God available to all in creation. Every natural person, without further revelation, can admire God's works of creation, preservation, and providence, and it is useful and even necessary to do so. To omit to praise God for this would be to sin gravely and rob him of his due, but to fail to go further and acknowledge his works of redemption, singing a new song to the Savior, would also be sinful. For a new song, however, a new spirit is necessary; the natural person must be changed.

> Just as a new song would be displeasing to God with an insincere, blameworthy disposition that is unbecoming to God, so a new, upright disposition that has been changed, amended, turned around through the grace of God is required for this praise. As it says several times in the Revelation of John, "See, the old has passed away, everything has become new." Thus, in order properly to sing of divine favors, we call upon God for a new heart, a new mind. When our heart is filled with the sense of new favors that come to us from God, our mouth will quickly and freely overflow with new songs and paeans to God.[35]

While this last sentence implies actual singing, this is not the primary significance of "new song" for Baumgarten. As with Francke, there is some ambiguity about whether worshipping in spirit and truth also includes an external component. Whereas Francke sometimes resolves this by saying that corporate worship is not to be neglected, Baumgarten leaves us questioning how strongly he would push believers to go to church. The fading importance of prophecy in his hermeneutics and a more modern sense of history led to increasing internalization of faith. Johann Salomo Semler moved even more decisively in this direction.

---

nicht selbst nach seiner Weisheit ein solches Wiederherstellungsmittel unserer Wohlfart erfunden und bewerkstelliget hätte."

[33] Baumgarten: Psalmen, Vol. 2, 372.
[34] Baumgarten: Psalmen, Vol. 2, 402.
[35] Baumgarten: Psalmen, Vol. 2, 1121: "Wie aber ein neues Lied mit einem alten, mit einem ungegründeten, verwerflichen und Gott unanständigen Gemüte, Gott unangenehm seyn würde; so gehöret zu diesem Lobe ein neues, aufrichtiges und durch die Gnade Gottes geändertes, ausgebessertes, herum gesetztes Gemüt; daß, wie es auch in der Offenbarung Johannis einigemal heisset: **Siehe das Alte ist vergangen, es ist alles neu worden,** wir also Gott um ein neu Herz, neuen Sin, götliche Wohlthaten recht zu besingen, anrufen. Wenn unser Herz vol Empfindungen der neuen Wohlthaten seyn wird, die uns von Gott wiederfaren: so wird unser Mund von neuen Liedern und Lobeserhebungen Gottes gar bald und ungezwungen überfliessen."

## 2 Johann Salomo Semler (1725–1791)

Baumgarten had chipped away at the belief in the unity of the Bible; Semler, who was first Baumgarten's student, then colleague, then successor and editor, struck down this unity decisively. The progression beyond Baumgarten can be observed in Semler's edition of Baumgarten's *Evangelische Glaubenslehre*. Semler's annotations on topics of biblical inspiration, revelation, and canon formation reveal his modifications of and deviations from Baumgarten's positions.[36] To say this is not to minimize Baumgarten's influence on Semler. As a student in Halle from 1743 to 1750, Semler was more closely affiliated with Baumgarten than any of the other faculty members. He lived in Baumgarten's house, utilized his extensive private library, tutored his children, and assisted in editing his publications. In his memoirs, he reported that he learned from Baumgarten that one might criticize the dominant theology of the time without doing harm to the Christian religion.[37]

Semler's research into the formation of the biblical canon led him to see how historically contingent it was.[38] He was not the first to question the inclusion of some of the books of the Bible: Luther had raised doubts about the books of James, Jude, and Revelation. Luther's followers, however, continued to accept these books as fully canonical and, as we have seen, some interpreters even regarded Revelation as essential to understanding God's plan of salvation. Semler's view of that book is evident already in the title of his publication: *Christliche freye Untersuchung über die sogenannte Offenbarung Johannis* ("Christian free Examination of the so-called Revelation of John"). His dismissive view is partly based on the difficulty of the text itself:

> It is quite strange to assert an important divine revelation on a topic and yet at the same time to admit that the matter itself is completely incomprehensible, useless, and irrelevant for capable and thoughtful Christians. [...] If such theologians themselves admit this, I do not know for what purpose this book should any longer be included in the number of canonical books.[39]

---

[36] For an extensive study of Semler's views in relation to Baumgarten, see Andreas Lüder: Historie und Dogmatik. Ein Beitrag zur Genese und Entfaltung von Johann Salomo Semlers Verständnis des Alten Testaments. Berlin, New York: De Gruyter, 1995, 43–116.

[37] Gottfried Hornig: Johann Salomo Semler. Studien zu Leben und Werk des Hallenser Aufklärungstheologen. Tübingen: Niemeyer, 1996, 5–6.

[38] On Semler's view of the biblical canon, particularly in relation to Luther, see Gottfried Hornig: Die Anfänge der historisch-kritischen Theologie. Johann Salomo Semlers Schriftverständnis und seine Stellung zu Luther. Göttingen: Vandenhoeck & Ruprecht, 1961.

[39] Johann Salomo Semler: Christliche freye Untersuchung über die so genannte Offenbarung Johannes, aus der nachgelassenen Handschrift eines fränkischen Gelehrten. Halle: Hendel, 1769, 104, fn. 79: "es ist ganz sonderbar, eine göttliche wichtige Offenbarung über eine Sache zu behaupten, und doch zugleich gestehen, die Sache selbst seye für fähige und nachdenkende Christen ganz unverständlich, unbrauchbar also und unerheblich. [...] Wenn solche Theologi es selbst gestehen müssen: so weiß ich nicht zu was für Nutzen und Gebrauch dis Buch in der Zahl der canonischen Bücher weiter mit begriffen wird."

Other objections concern the uncertain authorship of the book of Revelation as well as the nonbiblical sources of many of its concepts. Certainly, Semler would not take it as a key to understanding biblical prophecy.

The preface to this book on Revelation also explains Semler's larger view of the canon of the Bible. For some time, he notes, he had taken it upon himself to investigate whether all the books considered canonical really were of divine origin. The answer to this question should not be based on the tradition of inclusion but rather on the value of the content for all people in all times:

> In this investigation every thoughtful Christian and—even more—every teacher must be free to judge according to his conscience and to give precedence to the content, in respect to its general necessity and the usefulness for all people in all times, as the main criterion of a divinely inspired book.[40]

The genealogical lists found in the historical books of the Old Testament are of no practical use to people not belonging to the Jewish State. Furthermore, there is much in all parts of the Old Testament that does not serve for moral improvement. Attempts to apply a fourfold or a spiritual, mystical understanding are arbitrary and unconvincing. Semler sees no reason to struggle to find moral significance in books where it is not obvious:

> Or should a reader linger over his own thoughts and imaginings until he, for example, glimpses in the book of Esther the form of a new Christian person as in a clear mirror? Or until he can transform all the ever so coarse and sensual images and poetic descriptions of a bride in the so-called Song of Songs into clear images of Christian perfections? Or until he uncovers Christ beneath the heroic deeds of Samson?[41]

Semler rejects the approach, earnest though it may be, of turning all these texts into edifying Christian significance. In place of the view that the Christian message was continuous with the Jewish faith, though more complete, Semler regards it as discontinuous: the Jewish faith was particular, applicable only to a certain people in a specific place. The Christian religion, by contrast, is universal, applicable to all people in all places. This contrast pervades all of Semler's writings and results in a very negative portrayal of Jews and Judaism, in spite of his personal defense of the rights of Jews in his own day.[42]

---

[40] Semler: Christliche freye Untersuchung, A4a–b: "Bey dieser Untersuchung muß es einem jeden nachdenkenden Christen, und noch mehr jedem Lehrer freystehen, nach seinem Gewissen zu urtheilen, und den Vorzug des Inhalts, in Ansehung der allgemeinen Nothwendigkeit und Brauchbarkeit für alle Menschen aller Zeiten, zum Hauptmerkmal eines durch den Geist Gottes eingegebenen Buches, zu machen."

[41] Semler: Christliche freye Untersuchung, A5a–b: "Oder soll sich ein Leser so lange mit seinen eigenen Gedanken und Vorstellungen aufhalten, bis z. E. er aus dem Buch Esther die Gestalt des christlichen neuen Menschen, wie in einem hellen Spiegel, erblicket? bis er alle noch so groben und sinnlichen Bilder und poetischen Beschreibungen einer Braut, in dem sogenanten Hohenliede, in deutliche Vorstellungen von christlichen Vollkommenheiten verwandeln kan? Oder, bis er unter den heroischen Thaten des Simson, Christum entdeckt?"

[42] See the chapter on Semler in Anders Gerdmar: Roots of Theological Anti-Semitism. German Biblical Interpretation and the Jews, from Herder and Semler to Kittel and Bultmann. Leiden: Brill, 2009, 39–49.

## 2  Johann Salomo Semler

Not all parts of the Hebrew Bible were without value for Christians, however. The book of Psalms stands out as having immediate relevance for the Christian life, as Semler explained in his lengthy introduction to Baumgarten's Psalm commentary. Above all, the psalms show that the Jews believed there would come a person who would lead them to a higher level of morality:

> The old Jewish church, in its greatest and reasonable portion, never doubted that a person would some day arise in their midst who would excel all other teachers. This person would then impart knowledge and obligatory instruction to them and to other peoples concerning the whole of morality and a higher level of worship than had previously occurred from Moses himself and other respected teachers.[43]

If the Psalms were merely historical songs about the Jews' experiences, Semler reasoned, they would be of no more lasting value than the songs of other ancient peoples praising their gods or heroes. David was surely worthy of praise for his establishment of the kingdom in Jerusalem, but it was the analogy between David and a future Messiah that enabled the Jews to believe in a person who would lead them to a higher truth. Although the writers of the Talmud turned to foolish allegorical interpretations of the Psalms, as well as other parts of the Bible, the followers of Jesus understood the true, more sublime meaning of the Psalms in their prophecies of the Messiah. From the earliest times, Christians used the Psalms in their liturgies, even though they did not understand them as well as Semler thinks is possible in his own day. This is not to say that all differences of interpretation will be resolved, but these can be tolerated as long as the commentators approach the text with the right intention. Semler does not say that only the regenerate can truly understand the Bible, but he does ask that exegetes be in a frame of mind submissive to God.[44]

Semler did not write his own Psalm commentary, nor did he insert footnotes to Baumgarten's commentary where he might have had a different point of view. Only for Psalm 112, where Baumgarten's was missing, did Semler write the commentary.[45] Nothing in the psalm other than the opening "Hallelujah" lends itself to a discussion of music. Semler does say, in regard to "Hallelujah," that one cannot praise God enough and that God is to be recognized and loved "with sincere thanks and praise" as the originator of all happiness.[46] A somewhat more substantive comment on the musical aspect of the Psalms is found in Semler's *Ascetische Vorlesungen* ("Ascetic Lectures"), which followed in the Halle tradition of devotional periods of Bible study accompanied by hymns and prayers. In commenting on Psalm 8, Semler explained that the word "Gittith" in the superscript had

---

[43] Semler's preface to Baumgarten: Psalmen, Vol. 1, 9–10: "Die **jüdische** alte Kirche hat auch, ihrem grösten und vernünftigen Theil nach, nie gezweifelt, daß eine Person dereinst unter ihnen aufstehen würde, welche alle andere Lehrer übertreffen solte; die folglich von einer höhern Stuffe des Gottesdienstes und der ganzen **Moralität**, ihnen und andern Völkern, Belerung und verbindlichen Unterricht ertheilen solte, als von **Mose** selbst und andern ansenlichen Lehrern ehedem geschehen war."
[44] Semler's preface to Baumgarten: Psalmen, Vol. 1, 10–15.
[45] Semler reports this in the preface to Baumgarten: Psalmen, Vol. 2, fol. 2.
[46] Baumgarten: Psalmen, Vol. 2, 600.

been variously interpreted by rabbis as referring to a musical instrument, possibly related to the town of Gath, or as a melody, but there remained great uncertainty about the meaning even among the Jews. For the edification of his listeners, neither this term nor the Hebrew music itself mattered, only the evidence that music served to prepare an attitude of praise in the worshippers:

> We can say that the superscription of this psalm is very insignificant for our purposes. It relates, of course, to the erstwhile arrangement of music at that time, which is admittedly almost completely unknown to us but also actually quite inconsequential and insignificant. We can at least conclude from this, however, that already at that time they tried to put the common people in an attentive state of mind through the singing and the accompanying music. In this way they would lighten people's burden of coming together for public religious exercises and teach them by example how easy it is to gather reasons for continual praise and honor of God out of the great riches of blessings and the many signs of God's glory that are contained in what is for us the endless dimension of creation.[47]

Noteworthy in this citation is how quickly Semler moves from the specifics of public worship to a generalized awareness of the God of creation. He credits the author of Psalm 8 with expressing the sublimity of the universe in such lines as "You have set your glory above the heavens," and "how majestic is your name in all the earth" (Ps 8,1.9). Similarly, in commenting on Psalm 15, Semler regards David as implicitly criticizing the Hebrews' ritual distinction between priests and common people as a criterion for entering the tabernacle or temple. The distinction should instead be between morally upright persons and those who may practice the rituals but engage in immoral acts. David, he says, is adopting an invisible tent or tabernacle into which God accepts those whose character is pleasing to him, thus anticipating Jesus's saying to the Samaritan woman that God is to be worshipped in spirit and truth, not in a specific place. Such a principle was known even to many pagans, notes Semler, naming Plato, Pythagoras and Seneca.[48]

Psalm 19 provides Semler further opportunity to emphasize the universal over the specific. The claim of verse 9 that the fear of the Lord endures to eternity is for Semler a contrast to the changeable religious practices of the psalmist's time that would not endure. Semler finds no moral value in the practices of circumcision, ritual purification, and other outward ceremonies. Rather, the opening verses of

---

[47] Johann Salomo Semler: Ascetische Vorlesungen, zur Beförderung einer vernünftigen Anwendung der christlichen Religion. Halle: Hemmerde, 1772, 98. "Wir können sagen, daß die **Aufschrift** dieses Psalms für unsre Absicht sehr unerheblich sey. Sie bezieht sich allerdings auf ehemalige Einrichtung der Musik jener Zeiten, welche uns freilich meist ganz unbekannt, aber auch wirklich sehr gleichgültig und unbedeutend ist. Wir können aber vielleicht so viel daraus abnemen, daß man schon in jener Zeit gesucht hat, das gemeine **Volk** durch die Annemlichkeit des Vorsingens und einer dazu eingerichteten Musik in eine aufmerksame Gemütsfassung zu sezen, und den Menschen die Lust [NB: I am treating this as a misprint for Last, which seems to fit better in the context] zu erleichtern, sich zur öffentlichen Religionsübung einzufinden, und an solchen Mustern es zu lernen, wie leicht es sey, Ursachen des steten Lobes und Preises Gottes zusammen zu finden, aus dem grossen Reichtum der Wolthaten und der vielen Merkmale der Herrlichkeit Gottes, welche in dem für uns unendlichen Umfange der Schöpfung enthalten sind."

[48] Semler: Ascetische Vorlesungen, 127–128.

the psalm show that the psalmist went beyond these contingent laws to the realm of nature that gives witness of God's majesty to any who would listen. Though he never refers to the music of the spheres, Semler does bring out the auditory element in these verses, particularly verse 4, "The sound goes out through all the earth." Rejecting any Christological interpretation whereby this sound would refer to the preaching of the gospel, Semler regards it as the heavenly sound that may be heard by all, including the pagans, who are attuned to nature:

> As far as the heavens are stretched by length and width over the earth, thus far is heard this loud voice that speaks of the Creator's power and mercy. Indeed it can be seen along with the quite observable movements of air through the winds and in the rain, lightning and thunder, and so on, the effects of which are so discernible and so very familiar to people.[49]

Just as Semler appreciated those ancient Hebrews who had a broad vision of God that reached beyond Mosaic law, so also in his own time he recognized faith in persons of other religious communities regardless of the doctrines they espoused: "The fear of God in a sincere Papist, Jew, Quaker, Socinian, etc., must always be valued by us and considered worthy of respect. Their deficiencies or errors belong to their knowledge and not to their heart or will."[50] The truth of one's own beliefs must make a difference in one's own life before any claims are made about the superiority of those beliefs over other truth claims.[51]

Aware of the declining appeal of doctrinal religion, Semler wrote that traditional ecclesiastical language had lost its persuasive power.[52] While not rejecting historical Christianity, he found it insufficient and set private religion alongside it. Writing toward the end of his life, Semler reports that he had long attempted to fulfill his duties as a public teacher of religion and to enable his contemporaries better to understand the Christian religion. He had concluded, however, that the language of religion could not be limited to its public, organizational purposes. The conscience must not be subordinated to the social religious order but must be free to relate to God with a private religion. Not all Christians can be expected to use the same formulas for thinking and believing, for singing and praying. Even the professors of religion must be free to follow their hearts and consciences in teaching the riches of the Christian religion. They should first of all instill

---

[49] Semler: Ascetische Vorlesungen, 151–152: "So weit der Himmel in die Länge und Weite über die Erde ausgedehnet ist, so weit hört man diese laute Stimme, welche von der Macht und Güte des Schöpfers redet. Es kan allerdings hier mit auf die gar merklichen Bewegungen der Luft, durch Winde, und auf den Regen, Blitz, Donner etc. gesehen werden; deren Wirkungen den Menschen so kentlich und so sehr geläufig sind."

[50] Semler: Ascetische Vorlesungen, 137: "Furcht Gottes mus uns bey einem redlichen Papisten, Juden, Quaker Socinianer etc. allemal schäzbar und verehrungswürdig seyn. Die Mängel oder Feler in ihrer Erkentnis gehören nicht ihrem Herzen und Willen."

[51] Semler: Ascetische Vorlesungen, 155.

[52] Johann Salomo Semler: Ueber historische, geselschaftliche und moralische Religion der Christen. Leipzig: Beer, 1786, unpaginated preface: "Die alte Kirchensprache können wir nicht ferner geradeaus fortsezen; sie ist ohne Kraft und Samen; die Menschen sind nicht mehr da, welche damit zufrieden waren, daß sie durch die Kirche selig würden."

morality and should steer clear of the historical or biblical components that do not contribute to morality.

Morality is not simply ethics, however, but encompasses the pure truth of the gospel, the spirit and life of the teachings of Jesus, and the power of God for the moral blessedness of human beings. Semler uses the theological terms designating faith (πιστεύειν) and change of heart (μετανοεῖν) as the starting point of morality or moral religion. Because of historical change, the meaning of Spirit of God, for example, has been understood differently at different times and places. For this reason, there is no invariable definition of religious concepts that all can share. The followers of Jesus taught a universal religion that would not be limited as Judaism was, but the outward organization of church, creed, and sacraments could have a constraining effect on private religion. The historical formulation of creeds was an attempt to resolve differences of belief and to bring various groups together. This purpose was not, Semler claims, to promote Christian well-being or a more perfect religion and a higher level of virtue but rather to enforce the social uniformity of all church members. They professed that salvation depended on the language of these expressions of belief, "but thinking Christians always knew that this was not true, that everything depended on the moral actions or omissions of Christians."[53] Semler maintained that moral, Christian religion can spread equally well in various different church organizations, even if their teachings are not the same.

The higher level of religious awareness was not completely lacking among the writers of the Old Testament, particularly when referring to sacrifices: numerous passages contrast the common meaning of animal sacrifice with a higher understanding of personal sacrifice. Similarly, when Christ is called a sacrifice, this is also understood at different levels. Semler argues for taking both levels into consideration, but it seems clear that his understanding is not of a substitutionary sacrifice but of a priesthood of all believers who offer themselves to the service of God and others.[54]

Perhaps most remarkable is Semler's assertion that the Christian religion with all its vocabulary does not exist for its own sake or primarily for external purposes but for the sake of the general moral well-being of humans. Nor should one think that it has reached a stage of perfection, for all human proficiency will change, for better or for worse. Semler does recognize the value of institutional religion and uniform instruction for beginners in the faith, but this should not prevent the gradual growth that leads to private Christian awareness.[55]

To try to summarize Semler's religious position and place in history has proved difficult for even his contemporaries, not to mention subsequent historians. Johann August Nösselt, one-time student and later colleague, opened his essay on Semler with the sentence, "Of all the theologians of our time, there is hardly another who has traversed so many good and bad rumors at the same time as the blessed Dr.

---

[53] Semler: Religion der Christen, 19: "aber denkende Christen wusten es stets, daß alles auf das moralische thun und lassen der Christen ankomme."
[54] Semler: Religion der Christen, 37.
[55] Semler: Religion der Christen, 43–49.

Semler."[56] Both his admirers and his attackers found fault with his provocative style and immoderate passion in attacking positions he found erroneous, Nösselt recognized. Yet he was a "warm admirer of religion and of Christianity," and it pained him when he found himself charged with paving the way for the "zealots of unbelief" who were attacking the very basis of Christianity or even religion itself.[57] As a supporter of public order, he did not intend to undermine the institutional church; his goal, Nösselt believed, was to "awaken Christians and, actually, so-called teachers—who should always be improving—out of their indifferent lethargy."[58] The idea of "private Christianity" was a way of encouraging such persons to advance in their understanding of religion when they might otherwise reject the teachings of the church.

Another student and later colleague, August Hermann Niemeyer, saw Semler as struggling throughout his life with a double soul: on one side, he was inclined to mysticism and on the other to an intellectual standpoint that required a firm basis for any claims. As a result, both Orthodox and Pietists accused him of heterodoxy while the Rationalists derided his pious feelings.[59] In his feelings, Niemeyer wrote, Semler stood much closer to Pietism than many believed: "driven around on the barren fields of knowledge, he felt deeply Augustine's saying, 'the mind is restless until it finds rest in God'; he knew well that all knowing, digging and researching cannot satisfy the needs of the heart."[60] For this reason he found devotional practices, including the singing of traditional hymns, to be indispensable.[61] Even the distinction between public and private religion should not be shocking, according to Niemeyer, but is in accordance with Jesus' and the apostles' principle of giving no offence to the weak. From Niemeyer's perspective, this distinction prepared the way for the separation that would soon occur between the fields of academic and practical theology.

Subsequent generations were more inclined to view Semler's talk of private religion as subjectivist and a radical break from Reformation tradition. The history of Semler interpretation has been summarized by Andreas Lüder and is too extensive to review here.[62] Rather than beginning with Semler as the originator of a new direction in textual criticism, Lüder's own study looks for the roots of

---

[56] Johann August Nösselt: Leben, Charakter und Verdienste Johann August Nösselts. Pt. 2: Sammlung Nösseltscher Aufsätze und Fragmente. Ed. by August Hermann Niemeyer. Halle: Waisenhaus, 1809, 194.
[57] Nösselt: Aufsätze und Fragmente, 209–210.
[58] Nösselt: Aufsätze und Fragmente, 221.
[59] August Hermann Niemeyer: Die Universität Halle nach ihrem Einfluß auf gelehrte und praktische Theologie in ihrem ersten Jahrhundert, seit der Kirchenverbesserung dem dritten. Halle: Waisenhaus, 1817, lxxxiii–lxxxiv.
[60] Niemeyer: Die Universität Halle, xcv–xcvi.
[61] Although Semler had little to say about music in his writings, there is biographical evidence that he was trained in music. As a youth, he substituted on organ when the organist, also his piano teacher, became incapacitated. See Paul Gastrow: Joh. Salomo Semler in seiner Bedeutung für die Theologie mit besonderer Berücksichtigung seines Streites mit G. E. Lessing. Giessen: Töpelmann, 1905, 28.
[62] Lüder: Historie und Dogmatik, 8–42.

Semler's thinking. In so doing, he calls Semler a "self-conscious representative of Halle theology," building on the works of his teacher Baumgarten and then carefully working out his own distinct position. Although from the perspective of later history, Semler may seem to represent the beginning of a new era in biblical scholarship, his colleagues, recognizing his innovative scholarship, also observed the fervor of devotion that characterized the Halle Pietists in their quest for a practical faith not dictated by stringent doctrinal confessions.

## 3   Summary

Baumgarten and Semler moved away from the view of scripture as a unified whole with the Old Testament connecting to the New through typology. No longer influenced by Vitringa's periodization of salvation history, both thinkers regarded the Bible as a text to be approached like other texts, open to interpretation by both believers and unbelievers. Semler even questioned the canonicity of some biblical books, particularly Revelation, which had figured so prominently in the theology of Lange and Rambach.

Several elements of Baumgarten's thought remain close to Pietist thinking, making him difficult to classify historically. While the Bible may be understood by nonbelievers, the understanding is deepened through faith experience. Acts of praise are to be judged according to the intention of the worshipper, not by outward expression, which may be non-essential. Musical references in the Old Testament were often given general or spiritual meanings rather than serving as models for Christians. Nevertheless, Baumgarten did recognize the power of music both for the individual and for corporate worship.

At times Semler appeared to devalue the institutional church and its worship, finding moral religion more important than church organization. For him, the religion of the Old Testament was too narrow, not universally applicable, yet he found the Psalms to be relevant for Christians. While he wrote little about music, he was reported to find hymns personally indispensable. In his personal faith, he may have been closer to Pietism than his writings would indicate.

Chapter Five

# Elevating Religion through Poetry and Music: August Hermann Niemeyer (1754–1828), Literary Theologian

The integration of biblical commentary with artistic appreciation would be left to one of Semler's students, August Hermann Niemeyer (1754–1828). In his teen years, Niemeyer had been preoccupied with literature, enthusiastically reading English writers such as Milton, Richardson, and Young, admiring Lessing and almost venerating Klopstock. With his mentor and professor Johann August Nösselt, Niemeyer spent leisure hours reading and discussing literature. Nösselt taught New Testament at Halle University, and Niemeyer would go on to join the theology faculty also and, eventually, to preside over the Glaucha Anstalten, but his literary interests influenced his approach to theology and biblical studies. His multi-volume *Charakteristick der Bibel* is not a biblical commentary in the traditional sense, as it is organized around biblical characters rather than chapters and verses. To the extent that it covers most of the Bible, however, it is more thorough than the exegetical works of Francke, Rambach, Baumgarten, or Semler. He also wrote poetry, oratorio texts, and essays on the relationship of religion to poetry and music. All of these combined provide a comprehensive picture of the theological role of music in the thinking of a great-grandson and successor of August Hermann Francke. Surely, Francke would have been pleased with his great-grandson's work on behalf of the institutions Francke founded, but some aspects of young Niemeyer's approach to the Bible would have been quite disturbing for him.

## 1    On the Interpretation of the Bible

Looking back in later life on the middle of the eighteenth century, Niemeyer viewed it as a time of two great revolutions, the first in the area of taste, the second in theology. Of the first he seemed to be a full supporter: the efforts of Klopstock and Gellert to improve German literature had resulted in a purification of language and an ennobling of expression without doing any harm to the teachings of the church. The many efforts at improvement in the area of religion, on the other hand, had mixed results. The attempts at cleansing religious teachings of outdated dogmatic systems had made religion more a matter of the mind than the heart. When mystical language that was felt to be offensive was removed from hymns, the result was either that old hymns became unrecognizable or that new rationalistic hymns omitted those beliefs and feelings that gave nourishment to faith.[1]

We will return to Niemeyer's thoughts on hymnody later, but these reflections provide a context for his biblical interpretation. As a mere 21-year-old when publishing his first volume, his university education was fresh in his mind, and he was well informed about the latest developments in biblical research. The Bible was being studied with greater zeal and more successfully than ever before, he claims in his introduction to his first volume of the *Charakteristick*.[2] Biblical study was benefiting from a variety of perspectives, and in turn almost every branch of knowledge had gained from these approaches. Languages were better respected, ethics had been elevated, philosophy had been illuminated, history had been confirmed or supplemented, rhetoric was being strengthened, and poetry was indebted to the Bible for its most sublime works. What was missing in all this, he believed, was the study of characterizations. Our English cognate, characteristics, does not convey the full sense of his meaning when he says he will write a *Charakteristick der Bibel*. The English word connotes one or more aspects of a person, whereas the German "Charakteristick" has a fuller sense of "characterization, portrait, or portrayal of character." In other words, he intended to portray the moral character as well as the distinguishing characteristics of biblical personalities. Recognizing that in his day there were both friends and enemies of the idea of divine revelation, he hoped that his approach would appeal to both sides. His method, then, is not specific to the study of the Bible but, as he suggested, could be used to write a *Charakteristick* of philosophers, orators, poets, and others.

His target audience, then, is a general one, not biblical scholars or even Christians only. Rather than trying to persuade unbelievers with sermons or scholarly argument, he seeks to find common ground with opponents of Christianity by drawing on their shared humanity. Even a critic such as Rousseau expressed admiration for Jesus, Niemeyer recognizes, and while other biblical figures do not measure up to Jesus, they too can provide lessons in how to be more fully human and perhaps morally better: "Also, to view the Bible simply from this perspective—that it presents people so perfectly, so correctly, so precisely, just as they are—will gain more love, more respect; even if this is not exactly the way to becoming morally better, it can still be a means and an opportunity."[3] By looking

---

[1] August Hermann Niemeyer, "Ideen über geistliche Lieder und Oratorien," preface to A. H. Niemeyer: Geistliche Lieder, Oratorien und vermischte Gedichte. Halle: Waisenhaus, 1820, xv–xvi.

[2] August Hermann Niemeyer: Charakteristick der Bibel. Erster Theil. Halle: Gebauer, 1775, preface, 3–4. I will retain this spelling as used by Niemeyer rather than the modern "Charakteristik."

[3] August Hermann Niemeyer: Allgemeine Abhandlung über die Charakteristick der Bibel. In: Niemeyer: Charakteristick, Vol. 1, 1–20, here 15. "Die Bibel auch bloß aus dem Gesichtspunkt betrachtet, daß sie so vollkommen, so richtig, so genau **den Menschen**, den Menschen gerade wie er ist, vorstellt, wird mehr Liebe, mehr Achtung bekommen, und ob dis gleich der Weg nicht ist moralisch besser zu werden, so kann es doch Mittel und Gelegenheit seyn." Pagination begins again with the "Allgemeine Abhandlung," resulting in duplicate page numbers 1–25.

impartially at the essential character of individuals throughout biblical times, The reader may discover the core of humanity and how even a weak and limited creature can become a great and glorious work through the hand of God.[4]

Women are specifically included in Niemeyer's intended audience. They are the important part of humanity that is primarily responsible for forming the character of future citizens of the world. Although girls are often given books to read that make one blush rather than being given the Bible, there are still enough "female souls" who know that they are created for more noble and enduring pleasures. To take time for quiet study of the character of Mary or John and of moral beauty should be a blessing for the heart of his female friends, known and unknown.[5]

Niemeyer's purpose is clearly religious but not doctrinal nor in service to any particular party, though he anticipates objections from more traditional religious thinkers. For example, should one not seek God in the Bible rather than humans? This question provides Niemeyer with an occasion to explain his view of the Bible: he agrees that the books of scripture are divine and were written under the special influence of the Godhead in a much more sublime sense than all other books. To avoid contentiousness, he chooses not to advocate any particular idea of inspiration or *theopneustie* but to limit his observations to whatever degree of inspiration is described in the Bible itself. Without condemning anyone who disputes the authenticity of any of the books of the Old or New Testaments, he does not reject any of the books. Rather, he is grateful to God for their preservation, as they all contribute to the story of providence. Nevertheless, whatever immediate insights the biblical writers may have received from God, we should recognize that these writers—even the apostles who knew Jesus personally—wrote as human beings whose identities and characteristics are present alongside the divine content.

The second objection he foresees is that the important persons of the Bible should be treated as holy and not subjected to an analysis or judgment of their character. Surely, he responds, there will be no objection to presenting their good and honorable qualities and actions; the only objection could be to depicting their mistakes and weaknesses. We should not avert our eyes from their errors, he believes, but rather observe them at their best and their worst, learning to avoid their mistakes. If angels do not want to be worshipped, he asks, why should humans wish to be?[6]

Where does Jesus fit into this study of human characteristics, we must wonder. Would Niemeyer take this same approach to the character of Jesus? We cannot know for certain, but the fact that Niemeyer never managed to write the sixth volume that would have treated Jesus' life and character is noteworthy in itself.[7]

---

[4] Niemeyer: Allgemeine Abhandlung, 20.
[5] August Hermann Niemeyer: Vorrede. In: Niemeyer: Charakteristick, Vol. 1, 1–24, here 19–20.
[6] Niemeyer: Vorrede, 11–13. See also Niemeyer: Allgemeine Abhandlung, 17.
[7] In the preface to his fifth volume of *Charakteristick* (1782), Niemeyer wrote that an entire sixth volume would be devoted to the life and character of Jesus, but this never appeared; see August Hermann Niemeyer: Vorrede. In: A. H. Niemeyer: Charakteristick der Bibel. Fünfter Theil. Halle: Gebauer, 1982, III–XII, here XI.

From other writings we can conclude that, while Jesus' earthly life was indeed the focus of Niemeyer's attention, he nevertheless regarded Jesus with such awe that he was wary of writing a depiction of his character.

In a devotional work written a few years later, *Timotheus*, Niemeyer devoted a section to the connection between Jesus' resurrection and the truth and godliness of his teaching. Rather than saying that Christian faith is dependent on the miracle of resurrection, he preferred to see the resurrection as a corroboration of the truth and divinity of Jesus' teaching. Even if Jesus had not been raised from the dead, the great divine demands to live virtuously, honor God, love others, and view this life as a preparation for the next life would still be valid. That which is integral to the nature of being human cannot be changed by an extraordinary event. Right living is the only thing that can make us truly happy, and this cannot be contingent on the occurrence of the resurrection. Nevertheless, because Jesus foretold his death and resurrection, he would have been less believable if this had not turned out to be true. Stated more positively, by teaching "as if God himself were speaking to us," the fulfillment of his teaching confirms that God declared him to be the "most believable, incontrovertible witness" to divine truth.[8]

While this stops short of affirming the orthodox teaching on Jesus' divine nature, Niemeyer felt intense reverence for Jesus as a holy person. Not only is this a probable explanation for his failure to complete the promised volume of the *Charakeristick,* but it also suggests the reason why he did not include Jesus as a character in any of his dramas. He wrote disapprovingly of passion music in which a singer is chosen for the role of Jesus. He seems to say that the singing of Jesus' words diminishes their seriousness, but he may also be hinting at the earlier Pietist position that music must be sung or played out of a reverent heart, not just out of musical skill: "The person of the Redeemer is much too holy to be allowed to be represented by singers, among whom one can hardly choose and for whom a good voice is often the only good thing. Even the singing is to me a secondary idea that can easily weaken the sense of reverence."[9] As we will see, Niemeyer's solution to this problem was to write the story of Lazarus in which Mary and Martha speak of seeing Jesus and cite his words without his appearing in person. Even more unusual is Niemeyer's version of the passion story depicted as a commemoration by the disciples a year after Jesus' death. Niemeyer's other oratorios are from the Old Testament, which, because it showed more human weaknesses, offers the poet more freedom of invention, though it must still be treated with respect.

---

[8] August Hermann Niemeyer: Timotheus: Zur Erweckung und Beförderung der Andacht nachdenkender Christen. Zweyte Abtheilung. Leipzig: Weidmann, 1789, 31–32.

[9] August Hermann Niemeyer: Ueber das religioese Drama so fern es für die Musick bestimmt ist. In: A. H. Niemeyer: Gedichte. Leipzig: Weygand, 1778, 29–39, here 35. "Die Person des Erlösers ist viel zu heilig, als daß man sie von einem Sänger, unter denen man so wenig wählen kann, und bey welchen die gute Stimme oft das **einzige Gute** ist, könnte vorstellen lassen. Selbst das **Singen** hat mir da eine Nebenidee, die leicht die Ehrerbietigkeit schwächen könnte."

In sum, Niemeyer's biblical interpretation is informed by his academic training under Semler to the extent that he examines the historical context in which the books of the Bible were written and the human characteristics of the writers and other biblical figures. He is also well aware of differing views of the Bible and particularly of the skepticism of Enlightenment rationalists. What he shared with his Pietist predecessors was the conviction that moral character is a higher value than doctrinal certainty and that the heart was more crucial to faith than the mind. The most significant deviation from Francke, Lange, and Rambach, on the other hand, was no longer to view Christ as the key to all of scripture. The following sections on different themes or books in the Bible are chosen for their relation to questions of music and poetry.

## 2 Genesis: On the Origin of Music

In a section on the book of Genesis that Niemeyer labels "Archive of Ancient Customs," he discusses the organization of families and societies, then the transition from nomadic life to agriculture and the use of metal tools. Just as necessary to the fulfillment of human nature, however, is pleasure, and this is derived through music. Without commenting on the personal character of Jubal, the person credited with inventing music, Niemeyer attributes to music the power of touching both the understanding and the feelings as it leads the soul to the level of the sublime. Worth observing in this quotation are the roles of feeling and of the sublime, themes that will recur in his writings, as well as the added value of singing, which was not mentioned in the Genesis 4,21 verse but was important to Niemeyer as a poet and hymn writer:

> Fulfillment of necessity leads people who are capable of refinement to pleasure. Human nature has an aptitude for this, and it is natural that it be developed first. Expression of feeling through the voice and imitation of the voice through artificial tones lured out of wood or another material is the first basis for music, the most beautiful and most engaging of all the arts. It has elevated the vanquisher of hearts; through the rise and fall of its lofty and dulcet sounds, especially when accompanied by its lovely sister through song, every sublime and tender feeling streams into our souls.—Moses gives the honor of this invention to a certain Jubal.[10]

---

[10] August Hermann Niemeyer: Charakteristick der Bibel. Zweeter Theil. Halle: Gebauer, 1776, 404: "Erfüllung der Nothwendigkeit, führt Völker die der Bildung fähig sind, zum Vergnügen. Die menschliche Natur hat Anlagen dazu, und es ist natürlich, daß diese zuerst entwickelt werden. Ausdruck des Gefühls durch Stimme, und Nachahmung der Stimme durch künstliche Töne aus Holz oder andern Stoff hervorgelockt—ist die erste Grundlage zu der schönsten und liebenswürdigsten aller Künste der Musik, die den Verstand und das Gefühl des Menschen zu der Vollkommenheit erhöht haben, daß sie Bezwingerin der Herzen wird, und durch Steigen und Sinken ihrer hohen und schmelzenden Töne, zumal von ihrer schönen Schwester durch Gesang begleitet, jedes erhabne und jedes sanfte Gefühl in unsre Seelen strömt.—**Moses** giebt einem gewissen **Jubal** die Ehre dieser Erfindung."

## 3   Job

Of all the books in the Old Testament, Niemeyer finds the book of Job the most appealing, both because of its poetry and because of its important religious concepts. Like Semler, he criticized Mosaic religion for being too nationalistic and regarded the faith of the patriarchs, particularly Abraham, as purer. Though fully cognizant of theories asserting a much later composition for the book of Job, Niemeyer places its origin around the time and location of Abraham.[11] He wrote no oratorio telling Job's story, as he did for Abraham, perhaps because Niemeyer did not think of Job as a real historical person. Nor is there anything directly about music in Niemeyer's treatment of the book, but there is much about the literary art that was so closely associated for him with both religion and music.

Setting aside other scholars' attempts to identify a Hebraic meter pattern, Niemeyer is content to recognize a poetic intention in subject matter, language, and rhythm that differentiates it from other Old Testament writings. Anyone who cannot feel the poetry in its pictorial style is deserving of pity: "Poor insentient souls, who do not feel here the fire nor the flight of the poetic art!"[12] Like Homer's *Iliad* and *Odyssey* or Klopstock's *Messiah*, the book of Job is not meant to be read as an actual true history but as a poetic construct based on the experiences of one or more real persons. Never, claims Niemeyer, did a historian or a moralist write with such bold images. Again, admiring the writer's skill, he exclaims, "Whoever does not feel here the power and strength of poetic art—where will he ever feel it?" The great poets of the early modern age—Milton, Tasso, and Klopstock—could have learned from the author of *Job*, and he deserves to be grouped with such ancients as Homer, Pindar, Sophocles, and Euripides.[13]

The category Niemeyer is creating here is that of teachers of the sublime. The German word "Erhabenheit" or "das Erhabene" recurs throughout Niemeyer's lengthy study of *Job*, which he praises for both sublimity of thought and sublimity of expression. Referring to the ancient text on the sublime that is attributed to Longinus, he asks his readers if any of the five elements listed by Longinus are missing in *Job*:

> Is anyone unable, first, to find noble boldness in the representations of things? Is there anyone, moreover, who does not feel the passion, the inspiration, from which the poet speaks? Next, does anyone not see everywhere the felicitous application of figures of speech? Further, where is there any lack of splendor in expression, blossoming of language? And finally, how is it possible to concentrate the individual words in accordance with their whole strength and dignity better than this poet has done?[14]

---

[11] Niemeyer: Charakteristick, Vol. 2, 482–486.
[12] Niemeyer: Charakteristick, Vol. 2, 492: "Arme empfindungslose Seelen, die hier nicht Feuer, hier nicht Flug der Dichtkunst fühlen!"
[13] Niemeyer: Charakteristick, Vol. 2, 565: "Wer hier nicht die Macht, die Stärke der Dichtkunst fühlt—wo will er sie denn fühlen?"
[14] Niemeyer: Charakteristick, Vol. 2, 548–549: "Wer vermißt **zuerst** die edle Kühnheit in den Vorstellungen der Dinge? Wer fühlt ausserdem nicht die Leidenschaft, die Begeisterung, in welcher der Dichter spricht? **Dann,** wer sieht nicht überall die glückliche Anwendung der Figuren? Wo fehlt **ferner** das Prächtige in dem Ausdruck, das Blühende der Rede?—Und

Niemeyer points out images that demonstrate this sublimity, citing in particular chapter 26, verses 5–13, where, he says, one sublime idea presses on another. With images of the vastness and power of the cosmos, the poet expresses the concept of God's inscrutable ways. In footnotes, Niemeyer draws comparisons to the Odes of "our most sublime German poet," Klopstock.[15] Weather images are exceptionally suited to conveying God's awesome majesty, as when God speaks through thunder and wind in chapters 36–38. In another footnote, Niemeyer turns again to Klopstock's *Frühlingsfeyer*, which, next to this passage in *Job*, is for him the "most sublime and beautiful that has ever been said about thunderstorms."[16]

While Niemeyer often writes of the sublime and the beautiful in a single phrase, not everything that merits his admiration of the poet's expressive skill concerns matters we would consider beautiful. He praises, for instance, the way in which the poet can describe Job's misery with so many different images yet without bombast:

> What I most admire in this is the inexhaustible richness of the poet's thoughts and images concerning a single subject and how what is so characteristic in each term for **one** thing— the distinctness, suggestiveness, and resourcefulness—distinguishes **Job's** discourses so markedly from all that is turgid and simply verbose. What a fullness of imaginative power! What nearly inimitable variation on the **one** thought: "**I am miserable!**"[17]

As expressed in this quote, both the images and the concepts are necessary to convey the sense of sublimity. The concept in this case is of God's ineffable providence and self-sufficiency. God does not need the service or obedience of human beings, but the realization of the impenetrable darkness of his ways fills them with a holy shudder of deep reverence. What appears to be injustice as in the unmerited suffering of a good man serves as a lesson in humility: all human reflection concerning God's intentions is fruitless. Nevertheless, this is no cause for faithlessness or disobedience; rather, it teaches that one should pursue virtue for its own sake and not for the sake of reward.

---

    **zuletzt**, wie kan man die einzelnen Worte, nach ihrer ganzen Kraft und Würde, mehr zusammendrengen, als der Dichter getan hat?"

[15] Niemeyer: Charakteristick, Vol. 2, 552. Cited are Klopstock's *Frühlingsfeyer*, *Die Gestirne*, and *Die Zukunft*.

[16] Niemeyer: Charakteristick, Vol. 2, 554. For Niemeyer, the beautiful and the sublime form a single category rather than two distinct and even contrary concepts, as they were for the English writer Edmund Burke in his *Philosophical Inquiry into the Origin of our Ideas of the Sublime and Beautiful* (1757). The different ways in which 18th-century writers perceived the relationship between the sublime and beautiful are explored in Werner Strube: Schönes und Erhabenes. Zur Vorgeschichte und Etablierung der wichtigsten Einteilung ästhetischer Qualitäten. In: Archiv für Begriffsgeschichte 47, 2005, 25–59.

[17] Niemeyer: Charakteristick, Vol. 2, 561: "Was ich am meisten dabey bewundre, ist der unerschöpfliche Reichthum des Dichters, an Gedanken und Bildern, über einen einzigen Gegenstand, und das so sehr charakteristische aller Ausdrücke **einer** Sache, ich will sagen, das Bestimmte, Gedankenvolle, Ideenreiche, das **Hiobs** Reden so merklich von allem Schwülstigen und blos Wortreichen unterscheidet. Welche Fülle der Einbildungskraft! Welche fast unnachahmliche Mannigfaltigkeit des **einen** Gedanken: **Ich bin elend!**"

This is pure religion for Niemeyer and the basis for regarding the book of Job as superior to those Old Testament writings where religion is encumbered by laws and national ambition. The values he finds in this book are trust in God, purity of heart, just treatment, and love of others. Against those who say there is nothing in the Old Testament about love of others, Niemeyer brings this as evidence. The morals of this "enlightened man" are the pure morals of the gospel as taught by Jesus. The added force of the poetic expression used to convey these ideas gives the book special power:

> From this one can see how thoroughly capable this book was of retaining a very healthy, unspoiled knowledge of God and insight into moral behavior among human beings. Add to that, especially, that all these precepts are not told in a dry tone but rather almost entirely through strong expressions in a clear and striking manner.[18]

## 4   David

Niemeyer's depiction of David, which occupies nearly 300 pages in volume four of his *Charakteristick*, engages only implicitly with the Halle Pietist exegetical tradition. Explicitly, he refers to Pierre Bayle's entry on David in his *Historical and Critical Dictionary* and to responses to Bayle by British writers Patrick Delany and Samuel Chandler among others.[19] Expressing gratitude for the work done by his predecessors, he expresses his hope to avoid their errors and his intention to focus on the moral value of David's actions.[20] Thus, his interpretation reflects his own theology and his declared attempt to look into the character of the figures of the Bible.

In keeping with Semler's historical perspective on the Old Testament, Niemeyer portrays David as a man of his own time, not a type of Christ. Where many interpreters exalted David to a Messiah figure, explaining away his immoral acts, Niemeyer treats him as fully human, a man with both strengths and weaknesses. It is a mistake, Niemeyer charges, to mix our own preconceptions into the judgments of the Bible; his approach is to read the story of David as the opinions of one Israelite about another Israelite, noting the differences between the authors of First Kings and Second Samuel. Love of the Israelite nation may have influenced the author

---

[18]   Niemeyer: Charakteristick, Vol. 2, 597: "Man sieht daraus, wie überaus fähig dis Buch war, eine sehr gesunde unverdorbene Gotteserkenntniß und Einsicht in die Moralität unter den Menschen zu erhalten, zumal wenn man dazu nimmt, daß alle diese Vorschriften nicht im kalten Ton erzählt sind, sondern fast sämtlich durch starke Ausdrücke anschaulich und eindrücklich werden."

[19]   Patrick Delany: An Historical Account of the Life and Reign of David, King of Israel. London: Osborn, 1740; German translation: Historische Untersuchung des Lebens und der Regierung Davids des Königes von Israel. Hannover: Förster, 1748–1749; Samuel Chandler: A Critical History of the Life of David. London: Buckland and Coote, 1766; German translation: Kritische Lebensgeschichte Davids. Bremen: Cramer, 1777–1780. Another work Niemeyer mentions is Adolph Christoph von Aken: Glaube und Sitten Davids, des andern Königes im Volke Gottes. Leipzig, Stockholm: Kiesewetter, 1746.

[20]   August Hermann Niemeyer: Charakteristick der Bibel. Vierter Theil. Halle: Gebauer, 1779, 12.

of 1 Kings 15,5 to write such a glowing evaluation of David, and, furthermore, David looked particularly good in comparison with Saul. Certainly, the writers could not be expected to judge him according to Christian values and morals.[21] Niemeyer himself seems to fall victim to this fallacy, however, as he frequently criticizes David for his polygamy. On the other hand, Niemeyer recognizes that it is not merely the act of taking more wives but the immoral mode of acquiring them that is falling short of the moral code of his own time.[22]

In his extensive study, Niemeyer analyzes the many episodes of David's life to see what they reveal about his character. At several points Niemeyer inserts his own poetic paraphrase of a psalm that he thinks might have been written by David about that specific experience. Psalm 51, for example, expresses the conviction of sin that Nathan evoked from David in making him confront his misdeeds in relation to Bathsheba and Uriah. As his fortunes turned positive with military success and survival of his second son, he felt that he had been forgiven, and he wrote of God's mercy and protection in Psalm 32. Then in gratitude he praised God in Psalm 103. Observing the quick return to virtue by way of repentance, Niemeyer finds David more admirable than most rulers: by conquering his weakness, he found the depths of his inner goodness that had been obscured but not entirely lost. In saying this, Niemeyer is responding to those critics who placed David among the most hated of kings, not those who explained away his weaknesses.[23]

Niemeyer addressed both groups in the question of David's vengefulness as expressed in numerous psalms. Does this desire for revenge or for God to rid him of his enemies indicate a lack of mature faith or a righteous opposition to idolaters? For one, it is only fair to acknowledge that his feelings were quite natural. His was a fiery, not a patient temperament. Second, one should not expect a higher awareness of morality than was prevalent at the time. We should not impose our ideas of greater enlightenment in this matter but rather marvel at the stepwise movement of revelation. If God allowed polygamy at the time, it is not surprising that he had not yet taught people the distinction between hating the sin and loving the sinner. "The question is not," says Niemeyer, "whether there are not higher, more generous sentiments but rather whether, under his circumstances, with his temperament, and with his knowledge and concept of morality, David would have been able to come to that level."[24] To say this is not, however, to side with those who defend David by crediting him with acting as a defender of the faith against its enemies. He self-absorbedly speaks of the enemies, after all, more as his own than as God's, and asks God for revenge for himself.[25]

---

[21] Niemeyer: Charakteristick, Vol. 4, 386–387.
[22] Niemeyer: Charakteristick, Vol. 4, 152.
[23] Niemeyer: Charakteristick, Vol. 4, 260–269.
[24] Niemeyer: Charakteristick, Vol. 4, 165: "Die Frag' ist nicht, ob es nicht noch höhere, großmüthigere Gesinnungen gebe, sondern bloß ob **David** unter seinen Umständen, bey seinem Temperament, bey seiner Erkenntniß und Begriff von Moralität, bis dahin kommen **konnte**."
[25] Niemeyer: Charakteristick, Vol. 4, 166–167. Here Niemeyer cites Psalms 18, 54, 56, 58, 69, and 92 as examples.

David's character is for Niemeyer too complicated and ambiguous to side with either his detractors or his defenders. Seeking to balance critics Bayle and Tindal against defenders Chandler and Delany on David's behavior while living among the Philistines, Niemeyer finds insufficient evidence for an evaluation: "Anyone who has read this story impartially will hardly know what to think of David."[26] In this case, there is a lack of explanatory detail in the biblical account that might shed light on David's motives, but overall it is his changeable emotional state that makes him difficult to judge. Niemeyer writes of the ebb and flow of David's feelings ("Empfindungen") in the midst of the different circumstances of his life, as seen in the narratives and in the psalms. On the positive side, this emotional sensitivity allows him a great sense of joy, but he can also suffer greatly.[27]

Niemeyer recognizes that an openness to the senses, while resulting in religious and artistic expressivity, can also lead into temptations. Rather than distinguishing between individuals whose senses are pure and the impure unregenerate, as Pietists had done, Niemeyer sees conflicting inclinations within the individual: "There is many a **sensitive** feeling that seems to be pure immaterial joy; as advantageous as it may be for quick execution of decisions, it can be just as dangerous in temptations toward the wrong."[28] It is as if David often teetered on the brink of letting passion take over, yet he had enough reason and religion to keep from falling off the cliff. This was the case when he refrained from killing Nabal (though he managed to get Nabal's wife after either dissolute living or divine justice brought about Nabal's death): "Now this close case is itself a reminder how far passion can carry one away if reason and religion do not place a dam before it."[29]

It is for his religion that Niemeyer seems to appreciate David most, though even here the picture contains many grey tints. Overall, says Niemeyer, David's religion is that of his forefathers, at least in form and outward expression, yet through his experience and reflection, his spirit was more elevated. The history of his people and of the wonderful providence they had experienced filled his heart with expectation and drew him to faith in God. He found traces of God in everything, had a joyous faith and a sense of God's endless goodness. His acts of goodness and piety were done not out of duty or obedience to law but out of love of God and gratitude.[30]

---

[26] Niemeyer: Charakteristick, Vol. 4, 170: "Wer ganz unparteyisch diese Erzählung gelesen hat, wird kaum wissen, was er von **David** denken soll."
[27] Niemeyer: Charakteristick, Vol. 4, 290.
[28] Niemeyer: Charakteristick, Vol. 4, 222: "Es ist vieles **sinnliches** Gefühl, was reine geistige Freude zu seyn scheint, dessen Reizbarkeit, so vortheilhaft sie zur schnellen Ausführung edler Entschlüsse seyn mag, doch bey Versuchungen zum Unrecht eben so gefährlich werden kann."
[29] Niemeyer: Charakteristick, Vol. 4, 161: "Itzt ist selbst dieser nahe Fall Erinnerung, wie weit die Leidenschaft fortreissen könne, wenn ihr die Vernunft und Religion nicht bald einen Damm vorsetzt."
[30] Niemeyer: Charakteristick, Vol. 4, 380–382.

## 4 David

From this perspective, David's religion was different from Mosaic religion, which consisted of strict observance of many small regulations, resulting more in fear and anxiety than joy. Niemeyer, in contrast to Semler, does not reduce Israelite religion to mere legalism and ceremonialism, however. While observing that joyous, heartfelt worship was not taught or promoted, he recognized there were always a few Israelites whose faith was internal.[31] Already from his youth David had been exceptional in this respect. Trusting in God as he faced Goliath, David exhibited not just astonishing skill but a mentality that showed a higher than usual concept of God, a trust that linked him more to Abraham than to his contemporaries: "**To carry out deeds with God**—see here again a son of Abraham who has higher thoughts of his Jehovah than the crowd; even when they returned to the true God after their continual backsliding into idolatry, they had become unaccustomed, in their concepts and expectations of God, to all that is sublime and great."[32]

David was able to infuse a new sense of joy and trust into a cold dead religion, instituting what Niemeyer calls "almost a new founding of the religion."[33] This began with the ceremonial procession bringing the ark of the covenant to Jerusalem, accompanied by singing and dancing. The Bible names the string and percussion instruments that David and others played during the procession, but Niemeyer adds the specific psalms that he imagines were sung along the way. Significantly, these include Psalms 47, 68, and 24, which had been read by Niemeyer's predecessors as having explicitly Christological meaning. Rather than regarding them as prophecies of the future reign of Christ as king, Niemeyer sees them as a recounting of the deeds God had already done for his people and a celebration that God will dwell among them.[34]

The role of place in the sense of God's presence is somewhat ambiguous for David. Niemeyer writes that David wanted to have the holy ark near him as witness to the veneration of the patronal God of his people. The thought of dwelling close to Jehovah "raises him to the point of rapture," and he sees the value of the ark in building up his royal residence as a place of glory and gathering. Yet it is not as if God could be bound by a temple or tent: "I do not find the concepts in the Bible so paltry, least of all in David's hymns."[35] Niemeyer defends David against the "unworthy idea" that God actually dwells in a temple by citing the psalms in which he prays to the Omnipresent in the temple of nature and praises the works of God in streams, seas, storms, and stars. Niemeyer includes his own versions of Psalms 8 and 139 in the text and names several other psalms in the footnotes,

---

[31] Niemeyer: Charakteristick, Vol. 4, 217.
[32] Niemeyer: Charakteristick, Vol. 4, 130: "**Mit Gott Thaten** thun—siehe da wieder einen Sohn Abrahams, der es versteht, der wieder höher von seinem Jehovah denkt, als der Haufe, der durch die beständigen Rückfälle in die Abgötterey, auch dann, wenn er zu dem wahren Gott wiederkehrt, doch von allem Erhabnen und Grossen in den Begriffen und Erwartungen von **Ihm**, entwöhnt war."
[33] Niemeyer: Charakteristick, Vol. 4, 218.
[34] Niemeyer: Charakteristick, Vol. 4, 210–215.
[35] Niemeyer: Charakteristick, Vol. 4, 211: "so armselig find ich die Begriffe nicht in der Bibel, am wenigsten in **Davids** Liedern."

concluding with the summary statement, "Whoever thinks in this way about the Godhead does not want to enclose it within walls."[36]

Admittedly, the time of worshipping "in spirit and truth" had not yet arrived, but Niemeyer recognizes the appeal of ceremony as a way of expressing and encouraging religious feelings. Indeed, aside from the bloody sacrifices of Israelite worship, he compares their joyous exuberance favorably with the "cold, mechanical" worship of his own time. Implicitly criticizing an overly rational theology, he looks approvingly on those who have not yet unlearned how to experience that which is beautiful to the senses or made the unnatural demand that humans rise above the senses. David understood that sensual experience can lead to higher truths, and to this end he instituted the grandiose arrangement of priests and Levites to create splendid ceremonial worship. He appointed the most capable and inspired music leaders who would lead the musicians in an attempt at perfection, but it was David himself who provided the vision, the poetry, the music, and the instruction that would bind his people together and bring them to a higher level:

> David presided over all these arrangements with taste that was so pure and refined for his time. He himself was the first among these choirs, at the same time the first hero, the first poet of the people, the first harp player. How can we not expect a great deal for the culture of the people, and how much more for their moral formation! No song from him (and how quickly one learns song!) is without teaching. Many are actual instruction in virtue. That is a school for the heart; that is instruction that is not preached but is sung into the heart with all the magic of sounds.[37]

Niemeyer is quick to say, following this, that he does not mean to overstate praise of David. His piety was not consistent throughout his life, dependent frequently on his successes or failures. Both Jews and Christians have made him more holy than he was: "He falls far short of being the saint that the later Israelites and Christian readers of his history have made out of him."[38] What about the belief that he was directly inspired and had knowledge of the future coming of the Messiah? To this question, Niemeyer composes an elaborately non-committal response:

> I feel how difficult it is to be certain here when everything depends on the greater or lesser weight that one places on opinions about the **necessity of certain teachings** for salvation and on the often dubious explanations of a few passages that can decide **in advance** far

---

[36] Niemeyer: Charakteristick, Vol. 4, 323: "Wer so von der Gottheit denkt, will sie nicht in **Mauern** einschliessen."

[37] Niemeyer: Charakteristick, Vol. 4, 220–221: "Ueber allen diesen Enrichtungen waltet **Davids** für seine Zeit so reiner, gebildeter Geschmack. Er ist selbst unter diesen Chören der erste, zugleich der erste **Held**, der erste **Dichter** des Volks, der erste **Harfenspieler**. Wie viel ist davon nicht für die Cultur des Volks, wie vielmehr für die moralische Bildung zu erwarten! Kein Lied von ihm—und wie schnell lernt man Lieder!—ist ohne Lehre. Manches ist recht eigentlicher Unterricht in der Tugend. Das ist Schule für das Herz, das ist Unterricht, nicht vorgepredigt, sondern mit allem Zauber der Töne in das Herz hineingesungen."

[38] Niemeyer: Charakteristick, Vol. 4, 384: "Es fehlt ihm sehr viel, um der Heilige zu seyn, den die späteren Israeliten und die christlichen Leser seiner Geschichte aus ihm gemacht haben."

better than any deductions. Add thereto that we have no clear concept at all of the higher illumination that David owed to his closer walk with God. Also, we, for whom such an exceptional condition is unthinkable, cannot with any certainty determine what of it is **more** or **less** [illumined] and should be quite unsure also about the suppositions based thereon. Let us therefore research with modesty and mutual tolerance!³⁹

There remains the story of David playing the harp for Saul, a story that has served to elucidate an interpreter's view of the power of music and the source of its spiritual power, whether in the performer, in the text sung, or the musical tones. Niemeyer does not address these questions directly and pays little attention to the episode where Saul seems to be healed from his melancholy. He focuses instead on Saul's jealousy and even enmity toward David, mentioning the times when David's playing caused Saul to throw his javelin. The only mention of the initial encounter was that when David played at the suggestion of Saul's servants, Saul was pleased with David and made him his armor-bearer and constant companion.⁴⁰ There is no need, as far as Niemeyer is concerned, to look for any supernatural elements in the story. Saul was not possessed by an evil demon but afflicted by a melancholy that grew out of his dark temperament, which contained a mixture of insensitivity, lack of self-confidence, and secret fear. While his mental disturbance could be episodic, the underlying features would not change, whatever the temporary soothing effect of music might be.

In fact, in the next volume of his *Charakteristick*, Niemeyer inclines to think that music had less of a soothing than a stimulating effect on Saul. The soothing effect is too close to melancholy to have changed his mood; instead, the stimulation must have caused him joy. This elevation of the soul can lead to a form of inspiration, which frequently results from music.⁴¹ An example of this is seen in Saul's visit to Samuel's school for prophets. After the forces that Saul had sent there to kill David had fallen into rapture, Saul himself followed and also went into a state of rapture. Niemeyer writes that they were so taken by the songs being sung that they forgot their enmity and joined in the singing, but he also adds a footnote to assure his readers that they should not seek a supernatural explanation: "We have too little data to shed light on this obscure story. Certainly

---

39  Niemeyer: Charakteristick, Vol. 4, 354–355: "Ich fühle, wie schwer es ist, da bestimmt zu seyn, wo alles auf das grössere oder geringere Gewicht, das man den Meinungen von der **Nothwendigkeit gewisser Lehren** zur Seligkeit beylegt, und auf die oft so zweifelhafte Erklärung weniger Stellen, die doch weit besser als alle Schlüsse von **vorn her** entscheiden könnten, ankömmt. Setzen wir hinzu, daß wir von jener höheren Erleuchtung, welche **David** dem näheren Umgange mit Gott zu danken hatte, durchaus keine deutlichen Begriffe haben, also auch das **Mehr** oder **Weniger** darin, von uns, denen ein solcher ausserordentlicher Zustand ganz ungedenkbar ist, auf keine sichre Art festgesetzt werden kann, so möchten auch die darauf gegründeten Vermuthungen gar zu unsicher seyn. Laßt uns also mit Bescheidenheit und gegenseitiger Duldung forschen!"
40  Niemeyer: Charakteristick, Vol. 4, 98. Niemeyer does return to this episode in the context of the role of music in prophecy in volume 5, recognizing Saul's receptivity to David's harp playing. August Hermann Niemeyer: Charakteristick der Bibel. Fünfter Theil. Halle: Gebauer, 1782, 301–302.
41  Niemeyer: Charakteristick, Vol. 5, 301–302.

one must not think of anything supernatural in it. There could even be physical causes underlying it."[42]


## 5   Prophecy

In volume five Niemeyer commented further on this phenomenon of music connected with rapture. Another scriptural example is in 2 Kings 3,15 where Elisha asks for a musician to prepare him to receive the power of the Lord. In Niemeyer's own day he saw something similar in people with a lively power of imagination, which, he observes, is an essential trait in the soul of a poet. Communities of the Inspired, who were to be found in France and England as well as Germany, practiced a form of worship with bodily movement to music that induced a rapturous state. Rather than rejecting this as madness, as others had done, Niemeyer regards it as the natural response of persons of a "very delicate nervous structure."[43] It is appropriate to speak of them as inspired, but while this rapturous state is also associated with prophecy, it is to be distinguished from prophecy understood as an ability to foretell the future.

Where there is mention of having the Spirit of God or being seized by the Spirit, Niemeyer identified a gradation of experiences. In some cases, to prophesy simply means to teach. This is true of the schools of prophecy in the Old Testament. That these men who were knowledgeable in religious matters were thought to have the spirit of God is no different from Bezaleel being filled with the spirit in his ability to create artistic designs. In other words, one can be inspired in fields other than religion. In most cases, this does not entail any direct revelation from God.[44] The only activity specifically mentioned as carried out in Samuel's school of prophecy was the singing of religious hymns, but Niemeyer assumes that this entailed training in sacred poetry as well as reflecting on religion and communicating religious insight to others. The schools presumably produced some of the wisest teachers and the most sublime poets among the Israelites.[45]

The ability to foretell the future, which is the commonly understood characteristic of a prophet, would seem to require direct revelation from God as distinct from the inspiration involved in creative human activity. Even here, however, the lines are blurry. Many of the prophecies in the Old Testament, Niemeyer perceives, emerge from astute observation of the course of history; that is, the writers could see the decline of morals and religion and predict the dire outcome of this decline, or they could express the hope of better times if the people were to return to virtuous and devout ways. When the prophecies extend far into the future, it is difficult

---

[42] Niemeyer: Charakteristick, Vol. 4, 104, fn.: "Wir haben zu wenig Data, um die dunkle Geschichte aufzuklären. Gewiß muß man an nichts Uebernatürliches dabey denken. Es konnten sogar physische Ursachen zum Grunde liegen."
[43] Niemeyer: Charakteristick, Vol. 5, 303–304.
[44] Niemeyer: Charakteristick, Vol. 5, 306–307.
[45] Niemeyer: Charakteristick, Vol. 5, 254–255.

to determine whether there is a higher illumination. Niemeyer does not discount this possibility but doubts the likelihood of determining where one's own elevated spirit leaves off and higher illumination begins: "Perhaps they often got lost in one another."[46] Nor does he think it is of any benefit to make this determination: "and what would be gained in the end if we were now able to demarcate precisely the boundary between the divine and the human in the prophets?"[47]

Niemeyer considered it important, however, when interpreting the Bible, to differentiate the expectations of the Israelites from the meanings that have been superimposed upon the text by Christians. The hope of a king who would bring salvation was strong enough at the time of Jesus that he could apply the biblical prophecies to himself. Those who followed Jesus believed him to be the Anointed One of the Old Testament, but clearly not all accepted this interpretation. Niemeyer believes that Christians have made the error of looking for references to Jesus in the Old Testament rather than trying to understand how an Israelite understood the text. It may serve a homiletic or devotional purpose, he concedes, to claim that David had in his mind the whole passion scene of Golgatha, but such thinking does not follow rigorous exegetical methods.[48] Rather than expecting the prophets to speak of future historical events, Niemeyer prefers to find in them a spirit of truth, understanding and genuine devotion to God. Whether or not one considers them divinely inspired, they can in any case be regarded as having the Spirit of God.[49]

## 6 The Book of Revelation

A similarly moderate position characterizes Niemeyer's approach to the Book of Revelation. He admits that most of the images in the book are obscure and that previous efforts to clarify them have been unconvincing. It makes no sense, he notes, to read in the book prophecies about the fate of the Western church when the majority of the church of the time was in the East. Moreover, the images have been misused in sermons and hymns to create anxiety by those who fail to understand John's metaphorical thinking. On the other hand, those who equate the book with the Fourth Book of Ezra and think it was written by a fanatic Jew are overlooking the difference. The Book of Revelation communicates a greater sense of the forcefulness, sublimity, and greatness of the Divine. If it differs from John's other writings, that may be evidence that his own thinking and experience had been raised to a higher level, which could be a sign of its authenticity. Niemeyer thus explicitly endorses the Johannine authorship of the book while recognizing

---

[46] Niemeyer: Charakteristick, Vol. 5, 309.
[47] Niemeyer: Charakteristick, Vol. 5, 311: "und was wärs denn auch zuletzt gewonnen, wenn wir nun genau die Grenze des Göttlichen und des Menschlichen in den Propheten abzustecken vermöchten?"
[48] Niemeyer: Charakteristick, Vol. 5, 324–325.
[49] Niemeyer: Charakteristick, Vol. 5, 327–328.

that scholars whom he respects take a different position. He only asks that they be fair in reading his exposition or else skip over it.[50]

Describing John's character, Niemeyer says that he had a pure, innocent heart that was dedicated to God and to understanding the teachings of Jesus. Perhaps better than any of the other disciples, he embodied the saying of Jesus, "Whoever loves me will be loved by my Father, and I will love him and reveal myself to him" (John 14,21). Through his close and constant walk with God, John's spiritual powers were so elevated and perfected that he was capable of receiving an "extraordinary revelation." More than most of Jesus' followers, John understood the divine plan for blessedness of the human race, though admittedly he could not see into the distant future without higher wisdom. It is unclear whether Niemeyer thought John was given the ability to foresee the future, but, in any case, whatever ability he had is not transferred to his readers because he did not offer an interpretation of his own images. Be that as it may, Niemeyer finds much of value in the book, so that Christians should not neglect it just because much of it is unclear.

What Niemeyer finds of value in Revelation is primarily in the letters to the churches found in the early chapters of the book. After quoting extensively from these letters, Niemeyer returns to defending John's authorship, though in a rather indirect way: "Do we find John's favorite ideas missing here? Love, life, death—are they not woven in everywhere such that, if someone had wanted to imitate John, he would have used these expressions much more frequently and would have copied his style in a more obvious way."[51] It is possible, Niemeyer conjectures, that events predicted in the book came true during those early days and were thus understood at the time while opaque to us. Whatever may be thought of John's ability to see into the future, Niemeyer does not doubt that John felt he had received wisdom from God, especially as conveyed in the final chapter of Revelation:

> Finally, the solemn conclusion is too strong for a man—who was so religious and thought of himself so humbly and of God so sublimely as does the author of Revelation—to permit himself without feeling a higher impulse. For what could be bolder than to take life and death into his hands and threaten or promise people arbitrarily.[52]

John was Niemeyer's favorite among the gospel writers, and we will encounter him again when we look at Niemeyer's oratorio on Lazarus. By admitting that the imagery used in Revelation is difficult to understand, Niemeyer skips from the early chapters to the end, not providing us with an interpretation of the new song of the

---

[50] Niemeyer: Charakteristick, Vol. 1, 416–417.
[51] Niemeyer: Charakteristick, Vol. 1, 421: "Vermissen wir etwa die Lieblingsideen des Johannes? Liebe, Leben, Tod—ists nicht überall eingeflochten und so, daß wer den Johannes nur hätte nachahmen wollen, viel häufiger diese Ausdrücke gebraucht, viel offenbarer seinen Stil copirt haben würde?"
[52] Niemeyer: Charakteristick, Vol. 1, 422: "Endlich der feyerliche Schluß ist zu stark, als daß ihn sich ein Mann, der so religiös, so demüthig von sich, so erhaben von Gott dachte, als der Verfasser der Offenbarung thut, hätte erlauben sollen, ohne einen höheren Trieb zu fühlen. Denn was könnte kühner seyn, als Leben und Tod in seine Hände nehmen, und dem Menschen nach Willkühr drohen oder verheissen."

Lamb or the harp players surrounding the throne. We can be confident, however, that he would regard them as inspiring images without any literal application to an eschatological age.

## 7 Poetry, Music, and Religion

Niemeyer's love of poetry has been apparent throughout our glimpses into his *Charakteristick*, and while music does not feature prominently in his biblical commentaries, its close alliance with poetry and religion is explained in other writings. He published books of poetry containing biblical dramas, edited hymnals, and wrote essays on the relationship between religion and the arts of music and poetry. The content of the dramas as biblical interpretations will concern us in the next chapter. Here we will look at his general reflections on the religious importance of music and poetry.

In a 1777 essay entitled "Thoughts on the Union of Religion, Poetry, and Music" ("Gedanken über die Vereinigung der Religion, Poesie und Musik"), Niemeyer begins almost as if his first loyalty were to poetry and music, with religion as the most worthwhile companion to these: "Poetry and music—can a worthier, higher path be espied for these two twinned children of heaven than the path of religion?"[53] This, it turns out, is a roundabout means of appealing to Christians to strive for higher levels of artistry. If the Greeks could write hymns to their gods, how much better should be the hymns of Christians, who have received higher revelation with the most sublime truths that ever came into the human heart.

For someone who criticized the national focus of the Israelites, it seems inconsistent that Niemeyer then pits German accomplishments against Italian. Impressed by Pergolesi's *Stabat Mater*, he wishes for a composer to set Klopstock's *Messias*, specifically the 20th song, to music. Germany can, it seems, claim partial credit for Hasse's *Pelligrini* and Handel's *Messiah*, as the composers were German even if the texts were not. Ramler's *Tod Jesu* falls entirely to the credit of the German nation, and many chorales are masterpieces, including some of the newer melodies. Overall, there are in his view too few works that successfully combine poetry, music, and religion. As if to defend his nationalistic appeal, he admits to loving his fatherland and believes that the perfection of one people contributes to the perfection of humankind.

Recognizing that not everyone who has a feeling for religion has an ear for music or an appreciation of poetry, Niemeyer thinks that this may be due to insufficient education or inferior singing in churches. At its best, music combined with poetry makes a more lasting impression on the worshipper than a sermon, of

---

[53] August Hermann Niemeyer: Gedanken über die Vereinigung der Religion, Poesie und Musik. In: A. H. Niemeyer: Abraham auf Moria. Ein religiöses Drama für die Musik. Leipzig: Weygand, 1777, 3–62, here 5: "Poesie und Musik—läßt sich wohl für die beiden verschwisterten Kinder des Himmels, ein würdigerer, höherer Pfad ausspähen, als der Pfad der Religion?"

which the ideas may be quickly forgotten. Unlike his Pietist forebears, Niemeyer appreciates all kinds of music, even operas and humorous spoofs, but it is sacred music that moves him most and raises in him the joy of being a Christian:

> I know how to appreciate the beauty of all kinds of music; even bagatelles and cheerful happy jests provide me with joyful moments. I recognize what is pleasing in the mythology of Ino; I admire Alceste and high opera. But the power that religious music has cannot be compared with others. How deeply it all penetrates! How it gives birth to great thoughts and beautiful resolutions! How a Christian then feels what dignity it is to be a Christian![54]

Of this experience of sacred music, Niemeyer writes in mystical terms:

> All powers struggle to raise themselves up; all thoughts, however far they float around, unite for one great goal; all greatness and glow of the earth scatters like dust under the feet; there is a lively feeling of being human and of the grandeur of destiny; each truth of religion becomes omnipresent; it is as if God were walking in a soft whisper of sounds; the fire of heaven glows in the heart; one would like to sink down and worship the First and Most Sublime; death becomes sweeter than its image of sleep; in such moments one would like to lay down one's head and pass away peacefully; one already has the feeling of blessedness.[55]

The music need not be the most complex with large instrumentation to achieve this effect. Even a simple hymn accompanied by one instrument can have the same effect. As for the setting, Niemeyer wants people to recover a sense of the sacredness of place, but a place can become sacred through the worshippers, wherever they are. He recalled the joyful religious experience of singing hymns with a small group of companions:

> Oh, I know the consecrated hours when in a smaller circle of select brothers and sisters our sentiments became a song, when we intoned the God of love, the giver of joy, the one who endured, the resurrected one, the morning of our resurrection, and solemn eternity; when streaming tears of joy flowed into the melody of the lips and the entire soul felt more powerfully that the best and dearest that humans have is religion.[56]

---

[54] Niemeyer: Gedanken über die Vereinigung, 15: "Ich weiß die Schönheit von jeder Musik zu schätzen, selbst Kleinigkeiten und munterer fröhlicher Scherz machen mir freudige Augenblicke; ich kenne das Gefällige der Mythologie in einer Ino, bewundre Alceste, und die höhere Oper; aber die Gewalt, welche die religiöse Musik hat, weis ich keiner zu gleichen. Wie da alles so tief dringt! Wie da grosse Gedanken, schöne Entschlüsse gebohren werden, wie der Christ es da fühlt, was es für Würde sey, Christ zu sein!"

[55] Niemeyer: Gedanken über die Vereinigung, 15–16. "Alle Kräfte ringen, sich empor zu heben; alle Gedanken, wie weit sie auch umherschweifen, einigen sich zu einem grossen Ziel; alle Grösse und Schimmer der Erde schwindet weg, wie Staub unter dem Fuße; man fühlt so lebendig sein Menschseyn und der Bestimmung Hoheit; jede Wahrheit der Religion wird allgegenwärtig; es ist, als wandelte Gott im sanften Gelispel der Töne; Feuer des Himmels glüht im Herzen; man möchte hinsinken, und anbeten den Ersten, Hocherhabnen; der Tod wird süsser als sein Bild der Schlummer; niederlegen möchte man in solchen Augenblicken sein Haupt und hinüberschlummern; man fühlt sich schon selig."

[56] Niemeyer: Gedanken über die Vereinigung, 13–14: "Ach ich kenne die Stunden der Weihe, wenn im kleineren Kreise gewählter Brüder und Schwestern, unsre Empfindung zum Gesange ward, wenn wir sangen den Gott der Liebe, den Freudengeber, den Dulder, den Auferstandnen, den Morgen unsrer Auferstehung, und die ernste Ewigkeit; wenn in die Melodie der Lippe die rinnende Freudenthräne floß, und die ganze Seel' es gewaltiger fühlte, daß doch das Beste, Theuerste, was der Mensch hat, die Religion ist."

Niemeyer's concern is not limited to his own individual or small group experience, however. His hope is to improve the quality of hymnody for all, whatever their level of musical or religious sophistication. To that end, he does not prescribe the degree of feeling or the level of poetic accomplishment needed to write a new hymn, but he does ask that it come from a depth of feeling rather than a mere decision to set pen to paper. "Of how many of our new hymns is it evident that the poet had the thought, 'Now I will write a hymn'? How few pour forth from the inmost soul and are an expression of feeling, of gentler or stronger affects?"[57]

Sometimes the uneducated understand more sophisticated poetry than one would expect, but still there is a need for hymns that combine simplicity with sublimity. The test would be whether it leaves the poet with a warm feeling several days after its composition. Cold intellectuality is most to be avoided: "Just no cold reflections, no philosophical prayers, no mutilated religion!"[58] Significantly, Niemeyer regards hymnody as "relaxation for the mind, exertion for the heart" ("Abspannung für den Verstand, Anspannung für das Herz"). Far too many hymns are being published that lack the power to reach the heart, but this does not mean that poets should strive for great artistry. "Let our Christian song be forceful and unaffected, simple and sublime, gentle and overpowering."[59]

In the revision of this essay that appeared the following year as a preface to Niemeyer's *Gedichte*, it becomes clear that his goal is to revivify religion through improved poetry and music. The blame for the religious indifference of many may lie in inadequate religious upbringing or in the poor quality of the poetry and music to which one is exposed. If religion is presented just as a matter of beliefs and truth, the realm of feelings will be directed to other, lesser attractions. If the heart is to be won back to religion, it must perceive religion's beauty and loftiness.[60] The time has passed when religion could be defined as a system of teachings in scholastic format. In fact, true worshippers of God never thought of religion in that way. "What it actually is—indeed what it has been fundamentally throughout all centuries for all true worshippers of God—, is so different from that arbitrary construction of human invention and is manifestly something more than cold unrewarding speculation."[61] Religion, whether it is considered to be doctrine

---

[57] Niemeyer: Gedanken über die Vereinigung, 19: "Wie vielen unsrer neuen Lieder sieht man es an, daß der Dichter vorher dachte: 'Itzt will ich ein Lied machen.'—Wie wenige strömen aus der innersten Seele, sind Ausdruck des Gefühls, des sanfteren oder stärkeren Affekts?"

[58] Niemeyer: Gedanken über die Vereinigung, 21: "Nur keine kalten Betrachtungen, nur keine philosophischen Gebete, nur keine verstümmelte Religion!"

[59] Niemeyer: Gedanken über die Vereinigung, 23: "Kraftvoll und ungekünstelt, einfältig und erhaben, sanft und überwältigend, sey unser Christengesang." How this ideal of simplicity applies to Niemeyer's favorite poet Klopstock is hard for a 21st-century American to understand!

[60] Niemeyer: Ueber Dichtkunst und Musick in Verbindung mit der Religion. In: Niemeyer: Gedichte, 1–28, here 3.

[61] Niemeyer: Ueber Dichtkunst und Musick, 4–5: "Das was sie eigentlich ist, auch alle Jahrhunderte im Grunde allen wahren Verehrern Gottes gewesen ist, unterscheidet sich zu sehr von jenem willkührlichen Gebäude menschlicher Erfindung, und ist so augenscheinlich etwas mehr, als eine kalte unbelohnende Speculation."

or history, is nourishment for the soul's power of sensation. This is the area in which both poetry and music operate, needing only the right material, which can be supplied by religion. Thus, the three are natural comrades, or, in another way of thinking, religion is the leader of the other two.

One might object, Niemeyer recognizes, that religion could dissolve into mere sensation or that false teachings might be spread through poetry. Will not the reasonableness of religion lose more than it gains in this focus on feelings rather than doctrine? Niemeyer does not intend to abandon religious knowledge altogether in favor of feelings but to combine them, just as a scientist can be excited about a discovery.

> Does one not stumble upon points where, even in the driest of sciences (at least so called), observation changes over into rapture? May not the person who researches nature or the one who calculates the courses of the planets—precisely in those moments when he loses himself most deeply in the immensity—also bow down most deeply before the One who called forth everything out of nothing? And should only religion—only the strong, lively conviction of how true, how uplifting, how blissful it is—never come to such an outbreak of the highest feeling of joy?[62]

Because poetry and music make a more lasting impression on the mind than prose, it is all the more important to avoid communicating errors just for a better literary or musical effect. Poets should not take such poetic license that they add or subtract from the biblical substance. Niemeyer criticizes Milton for bringing references to Greek and Roman gods into the temple of the One Eternal God. While the poet needs to find variety of expression, he should not wander too far from biblical language or insert too many of his own thoughts into religious poetry. What is needed is a kind of imitation of religion but one that allows for the skill of an original genius. Here Niemeyer praises both Milton and Klopstock and, on the subject of imitation, makes reference to the latter's essay on sacred poetry.[63] In terms reminiscent of Pietists' insistence that only the regenerate can truly understand the Bible, Niemeyer insists that the poet, before using biblical subject matter, study the Bible with inner involvement of the heart:

> Biblical stories may be re-worked, may even be embellished, but with modesty, a delicate sense of truth and appropriateness, and self-denial, and only for the sake of a higher value of the historical account that could be gained through thinking, in a word, with the actual spirit of religion. Only the study of the Bible and inward participation of the heart in its teachings can provide this.[64]

---

[62] Niemeyer: Ueber Dichtkunst und Musick, 10: "Stößt man nicht selbst in den allertrockensten Wissenschaften (wie man sie wenigstens nennt) auf Puncte, wo die Betrachtung in Entzückung übergeht? Möchte der Forscher der Natur, möchte der Berechner des Laufs der Welten nicht gerade in **den** Augenblicken, wo er sich am tiefsten im Unermeßlichen verliert, auch am tiefsten sich hinbeugen können vor dem, der alles aus dem Nichts rief? Und nur die Religion, nur die starke lebendige Ueberzeugung wie wahr, und wie erhebend, und wie beseligend sie sey, dürfte nie zum Ausbruch des höchsten Gefühls der Wonne kommen?"

[63] Niemeyer: Ueber Dichtkunst und Musick, 13. For a modern edition of Klopstock's essay, see Friedrich Gottlieb Klopstock: Ausgewählte Werke. Munich: Hanser, 1981, 997–1016.

[64] Niemeyer: Ueber Dichtkunst und Musick, 13–14: "Biblische Geschichten dürfen bear-

## 7  Poetry, Music, and Religion

Without labelling poetry as a sacred vocation, Niemeyer nevertheless writes of the seriousness of the poet's purpose in terms that could very well apply to clergy. Moreover, without using the term regenerate, he writes as if only the person who has experienced the profundity of religion is able to convey its power to others in poetry. In a single extra-long sentence demonstrating his own literary skill, Niemeyer issues a charge to poets:

> In general, if the sacred poet never takes his eye off his great purpose of producing noble, virtuous, godly sentiments with all the force of highest eloquence, as one might call the art of poetry, to affect others, to shake their souls, to convince, to move, to remind people what it is to be human and to what dignity and sublimity our faith raises humanity, to stir up gentle or fiery feelings, to give wing to the all-too-slow pace on the runway of virtue, or to pull the restless flight of the spirit back with gentle force from the frenzy of vanity—when, I say, he does not lose sight of this purpose, when he keeps in mind the importance of his subject and the possibility of becoming the friend and consoler of many unknown brethren, perhaps in their most serious and solemn hours, when he thinks vividly and does not in the end forget that he himself can do not a little thereby toward commending and making that which is dearest to him attractive—this will all teach him how he should work and will protect him from every discordant note and thus show every complaint that religion may endure to be unfair.[65]

Creators of sacred poetry, Niemeyer thinks, need more encouragement than composers of sacred music. The poets are not sure whether anyone reads their works, but religious music is appreciated more than other music because it is based on texts that are familiar and well understood. The task of composers is also easier because the text is provided to them, and they have only to set it to music. Still, they too must forego the self-centered desire for personal success in order to attain the higher purpose. They must not merely identify the affect of a text but must understand the source of the affect, lest the music sound more suited to an opera: "Yet as long as they also do not search out the character of religion with constant

---

beitet, dürfen auch ausgeschmückt werden, aber mit der Bescheidenheit, dem feinen Gefühl für Wahrheit und Schicklichkeit, der Selbstverleugnung, wenn man **nur** auf Unkosten der höhern Würde des Geschichtbuchs, durch einen Gedanken gewinnen könnte, mit einem Wort, mit dem eigenthümlichen Geiste der Religion, den nur Studium der Bibel und innige Theilnehmung des Herzens an ihren Lehren, geben kann."

[65] Niemeyer: Ueber Dichtkunst und Musick, 15–16: "Ueberhaupt, wenn der heilige Dichter nie seinen grossen Zweck, edle, tugendhafte, gottselige Gesinnungen hervorzubringen, mit aller Stärke der **höchsten Beredtsamkeit**, wie man die Dichtkunst nennen könnte, auf andere zu wirken, Seelen zu erschüttern, zu überzeugen, zu rühren, den Menschen zu erinnern, was es heißt, ein Mensch seyn, und zu welcher Würde und Erhabenheit unser Glaube die Menschheit emporhebt, sanfte oder feurige Gefühle rege zu machen, dem zu langsamen Schritt auf der Laufbahn der Tugend Flügel zu geben, oder mit sanfter Gewalt den rastlosen Flug des Geistes aus dem Taumel der Eitelkeit zurück zu ziehen—wenn er diesen Zweck, sag' ich, nie aus dem Auge verliert, sich die Wichtigkeit seiner Gegenstände vorstellt, die Möglichkeit vielleicht in den ernstesten und feyerlichsten Stunden, so der Freund und Tröster vieler auch unbekannter Brüder werden zu können, ganz lebhaft denkt, endlich auch nicht vergißt, daß er selbst dadurch zur Empfehlung und Liebenswürdigmachung dessen, was ihm das theureste seyn muß, nicht wenig thun kann—so wird schon dis alles ihn lehren, wie er arbeiten soll, ihn für iedem Mißton bewahren, und so iede Klage, die Religion leide, ungerecht machen."

diligence and set this in their works, if one happy sensation is expressed just like another without regard to its source, too much of an operatic nature still remains in the larger pieces."[66]

There is, then, a clear difference between sacred and secular music, and Niemeyer exhorts the German princes to provide more support for the teaching of church music in order that singing regain its "almost lost beauty and harmony." If children are taught good songs, they learn a sensitivity to music, and the songs embedded in their memories will serve them well later in life. Niemeyer has in mind, however, not the specific teachings of Christianity but the general positive influence of religion for the betterment of society.[67]

As a pedagogue, many of Niemeyer's publications were focused on education of the young, and in fact his 1796 educational tome, *Grundsätze der Erziehung und des Unterrichts für Eltern, Hauslehrer und Erzieher* ("Principles of Education and Instruction for Parents, Tutors, and Educators"), was his most influential and most reprinted work.[68] Motivation for writing this came from his responsibilities as administrator and instructor at the Francke Foundations, and a similar motivation led him to publish a hymnal for schools, *Gesangbuch für höhere Schulen und Erziehungsanstalten* ("Hymnal for Secondary Schools and Educational Institutions"), first published in 1785 and subsequently reissued numerous times through 1825.

In his preface to the first edition of the hymnal, Niemeyer acknowledged that many schools held assemblies that include prayer and song with the purpose of furthering devotion in young people. Too often, he charges, these gatherings are counterproductive because of mechanical repetitions, lengthy sermons that fail to address students' interests, and prayers that may be in an incomprehensible Latin. Even the instructors often show that they find these periods burdensome, which does not go unnoticed by the students. Niemeyer seeks to replace these religious exercises with a better integration of religious content into the rest of the curriculum and shorter devotional periods better suited to speak to the hearts of the students.

A component of these periods would be singing, for which purpose he compiled this hymnal for "higher schools." Because it is intended for upper-level students, it differs from a children's hymnal but also from a hymnal for rural or general elementary schools. He assumes a higher level of culture and literary sophistication and seeks to adapt the hymns to the taste and sensibilities of their class and educational level. For this reason, without wishing to denigrate old familiar hymns, he selected poems mostly from his own century and wrote a large portion himself. In addition to Klopstock, other well-known

---

[66] Niemeyer: Ueber Dichtkunst und Musick, 26: "Doch so lang auch sie nicht mit dauerndem Fleiß den Charakter der Religion ausforschen und diesen in ihre Werke legen, wenn **eine** freudige Empfindung wie die andre, ohne Rücksicht woraus sie entsteht, ausgedruckt wird, noch immer in den grössern Stücken zu viel Opernmäßiges bleibt."

[67] Niemeyer: Ueber Dichtkunst und Musick, 27–28.

[68] For an appreciation of the historical significance of this work, see Klaus Zierer: On the Historical Oblivion of August Hermann Niemeyer, A Classic Author on Education. In: The Journal of Educational Thought (JET) / Revue de la Pensée Éducative 43, Winter 2009, Issue 3, 197–222.

poets of his time such as Johann Kaspar Lavater, Christian Fürchtegott Gellert, and Johann Andreas Cramer, were heavily represented. A smaller number of seventeenth-century hymn writers such as Joachim Neander and Paul Gerhardt were represented, but their texts were drastically rewritten and sometimes only recognizable in a single strophe. Even the poems of his contemporaries were not exempt from reformulation; biographer Karl Menne notes that Lavater and Klopstock themselves modified older hymns for inclusion in their own collections.[69] From Menne's twentieth-century perspective, Niemeyer had diluted the vivid imagery of familiar hymns into bland propriety, but the success of the hymnal may indicate that it appealed to the taste of the time.

As with most hymnals of the time, no music is included in this hymnal, only the indication of the tune to be used. Niemeyer made few remarks about the tune selections, just that his criteria were beauty, appropriateness, and variety. Perhaps an unmentioned criterion was familiarity, as, in contrast to his texts, most of the suggested melodies were standard repertoire for Lutherans of the time. The majority came from the seventeenth century with a few from the sixteenth or the early eighteenth centuries. To those who think of "Ein feste Burg" ("A Mighty Fortress") as quintessentially Lutheran, it may come as a surprise that it was suggested as a tune only once (without any reference to the original text). By far most frequent, with 25 mentions for the hymnal's 328 texts, was Georg Neumark's 1641 melody "Wer nur den lieben Gott" ("If You But Trust in God to Guide You"), though again his text was not used.

With regard to the subject matter of the hymns, relevance to the lives of young people was foremost in Niemeyer's mind, and for this reason the section on trust in God in times of suffering was shorter than in general hymnals. He felt that most hymnals did not give sufficient attention to Christian duties and, accordingly, devoted a third of the work to the section he labelled "Christian attitudes, duties, and virtues." This included not only the duties toward God and neighbor but also to oneself, both soul and body. It is here that we find topics that his predecessors would have placed under the category "sin and repentance." There is little sense that one might risk eternal damnation by remaining in a sinful state, but surely one would fail to experience the fulfillment of a trusting relationship with God.

As Niemeyer himself had written, significant changes had taken place in the course of the eighteenth century, some of which he endorsed, some of which he regretted, but all of which affected his writings. The Christocentric reading of the Old Testament had to give way to a historical reading of the text, but scripture should still be read with devotion, not dispassionate intellectual comprehension. The hymnody that had always been central to the Pietist cultivation of devotion became infused with the aesthetic values of the leading poets of the time. Doctrine, which had for Pietists always been subordinated to living faith, gave

---

[69] Karl Menne: August Hermann Niemeyer: Sein Leben und Wirken. Halle: Niemeyer, 1928, 111.

way to a more general idea of religion as a feeling of the sublime. Poetry and music were some of the best means of conveying this feeling; when presented through the means of biblical character study, as in Niemeyer's oratorios, the demands of late-eighteenth-century society might coincide with the devotional ideals of early Pietism.

## 8     Summary

Born after the mid-point of the century, Niemeyer's intellectual context was that of the European Enlightenment and German poetry and literature. His approach to the Bible was an attempt to respond to the secularism of the age by, on the one hand, admitting the imperfections and natural limitations of biblical personalities, but also commending their sense of the sublime and their insights into divine wisdom. Niemeyer did not claim any supernatural inspiration for the prophets or other biblical authors, and he rejected attempts to apply biblical prophecies to actual historical events. Music and poetry are human skills but are very closely linked to religion.

Niemeyer criticized the theology and hymn writing of his time for being directed to the mind rather than the heart. While not saying that only the faithful could produce valid hymns, he did ask that poets write from their souls more than their intellect. Congregational singing was in need of more beauty and artistry, but simple hymns could make as profound an impression as complex musical compositions. In this, as in the elevation of feeling over doctrine, Niemeyer endorsed the values of his Pietist predecessors.

Chapter Six

# Love, Trust, Constancy, and Humanity in Biblical Characters: Niemeyer's Oratorios, or Religious Musical Dramas

While Niemeyer's hymnal editions merit further examination, they would not add as much to our understanding of his biblical interpretation as will his oratorios. These, he explains, belong in a different category from hymn texts, as they not only require greater art from the poet, but they are meant for a more exclusive audience than a general church congregation. Displaying his nationalist inclinations, he regretted that Germany had so far produced few good works in this category. The two that he found worthy of mention were Johann Heinrich Rolle's *Death of Abel* and C. P. E. Bach's *Israelites in the Desert*. For librettos, he admired Pietro Metastasio, an Italian who spent most of his career in Vienna and whose opera librettos were set by numerous well-known composers. Had Niemeyer known Metastasio's version of the Abraham story before writing his own, he admits, it would have been difficult for him not to copy parts of it. The drawback to Metastasio's sacred texts, in Niemeyer's view, is that he was bound to theological ideas that Niemeyer did not necessarily endorse, one example of which was to regard Isaac as a figure of Christ.[1]

Finding no theory of religious musical drama to draw on, Niemeyer outlined some defining factors and guidelines. While the genre shared characteristics with both drama and opera, or *Singspiel*, the rules for opera set forth by Johann Georg Sulzer in his *Theorie der schönen Künste* were not entirely applicable to sacred musical dramas. Hence, Niemeyer put forward in a second preface to his *Gedichte* the principles that guided the writing of his own oratorio texts.

First, all the obligations incumbent on a religious poet are applicable here except for the requirement of simplicity. Because the audience is more educated, poetic beauty trumps comprehensibility. In manner of expression, the poet should be allowed freedom, but when presenting a biblical story, freedom should be limited to omitting secondary elements of the story, not to changing any of the essential elements. Because the stories are commonly regarded as holy, the poet should respect the faith of believers.

In cases where a drama is based on a single circumstance, however, the poet needs to fill out the story with invented details. These should be determined, as in any drama, by propriety, plausibility, and interest, but in the particular case of religious drama, each of these factors is in turn determined by the religious factor.

---

[1] Niemeyer: Ueber das religioese Drama. In: Niemeyer: Gedichte, 42–43.

The boundaries of plausibility may be wider in religious matters, and skeptics should allow religious poets this flexibility.

Religious dramas may be derived from both Old and New Testaments, but the Old Testament is a more abundant source of stories about ordinary, fallible people in everyday circumstances. Audiences will be more accepting of literary license in Old Testament stories than when portraying the holy persons of the New Testament. As noted in the previous chapter, Niemeyer disapproved of passion music in which Jesus is represented by a singer, and for musical dramas he wanted to prohibit such appearances. A singing Jesus is inappropriate and detracts from the reverence that is due him. Against the hypothetical objection that this makes the great stories from the Evangelists unusable, Niemeyer responds that it merely depends on the poet's creativity. The usual practice of narrating events through recitatives is in any case not dramatically satisfactory, as it underlines the awareness that it is an imitation, not the event itself.

A drama without action is not a drama, Niemeyer observes, though it is not his intention that the religious musical dramas actually be staged. This has the advantage that the unnaturalness of sung conversations is less noticeable. Also, too much action can be a distraction from the effects of the music and poetry. The poet must always keep in mind the musical requirements for a good drama, for instance that there be variety of tempo and affect. The attention of the audience cannot be sustained in a single mood. "The greatest solemnity can never be maintained equally in all parts; constant lament is wearisome; and joy undimmed by pain or sorrow is like a concerto with only Allegro and Vivace."[2]

In addition to musical dramas derived from the Bible, there can be religious dramas based on legends or on stories of the saints. Niemeyer places his *Thirza* in this category, as it is based on an apocryphal book and on the ancient historian Josephus. In these cases, the poet has more freedom to introduce secondary ideas and perhaps even to consider actual staging. The main rule is always to consider the narrative from the standpoint of religion. When the characters are influenced by godly religion, this is exhibited in their love, trust in God, faith, constancy, patience, and humanity; when characters are indifferent toward religion, they manifest the opposite qualities.

Three of Niemeyer's dramas were published in his 1778 collection of poetry entitled *Gedichte*, where they were labelled "Religious Dramas." In his 1814 collection entitled *Religiöse Gedichte*, the same three were republished along with two more, this time labelled "Oratorios." These genre labels need not concern us here, but readers wishing a deeper understanding of the use of genre terms by Niemeyer and his circle may consult the research of Janet Best Pyatt, Christine Blanken, and Andreas Waczkat.[3]

---

[2] Niemeyer: Ueber das religioese Drama, 37: "Die höchste Feyerlichkeit kann sich nie in allen Theilen gleich erhalten; stete Klage ermüdet, und Freude, ohn' alle Dämmrung des Schmerzes oder der Wehmuth, gleicht einem Concert von lauter **Allegro** und **Vivace**."

[3] Janet Best Pyatt: Music and Society in eighteenth-century Germany: The music dramas of Johann Heinrich Rolle (1716–1785). Diss. phil. Duke University 1991; Christine Blan-

# 1 Abraham auf Moria (1776)

The first of Niemeyer's religious dramas was *Abraham auf Moria*, which, set to music by Rolle, was first performed in November 1776 in Magdeburg. The work was received with acclaim, performed again in Magdeburg the following spring and in numerous other locations in succeeding years.[4] Niemeyer was very pleased with Rolle's work, and the success of the performances is undoubtedly due as much to Rolle's skill as to Niemeyer's. Niemeyer seemed to recognize this when he wrote in his preface to the 1777 publication of the text that he was "almost a little proud to have given him the occasion for such an outstanding work of art."[5]

The title page of this publication, interestingly, does not give Niemeyer's name but identifies him as "the author of the *Charakteristick der Bibel*." Indeed, Niemeyer's intention was to depict in dramatic form the same Abraham that he had described in his book. Certain adaptations were necessary, though, in order to make the short biblical narrative into a drama. The variety of affect that he considered desirable in a musical drama led him to conclude the first act with an aria for Abraham that, he admitted, might seem too cheerful for a man who was committed to sacrificing his son. At Klopstock's suggestion, Niemeyer also introduced additional characters to avoid the monotony of dialogue simply between father and son. Sarah, who is not mentioned in the account in Genesis 22, plays a major role in Act 1, and some pilgrims appear in Act II to form a chorus of sympathetic observers. These additions, Niemeyer believes, have dramatic plausibility that does not contradict the sense of the biblical account.[6]

## 1.1 Abraham and Sarah

Niemeyer's expressed goal in writing the drama and in depicting Abraham's character in the *Charakteristick* was to encourage others to attain the same degree

---

ken: Franz Schuberts *Lazarus* und das Wiener Oratorium zu Beginn des 19. Jahrhunderts. Stuttgart: Steiner, 2002; Andreas Waczkat: Johann Heinrich Rolles musikalische Dramen: Theorie, Werkbestand und Überlieferung einer Gattung im Kontext bürgerlicher Empfindsamkeit. Berlin: Ortus Musikverlag, 2007.

[4] Menne reports on the early performances in Magdeburg and Leipzig; see Menne: August Hermann Niemeyer, 95–96. Librettos published for performances in 1777 in Hamburg, Freiberg, Berlin, and Wernigerode are listed in the *Gemeinsamer Verbundkatalog* (GVK), as are later publications from other locations such as Wolfenbüttel and Regensburg through 1795. In the following century, composer Franz Danzi wrote his own musical setting of Niemeyer's text, the libretto to which was published in Berlin in 1816. Austrian composer Ignaz von Seyfried also used Niemeyer's text but with considerable modification for a musical drama published in Vienna in 1818.

[5] Niemeyer: Abraham auf Moria, 71.

[6] Niemeyer: Abraham auf Moria, 66–70.

of obedience that Abraham exhibited.[7] Yet Niemeyer was not advocating blind obedience, nor did he think that Abraham obeyed without inner struggle, even if the biblical account gives no indication of struggle. It is left to the reader, Niemeyer says, to imagine the conflict Abraham faced between his fatherly feelings and his determination to obey God. To struggle against the natural instinct to protect one's family does not diminish the strength of his will to obey; rather, such struggle shows his will to be all the stronger for having overcome his doubts. "It belongs to strength of spirit to bear the most powerful pain; and when all the forces of the soul are driven to their extreme and yet do not succumb, that is indeed strength."[8] Powerful emotions, then, are not evidence of weakness but of strength. In a footnote, Niemeyer asserts that "one will not see common people who are in no respect extraordinary rise to the highest degree of affect. The weaker, the more lacking in affect."[9]

While Abraham may be described by the qualities of quiet greatness and peaceful sublimity, this is not to be confused with Stoicism. Not resignation to fate but trust in God's providence is the basis of his tranquility in facing the darkest night imaginable. The placidness ("Gelassenheit") of the Stoics comes from deadened senses, from a lack of feeling, which is far different from Abraham's experience:

> The quietude of which we speak, which we have seen in Abraham, was of a different sort. It was this that maintained equanimity in the face of the most susceptible pains of a father's heart, so that he did not founder in misery, so that in the end faith was victorious and Abraham himself had to see how great a person can become with God [...].[10]

Both the strong trust and the pain of the struggle are effectively conveyed in the opening scene of *Abraham auf Moria*.[11] An opening chorus of shepherds sets the mood of reverence toward a holy God who created the universe and maintains it through his power.

---

[7] The republication of the *Charakteristick* after the drama had been written makes this comment. August Hermann Niemeyer: Charakteristick der Bibel. Vol. 3. Expanded ed. Schaffhausen, 1779, 193.

[8] Niemeyer: Charakteristick, Vol. 3 (1779), 186: "Es gehört Stärke des Geistes dazu, den mächtigsten Schmerz zu tragen, und wenn auch alle Kräfte der Seele bis aufs äusserste getrieben werden—erliegen sie nicht—so ists doch Stärke."

[9] Niemeyer: Charakteristick, Vol. 3 (1779), 186, fn.: "Man wird bey gemeinen Seelen, die in keiner Absicht ausserordentlich sind, auch keine Affect auf den höchsten Grad steigen sehen. Je schwächer, desto affectloser!"

[10] Niemeyer: Charakteristick, Vol. 3 (1779), 200; also Niemeyer: Charakteristick, Vol. 2, 166–167: "Die Ruhe, von der wir reden, die wir in Abraham gesehen haben, war eine andre. Sie war es, die dem allerempfindlichsten Schmerzen eines Vaterherzens das Gegengewicht hielt, daß es nicht versank in seinem Jammer, daß endlich der Glaube siegte, und Abraham es selbst fühlen mußte, wie groß ein Mensch durch Gott werden kann [...]."

[11] Johann Heinrich Rolle's musical setting of this oratorio is held as Mus.ms.18701 at the Staatsbibliothek zu Berlin Preußischer Kulturbesitz in the Musikabteilung. This manuscript was the basis for the modern edition: Johann Heinrich Rolle: Abraham auf Moria: Musikalisches Drama, für Solisten. Ed. by Norbert Klose. Haale: Renaissance-Musikverlag, 2002. Page numbers in the text refer to this edition.

## 1 Abraham auf Moria *(1776)*

> Heilig, heilig, heilig Gott,
> Der die Welten schuf!
> Werdet! Rief Gott Zebaoth,
> und die Welten hörten seinen Ruf!
>
> Wie sie schimmern in der Ferne,
> in der stillen feyernden Nacht!
> Jehovahs Ruhm schwebt höher als die Sterne
> Groß wie sein Name, seine Macht! (1–16)[12]

Next to sing after the shepherds is Sarah, whose role in the drama is to reflect Abraham's moods, quite apart from any role she played in the biblical narrative. She continues the shepherds' joyous praise of God the Creator until she realizes that Abraham is late to return home from his daily prayers. Off to the side, without being seen or heard by others, Abraham appears and sings an agonized recitative about his terrifying encounter with God. Here the imagery of *Sturm und Drang* poetry with God's thundering voice causing knees to shake expresses the inner turmoil of Abraham's soul:

> Ich habe Gottes Stimme vernommen,
> Gesehen Gott von Angesicht!
> Ach, trüb und dunkel war Gottes Antlitz,
> daß noch mein Gebein mir bebt,
> da sank mein Knie hin in den Staub
> und bänger als es je mein Herz empfand,
> rang ich in tiefem Gebet mit Gott
> "Zum Opfer gib ihn mir!" — Noch donnert sie
> Noch des Allmächt'gen Stimme meinem Ohr, —
> "Gib deinen Sohn, den Ein'gen, gib ihn mir!" (39–40)[13]

In the aria that follows, it appears that Abraham has become reconciled to the sacrifice God demands of him: "The One who gave him should have him back. His will is good, his word is love" ("Er soll ihn haben, der ihn gab! Sein Will ist gut, sein Wort ist Liebe"). Rolle's setting is a tranquil E-flat major with harmonious instrumental thirds and sixths accompanying and also alternating with the solo voice. Only occasionally, as when Abraham sings "His way is night" ("Nur Nacht sein Weg"), does dissonance underline Abraham's conflicted feelings (41–52).

By the time the aria is finished, Abraham has come close enough that Sarah sees his disturbance in his face, and she has also heard enough to know that God has made a demand of her husband. Slowly she begins to suspect that the demand is the sacrifice of her son, and in anguish she asks that God take her instead of

---

[12] "Holy, holy, holy God, / who created the worlds! / The God of Sabaoth called out, 'Become!', / and the worlds heard his call. / How they shimmer in the distance, / in the quiet celebratory night! / Jehovah's fame floats higher than the stars, / his power as great as his name!"

[13] "I have heard God's voice, / seen God face to face! / Oh, God's countenance was so dark / and gloomy that my limbs still shake. / My knees sank into the ground, / and with more fear than my heart had ever felt / I wrestled with God in deep prayer. / 'Give him to me as a sacrifice!' / The voice of the Almighty still thunders in my ear: / 'Give your son, your only son, give him to me!'"

Isaac. In Rolle's setting, Sarah moves from a simple recitative through an orchestral recitative characterized by tempo and dynamic contrasts and wide vocal intervals to a fast aria with agitated string parts and a high-pitched vocal line that resembles screams. This is the end of Sarah's appearance in the drama, though toward the very end Isaac credits her with having helped to gain his release: "The Lord saw the pleas of my mother" ("Der Herr sah meiner Mutter Flehen", 277).[14] This single line is surely intended by Niemeyer to tie up a dramatic loose end rather than to imply that humans can influence God's will. If Sarah is not to re-appear, there needs to be at least some recognition of the obvious relief she will feel when Isaac returns. None of this, however, is found in the biblical account, and in Niemeyer's brief treatment of Sarah in the *Charakteristick* he admits that it is impossible to form a complete picture of her character based on her limited appearances in the Bible.[15]

### 1.2 Isaac

The biblical appearances of Isaac are much more extensive and provide the basis for Niemeyer to characterize him as "good, pious, upright, and virtuous but without sublimity of spirit."[16] In contrast to his father, Isaac did not have "sublime concepts of the blessings of the Godhead," nor did he receive as many appearances from God as did Abraham. Still, when God did appear to him, he celebrated by erecting altars of thanksgiving, and he was intent on spreading the true knowledge of God.[17] The desire to see God is the theme of Isaac's first aria in *Abraham auf Moria*, sung before he understands what his father means when he tells Isaac that he will soon see God's face. Imagining only that his experience will be like Abraham's encounters with God, Isaac expects "holy ecstasy" and a preview of the life to come. In a lovely E-major aria, Rolle stretches the word "Wonne" ("bliss") over eleven measures of an ornamented swoon-like vocal line with strings expressing excitement in arpeggiated 16th notes and an ascending scale that leaves Isaac suspended alone in rapture at the end of the phrase (62–64). This aria is the longest and only true da capo aria in this drama; combined with several arias and recitatives in Act II, the effect is to make Isaac's role equal in importance to Abraham's.

Thematically, Isaac serves to demonstrate the faithful person's confidence in the life to come. In the *Charakteristick*, Niemeyer briefly asserts, in apparent opposition to those who may have objected that immortality was not a Hebraic expectation, "I do not comprehend how anyone can doubt that Abraham knew the concept of immortality."[18] In *Abraham auf Moria*, Isaac is the one who has most

---

[14] In the 1777 version of the libretto, the sentence reads "Der Berg sah meiner Mutter Flehen," as in the context Abraham and Isaac are naming the mountain Moria (p. 45). In later editions, as in the musical performance, the subject was changed to "Der Herr."
[15] Niemeyer: Charakteristick, Vol. 2, 168.
[16] Niemeyer: Charakteristick, Vol. 2, 196.
[17] Niemeyer: Charakteristick, Vol. 2, 198.
[18] Niemeyer: Charakteristick, Vol. 2, 167: "ich begreiffe nicht, wie man daran hat zweifeln können, daß Abraham die Lehre von der Unsterblichkeit gekannt habe."

*1 Abraham auf Moria (1776)* 151

fully internalized this belief, even after he learns that he is to be the sacrificial offering. In the aria of Act I, when he still thinks his vision of God will be in this life, he already knows that the glories he experiences in the natural world are just precursors to the joys to come:

Du o herrliche Natur,
Bist des Tempels Vorhof nur.
Ewge Wonne wird mir dann gegeben
Wenn der Geist der Erd' entflieht! (82–85)[19]

The imagery of the spirit rising high above the created world recurs in the aria Isaac sings after his near-death experience:

Schon sah ich mit gestärkten Blicken
Des Himmels wonnevoll Entzücken,
und Orionen unter mir. (242–247)[20]

Rolle lets Isaac sing these words four times with melismas on "gestärkten" ("strengthened") and graceful triplets on "Himmel," "voll" and "Entzücken," ending with five more repetitions of the word "Orionen," as if he were suspended above the stars. Nevertheless, the earth is sanctified as the place where Isaac has seen God, and he expresses no regret in returning to his friends on "motherly earth." In apparent allusion to the claim in Exodus 33,20 that no one who sees God will live, Niemeyer has Isaac say, "Here I have seen God; I have seen the Lord, and I am still alive!" ("Hier hab' ich Gott gesehn, gesehn den Herrn, und lebe noch!", 241)

The beauty and sanctity of nature is a theme of Isaac's observations throughout the drama. In the first act, Isaac reported that he had felt God's presence that day in the shade of the forest and had pleaded to see God in the sacred grove as his father had done. When father and son arrive at the hill of sacrifice in the early morning, Isaac sings of how the splendor of nature overcomes the star-filled night in the morning. With irrepressible cheerfulness, he laughs at how he as a seed from God will slumber in the grave awaiting the dawn of Resurrection. The lines of his lilting melody alternate with instrumental phrases resembling bird song (141–152). He reports to Abraham that he has decorated the altar with roses, and, though puzzled by the absence of the sacrificial lamb and by his father's enigmatic answer, rejoices to greet pilgrims who approach, regarding them as witnesses to the sacrifice who will add to the effectiveness of their prayers. Even the eventual word that he himself is to be the sacrifice only momentarily shatters his mood; he quickly declares his willingness to die joyfully, entering a better life, and urges his father to take comfort. The nature theme returns when Isaac is bound and ready; he sees the heavenly palm tree waving toward him. He is not insensitive to Abraham's disturbed soul; like their shepherd Abimael, Isaac wonders why

---

[19] "You, oh glorious nature, / are just the forecourt of the temple. / Eternal delight will be given to me then / when the spirit escapes the earth!"

[20] "Already I saw with strengthened glances the delightful bliss of heaven and Orion beneath me."

Abraham appears so troubled, and after he learns the reason, he prays that God will console his father. Yet Isaac's own equanimity is perhaps Niemeyer's way of demonstrating his point from the *Charakteristick* that Isaac does not have the same sense of sublimity as his father. If so, what is missing in Isaac is not the sense of sublimity as beauty but sublimity as awe and terror.

### 1.3  Literary Themes

For Abraham the theme of darkness is predominant in this drama. Already in his first recitative, Abraham reports that God's face was sad and dark ("trüb und dunkel war Gottes Antlitz"). Upon seeing Abraham, Sarah comments that his look is sad and his forehead turning dark. After Isaac's song of ecstasy described above, Abraham, in stark contrast, announces his intention to retreat to the stillness of the night to be alone with God. Sarah, sensing clouds moving into her soul, says she is thirsting for light. Abraham asks her to be patient and to follow God's path that, though appearing dark, will end in daylight. She is not reassured and sings the tormented aria described above, but Abraham finds relief in a scene reminiscent of Jesus in the Garden of Gethsemane. The "night of suffering grows brighter to me" ("diese Nacht der Leiden wird mir heller"), he says as he prays: "If it be possible, Lord —no, not my will, but Thine be done" ("Ists möglich, Herr!—Nein, nicht mein Wille, der Deine soll geschehen", 106–108). Musically, this scene moves from the starkness of these unaccompanied recitative lines through an orchestral interlude in G minor—one of the few minor passages—to another sparse recitative during which Abraham regains his faith that, even if Isaac must be sacrificed, God's promise will come true. The transition from darkness to light coincides with a move from minor to major, leading to an F/B flat major aria that concludes Act I (105–121).

Musical and dramatic demands rather than logical consistency lead to this positive ending to the first act. The biblical text that provides the basis for the aria does not come until the end of the story (Gen 22,17), after God has provided an alternate sacrifice, and the original promise to bless Abraham's seed (Gen 15,5) becomes credible again. But it is also credible that Abraham remembered this promise even in his dark night of despair, as he is given to sing,

> Wer zählt der Welten Heere?
> Wer hat mit Namen die Sterne genannt?
> Wer zählt am Gestade der Meere
> Nach Millionen den Sand?
> Der zählt auch meiner Kinder Schaar,
> die meines Glaubens Erbin war. (109–111)[21]

These words, set in a somewhat pensive Largo or Larghetto tempo, are then followed by a rapturous Allegro finale to the lyrics

---

[21] "Who counts the multitudes of worlds? / Who gave the stars their names? / Who counts the millions of grains of sand on the shores of the seas? / He also counts the host of my children / who were heirs of my faith."

## 1   Abraham auf Moria *(1776)*

> Ich sehe mit trunk'nen Blicken
> die Kinder meines Glaubens stehn!
> Entzücken! Entzücken!
> Sie werden, was ich glaubte sehn. (115–121)[22]

Rolle must have known how important the theme of faith was for Niemeyer, for not only are these lines repeated several times, but "Glaubens" and "glaubte" are lengthened, sometimes taking up only one measure, sometimes more, the longest stretch taking nine measures of stepwise eighths and half-note leaps. This joyous ending to the act was surely satisfying to the audience and fortified them for the disquiet to follow.

The theme of darkness reappears early in Act II when Abimael, in an aria that begins in F major, then switches to F minor to sing:

> Ach Ernst und lastender Kummer ruhte,
> wie finst'res Gewölk
> dir auf der denkenden Stirn. (125–127)[23]

Seba, the other accompanying shepherd, responds with a petition that peace, like the brightness of daylight, will return to Abraham at the holy altar. The alternating themes of this duet are later reflected in Abraham's aria that follows his recitative asking God to give Isaac courage to follow the dark path along which both are being led. In the course of the aria, Abraham proclaims his steadfast faith in spite of the fearsome demands he faces. In a modified da capo form, the expression of fear takes middle place between the opening and closing expressions of confidence. This is still a conflicted confidence, however, and Abraham twice states that he has gained strength while Isaac and the chorus of pilgrims serve to support and assure him. In the end, he sings that the dark night of suffering was a fleeting moment: "Was ist die Nacht durchkämpfter Leiden? / Ein hingeschwundener Augenblick" ("What is the night of sufferings that have been fought through? / A moment that has vanished away", 254–255). Yet now the image of darkness is transferred from Abraham's trial to God's nature. As the choir had sung of God as "Unerforschter" ("the unfathomed one"), now the choir sings, "Preist von Geschlechten zu Geschlechten / Ihn, der im heiligen Dunkel wohnt" ("Praise Him from generation to generation who lives in sacred darkness", 263–264). The concluding lines of the drama extol the triumph of light over darkness, but the light is the light of faith rather than illumination of God's mysterious ways: "Sein dunkler Pfad führt doch zum Licht / Und wer ihn glaubt, den läßt er nicht" ("His dark path leads indeed to light, and he does not leave the one who believes in him", 285–293).

Rolle sets these words with clear contrast between the dark path, which in chordal half-note phrases leads from dissonance to consonance, and the light, which moves in sprightly 8ths and 16ths to a soprano high A. The final line about

---

[22] "With drunken glances I see / the children of my faith standing! / Rapture! Rapture! / They will see that which I believed."
[23] "Oh, solemnity and oppressive grief rested / like dark clouds / on your pensive forehead."

faith turns to a fugal form with a Baroque feel that conveys confidence without excessive gaiety. The Bachian or Handelian style may be intended to instill a sense of tradition or endurance of faith from generation to generation.

There is much in the drama that is reminiscent of Job, which may be no coincidence given that in his *Charakteristick* Niemeyer had placed Job at the time of Abraham. At one point he has Abraham say, "You gave him to me, you take him from me, may your name be praised!" ("Du gabst ihn mir, du nimmst ihn mir, Dein Name sei gepriesen!"), a clear allusion to Job 1,21. In the ending scene, Abraham and Isaac do not say, like Job, that they have seen the Lord but rather that the Lord has seen the mountain, which shall then be holy. The response of the chorus, though, is, like Job (42,6), to kneel in dust: "Most Holy One, we worship you and sink down low in the dust" ("Hochheiliger, wir beten an / Und sinken tief zum Staube nieder!", 280–281).

## 2      Lazarus (1778)

The next oratorio text Niemeyer wrote was *Lazarus*, first performed with Rolle's musical setting in 1778. This has received the most scholarly attention, largely because Franz Schubert also used Niemeyer's libretto for an oratorio. The lengthiest study, Christine Blanken's *Franz Schuberts "Lazarus" und das Wiener Oratorium zu Beginn des 19. Jahrhunderts*, contains an extensive section on Niemeyer, his *Lazarus* text, his theology, and its 18th-century context as well as the reception of the drama and its later adaptations. Blanken does not, however, discuss Rolle's musical setting. Howard Smither devotes an extended section in his *A History of the Oratorio* to Rolle's *Lazarus*, complete with lengthy musical examples.[24] In contrast to my character-based examination, Smither gives a detailed plot summary as well as musical analysis.

We have already learned that John was Niemeyer's favorite gospel writer, and it should not then surprise us that he chose a story from John's gospel as the subject for a musical drama. In his *Charakteristick*, Niemeyer had said that the story of Jesus raising Lazarus from the dead served as "a means toward the goal of representing Jesus as life, as the one who brings to life, as the one who conquers death, as the Son of God."[25] He also said that John was endowed with *Empfindsamkeit* that he was able to express very well as a writer, particularly in the story of Lazarus.

---

[24] Howard E. Smither: A History of the Oratorio. Vol. 3: The Oratorio in the Classical Era. Chapel Hill, NC: University of North Carolina Press, 1979, 463–487.
[25] Niemeyer: Charakteristick, Vol. 1, 405: "Mittel zu dem Zweck, Jesum als Leben, als Lebendigmacher, als Ueberwinder des Todes, als Gottes Sohn darzustellen."

## 2 Lazarus *(1778)*

### 2.1 Mary and Martha

The main characters in the biblical story are, in fact, sisters Mary and Martha, not Lazarus himself. They are the ones, therefore, who merit a separate section in the *Charakteristick*, where Niemeyer deals not only with the Lazarus story but with the well-known visit of Jesus when Martha is the perturbed hostess while Mary quietly listens to Jesus' teaching. The same contrast of personality is found in their different responses to Lazarus' illness and death. Their contrasting reactions are for Niemeyer a key to their differing characters, especially from the perspective of the depth of feeling:

> Martha talks a lot, shows more outward sadness, is without hope, and pours out her pain in loud laments. Mary says less, remains full of melancholy within the circle of her friends and appears not to notice the first rumor of Jesus' arrival. Her feelings were indisputably deeper than [Martha's]. For the pain is, to be sure, more visible with the fiery character, but more fleeting. The quiet, melancholic soul speaks little, but the wound bleeds all the longer and buries itself deeper in the soul.[26]

In later, expanded editions of the *Charakteristick*, Niemeyer elaborates on the seeming lack of feeling that belies Mary's deeper sensitivity.

> Anyone who is not familiar with pain or with the human heart considers it hardheartedness, yet in reality she borders close to the highest of pains. The one who dissolves in tears appears to suffer most if one doesn't know that in the greatest suffering all the sources of tears dry up.[27]

In a footnote, Niemeyer reinforces this point with a poem, unidentified but actually from Klopstock's "Der Königin Luise":

> Wer sonst nicht Thränen kannte,
> Ward blaß—erbebt' und weinte laut.
> Wer mehr empfand, blieb unbeweglich stehen,
> Verstummt' und weint' erst spät.[28]

---

[26] Niemeyer: Charakteristick, Vol. 1, 39–40: "Martha spricht viel—zeigt mehr äußere Traurigkeit—ist ohne Hofnung und ergießt ihren Schmerz in laute Klagen. Maria sagt weniger, bleibt voll Wehmuth in dem Creiß ihrer Freunde und scheint das erste Gerücht von der Ankunft Jesu nicht zu bemerken. Im Grund empfand sie ohnstreitig mehr als jene. Denn der Schmerz ist zwar bey dem feurigen Charakter sichtbarer, aber vorüberrauschender. Das stille melancholische der Seele sagt wenig, aber die Wunde blutet desto länger und gräbt sich tiefer in die Seele ein."

[27] August Hermann Niemeyer: Charakteristick der Bibel. Vol. 1. 4th, improved ed. Halle: Gebauer, 1780, 63: "Wer nicht mit dem Schmerz oder dem menschlichen Herzen bekannt ist, hält es für Fühllosigkeit, und würklich gränzt auch der höchste Schmerz dicht an sie. Wer in Thränen zerfließt—scheinet dem am meisten zu leiden, der es nicht weiß, daß im höchsten Leiden alle Thränenquellen versiegen."

[28] Klopstock's poem was written in 1752 in memory of Louise of Great Britain, who became Queen of Denmark and Norway through her marriage to Frederick of Denmark but died in childbirth in 1751 at the age of 27.

The personality contrasts between the sisters are based in the biblical accounts, but for dramatic purposes and to convey his view of religious feelings, Niemeyer magnifies their differences in his *Lazarus* libretto. As Eckart David Schmidt observed,

> The contrasting figures of Martha and Mary are fashioned in a more extreme manner by Niemeyer than in the Gospel of John and yet, one might say, in the same direction as presented in the biblical text. Martha has become still more extroverted and driven, even hyperbolically combative by the end of the second act. By contrast, Mary has become even more tear-filled but also ready to accept the circumstances willingly.[29]

Already in the first scene the contrast, even the tension, between Martha and Mary is on display. Lazarus has asked for rest in his last hour and instructed his sisters not to weep, for life is a brief moment, and after that moment he will see them again. Martha disagrees with his sense of time, lamenting that hours without him will be an eternity, nor will she cease weeping; rather, her song of mourning will resound from her lonely cottage to his grave in desolate nights. Rolle sets this recitative in a high tessitura, rising to its highest point on the word "Jammerlied" and descending only at the mention of graves.[30]

Mary, singing as an alto in calm phrases, asks Martha to give Lazarus the rest he requested. She acquiesces to a higher wisdom and here already at the beginning of the drama—rather than at the end as with the chorus in *Abraham auf Moria*—she prays "bowed deeply in the dust to the Most Sublime" ("Ich verstumme vor des Weisen Führung, bet' im Staube, tief gebückt, den Hocherhabnen an!", 8). Lest Martha think her unmoved, Mary assures her that she feels Lazarus' impending death just as deeply, but she considers him fortunate to be shaking off the dust of earth. In the quietly flowing aria that follows this recitative, Mary prays that his soul may be full of sweet peace in this last battle (9).

Although Lazarus sings that he has indeed found peace in facing death, and his friend Nathanael regards his calmness with admiration, Martha finds no consolation, only thoughts of horror and dreadful visions of death. Mary sympathetically tries to quiet her by saying that God is being transfigured in Lazarus,

---

[29] Eckart David Schmidt: "Lazarus, oder die Feyer der Auferstehung": Die Erzählung von der Auferstehung des Lazarus im Johannesevangelium und ihre Interpretation durch den Dramatiker August Hermann Niemeyer und den Komponisten Franz Schubert. In: Theologische Quartalschrift 196, 2016, Issue 2, 170: "Die Kontrastfiguren Martha und Maria sind bei Niemeyer noch extremer als bei Joh[annesevangelium] gestaltet, doch, so will man meinen, in der vom biblischen Text vorgegebenen Richtung. Martha ist noch extrovertierter und initiativer geworden, am Ende des 2. Aktes sogar hyperbolisch kämpferisch ('Hebt mich, der Stürme Flügel'), wohingegen Maria noch tränenreicher geworden ist, aber auch bereit, die Umstände willig zu akzeptieren."

[30] Johann Heinrich Rolle: Lazarus, oder die Feyer der Auferstehung, ein musikalisches Drama, in Musik gesetzt, und als ein Auszug zum Singen beym Klaviere herausgegeben. Leipzig: Breitkopf, 1779, 7. Subsequent page numbers in this section will refer to this edition. A modern transcription is also available: Johann Heinrich Rolle: Lazarus oder die Auferstehung am Grabe Lazari. Ed. by Norbert Klose. Embühren: Renaissance-Musikverlag, 2000. This edition, however, is based on an unidentified manuscript from the nineteenth century.

who is suffering patiently. Lest this seem to be shallow platitudes, she then sings a long recitative in which she depicts the agony of one who approaches death without the confidence of life after death. Rolle punctuates her lines with quick syncopated orchestral cadences culminating in the line "die athemlose Brust mit jedem Hauch ein neuer Dolch durchdringt!" ("A new sword penetrates the gasping breast with every breath!", 16). Here, every breath is felt in repeated chords and the loud descending syncopations give expression to the dagger's thrust. The person who trusts in God's love, however, will not sink in the storms of life. The aria that follows this turbulent recitative returns to a peaceful regular rhythm, though the orchestra rises in arpeggiated sixteenths when depicting the waves of the sea. Against these stormy waves, the believer holds on to the rock of God's love.

Toward the end of Act II in the aria mentioned by Schmidt, we see Martha not anchored by this rock but in her imagination flying high on the wings of the storm, following Lazarus beyond the stars, pushing through the ranks of angels to claim Lazarus for herself. Unable to think of life without him, she asks to die with him; the only love she names is her love of Lazarus, not the love of God. In keeping with the libretto, Rolle's music is filled with rising arpeggios in the voice and rising scales in the instruments. The high tessitura with numerous high As conveys the sense of flying into the stratosphere, and the extremely long melisma on the word "Sternenbahn" ("orbit of stars") circles up and down in fast runs and turns (44). This time it is not Mary but Nathanael who tries to bring Martha back to earth and to accept the temporary separation from her brother but with the expectation of eternal reunion.

We next meet the sisters at the beginning of Act III. Mary is walking around pensively when Martha hurries in with the report of her encounter with "the Holy One of God" ("den Heiligen Gottes", 57). In keeping with Niemeyer's belief that Jesus should not be portrayed by a singer or actor, Martha reports the conversation, which corresponds roughly with the biblical text though with somewhat modified wording. Jesus does not say he is the resurrection but "the one who awakens" ("der Auferwecker"), and in a phrase characteristic of Niemeyer, Jesus is reported to say, "Immortal life is the reward for faith" ("Unsterblich Leben ist des Glaubens Lohn", 58). The second-hand report of the conversation allows Martha to convey her enthusiasm:

> Auf einmal ward in meiner Seele Tag,
> So fühlt' ich seine Herrlichkeit,
> Sank tiefer vor ihm hin, tieff mit Entzücken. (58)[31]

This account brightens Mary's spirit and reawakens the hope that had apparently been wavering, though unexpressed. Now she is able to sing of the one who awakens and of the consolation that faith brings when faced with death. As in *Abraham auf Moria*, Rolle gives the word "Glauben" long melismas along with

---

[31] "At once day dawned in my soul / as I felt his glory / and sank deeper before him, in deep rapture."

several repetitions of the phrase "des Glaubens Lohn." (59–60) Word painting is especially obvious in the middle section of this da capo aria with a rising, sighing melody for the line "Aus des Jammers Nacht erheben sich" ("rise up from the night of misery") followed by quick moves and turns in the setting of the phrase "und die Seele jauchzt ihm wieder" ("and the soul exults in him again", 61). Significantly, the raising of Lazarus has not yet occurred at this point, but the report of Jesus' approach is sufficient to overcome Mary's melancholy. Martha now takes the lead as the sisters go with high hopes to join the group that has gathered around the grave. With one more short aria by Mary that employs the metaphor of the dew of Hermon to sing of nature coming back to life, the roles of Mary and Martha recede into the background.

Although the sisters are the only named persons in the biblical account other than Lazarus, Niemeyer's drama includes three other characters: the friend Nathanael, a girl derived from a separate gospel story who is given the name Jemina, and a Sadducee named Simon. Lazarus, who does not get a speaking part in John's gospel, becomes a much more fully developed personality through Niemeyer's imagination. As Schmidt observed, the three invented characters along with the more extensive characterization of Lazarus carry almost more of the message of the drama than Mary and Martha.[32]

### 2.2 Jemina

For the character of Jemina, Niemeyer reaches outside John's gospel to a story told in the other three gospels of an unnamed girl who was thought to be dead. Jesus told the parents that she was not dead, just asleep, and at his word she awakened. She enters the *Lazarus* drama as if she already knew all the other characters and has hurried to be with them, having heard of Lazarus' impending death. Lazarus welcomes her as "daughter of the resurrection" and asks her to sing a song of death and resurrection as she had often done in moonlit summer nights accompanied by her string playing. Jemina accommodates his request in a quite literally flowery aria that recounts her falling to sleep:

> So schlummert auf Rosen die Unschuld ein!
> Wo sanfte Lüftchen säuselnd mit Blüte sie bestreun.
> [...]
> So schlummert' ich und die Gespielen
> Streuen die Rosen Sarons über mich! (20–22)[33]

Rolle's graceful setting ends with repetition of the words "So schlummert' ich" followed by a soft string descending line to a single low A. Suddenly, though,

---

[32] Schmidt: Lazarus, 171.
[33] "Thus does innocence fall asleep on roses! / Where soft breezes, rustling, bestrew her with blossoms. / [...] / Thus did I sleep, and the playmates / scattered the roses of Sharon onto me!"

the orchestra bestirs her with rapidly ascending arpeggios; as if she has been taken up to heaven, she is greeted by angels welcoming her. Before she can settle into heaven, she hears a voice from earth telling her to awaken. Hearing the last sounds of weeping around her bed, she sees the face of the Mediator and, far from regretting her return to earth, proclaims that heaven's bliss is not greater.

At this point Lazarus utters his last words which, in contrast to Jemina's upbeat message, tell of the dark path he faces and the footsteps of death he hears. Lacking the confidence that Jemina intended to instill in him, he asks the Lord as his shepherd to lead him, to be gracious and not reject him. Nathanael, Jemina, Mary, Martha, and the chorus of friends then close out Act I with a dirge-like prayer for mercy that they not be abandoned in their last hour. Perhaps because there are two more acts in this drama, Niemeyer did not need to end this act with an upbeat chorus, but, even if his aim is to allow the audience to experience the depth of emotion, the text as well as the music conveys the feel of a more traditional view of death as an occasion for fear. The slow C minor with pulsating repeated bass notes resembles the ending of a passion story depicting last breaths. Indeed, Rolle's last three measures seem to express a fading away of life; after a predictable i-V-I cadence on the word "hour," Rolle tacks on a harmonically indeterminate downward line repeating the phrase "in the last hour," ending with a surprising C major chord (28).

Jemina appears again toward the end of Act II in a duet with an unnamed young man, singing of a holy valley of rest for the faithful. The thought of immortality fills them with heavenly rapture ("himmlisches Entzücken") in words reminiscent of Isaac's vision in *Abraham auf Moria*. The chorus that follows the duet also uses the imagery of the soul hovering high, this time not over the stars but over the grave. They picture Lazarus surrounded lovingly by angels, and they look forward to a rapturous reunion with him. This act does end with a joyful chorus accompanied by many measures of rising orchestral arpeggiated chords (53–56).

Parallel to this duet and chorus of Act II, Jemina sings another duet toward the end of Act III, this time with Lazarus. The pair have each had their experience of the glories of eternity, which makes them eager to fill earth with praise. Gone is any fear of death or judgment, and even the idea of sleeping until a final resurrection is absent; they sing of life flowing into the sea of eternity, as if without interruption. Now it is the word "immortality" ("Unsterblichkeit") to which Rolle sets extended melismatic lines that weave between the two soloists (97–102).

## 2.3   Simon the Sadducee

The drama does address the fear of death, however, in the person of another invented character named Simon. While all the other characters believe in immortality from the outset, Simon is identified as a Sadducee, a member of the Jewish sect that is said in the gospels to reject the idea of resurrection. In Niemeyer's libretto, however, he appears as one who has formerly found consolation through belief in resurrection and judgment but now is terrified. Entering after Lazarus' grave has been dug, Simon fears that the grave is for him. Nathanael, addressing him as a friend, tries to reassure him and hopes that the song the friends will sing around the grave will give Simon a glimpse of immortality. Simon slips away as the friends bring Lazarus' body to the grave, singing of the rest that may be found in that shade.

While Simon only reappears well into Act III, his time has been spent in restlessness and disorientation. Not sure whether hours or only minutes have passed, he is in a cold sweat, overcome with the fear of bodily decomposition. Falling in despair onto a tombstone, he cries out to be released from his misery. At this point nature itself communicates the supernatural event that is occurring, though he fails to understand. Sensing a "holy stillness," he sings that new life is being breathed into nature. The stillness is broken, however, by thunder and the sinking of graves beneath him. Fearing that God is destroying the earth, he runs away wildly while calling out for rescue (63–65).

This is the point, of course, when Lazarus rises from the dead, and with the imagery of all nature growing silent and graves quaking, Niemeyer has added dramatic elements not conveyed in the biblical story. Simon, who reappears after the resounding chorus of thanksgiving, thinks that Nathanael is deluded when he speaks of a miracle. Upon seeing Lazarus and, moreover, being told that Lazarus has seen Simon's long-deceased family, Simon comes to believe and to overcome his fear of death. Explaining that he had been launched into a labyrinth of despair when his virtuous father had died unappreciated, Simon can regain his joy, knowing that his father has been rewarded in eternal life. In a long aria he sings of the day of judgment when the earth shakes, thunder roars, and sounds of wailing are heard throughout the world; virtue, by contrast, has no fear of judgment but, certain of its reward, looks upon the throne and shouts with joy (91–96).

Schmidt regards Simon as a prototype of the converted Pietist,[34] and Simon does say that he has been reborn, but several elements of Pietist conversion are missing. There is no mention of sin, repentance, or Jesus' substitutionary atonement. In fact, Simon does not speak of Jesus or encounter him. He comes to belief through Lazarus' testimony, but it is a testimony of seeing his own father, not the Divine Father. His belief is that virtue will be rewarded in the life to come, a much-reduced content in comparison with Pietist conversion experience.

## 2.4   Nathanael

The third character not included in the John 11 narrative is Nathanael, who, as mentioned above, is identified as a friend. He has come from hearing Jesus say that Lazarus' illness is not unto death, calling it "rest in the grave." In the biblical account, Jesus first said that Lazarus had fallen asleep but, when the disciples misunderstood, clarified that Lazarus was dead but that he was going to reawaken

---

[34] Schmidt: Lazarus, 170.

him in order to bring them to belief. No mention is made of Nathanael in this chapter, but he appears in the gospel of John in two other chapters, though he does not appear at all in the synoptic gospels, unless he is equated with Bartholomew. In any case, his role in Niemeyer's drama is to serve as messenger from Jesus and a steadying force for the other characters. Schmidt calls him "the most reliable evangelist and adviser, a pastor who prays for the sick and is always prepared to dispense comfort to others."[35] Blanken points out that Klopstock in his *Messias* had given Nathanael lines very similar to those that Niemeyer gives him, though the circumstance in *Messias* was not the death of Lazarus but of his sister Mary.[36]

There can be little doubt that Klopstock's influence carried over into Niemeyer's librettos and even into his understanding of the Bible. Niemeyer said so explicitly in a footnote to his treatment of the disciple Thomas, thanking Klopstock effusively for stimulating so many insights into biblical characters.[37] The next section after Thomas in the *Charakteristick* is about Nathanael and, remarkably, these are the only two disciples other than Judas who are singled out for separate study. Niemeyer regrets that there is so little biblical material for knowing Nathanael, but the exchange with Jesus in John 1,43–51 is enough for Niemeyer to esteem Nathanael highly. In the encounter with Jesus, Nathanael, according to Niemeyer, "feels all the divine sublimity that lies in Jesus' answer"; without hesitation or delay, Nathanael then gives "the most remarkable testimony of the person of Jesus."[38] This is the steadfast character who guides Mary, Martha, and Simon in the drama through the emotional turmoil they are experiencing.

Because of his steadfastness, Nathanael is less interesting from a dramatic standpoint, as he does not struggle with doubts. Musically he functions almost as a narrator to the extent that most of his lines are recitatives, and several times he asks other characters to sing. His one aria occurs soon after he has arrived and has seen how peacefully Lazarus is facing death. Nathanael expresses the hope that he will approach his own death just as peacefully. The high point of the aria is on the word "Herrlichkeit" ("glory") in the phrase "wenn des Triumphes Wonnetag in seiner Herrlichkeit erscheint" ("when the blissful day of triumph appears in its glory", 12). Already we have a glimpse of victory over death, even though the drama must proceed through death and mourning.

## 2.5  Lazarus

What, finally, is the role of Lazarus? We have seen his desire for rest and a peaceful death. While the drama is short on Christological claims, Lazarus does allude to the impending suffering of Jesus. After Mary praises Lazarus' patience and sees God being transfigured in him, Lazarus deflects praise onto the one who

---

[35] Schmidt: Lazarus, 170.
[36] Blanken: Franz Schuberts "Lazarus", 130.
[37] Niemeyer: Charakteristick, Vol. 1 (1775), 64, fn.
[38] Niemeyer: Charakteristick, Vol. 1 (1775), 68–69.

will endure much more, the one who has taken human sickness upon himself and shown the way to the Father:

> Mehr, viel mehr wird einst, der unsre Krankheit auf sich nahm,
> der uns den Weg zum Vater lehrte,
> Ach, der uns liebt, durch den wir selig sind,
> viel mehr wird er erdulden! Jedes Leiden,
> Kommt's nicht von dem, der Lieb', ach, der ganz Lieb' ist? (15)[39]

Lazarus' other Christological statement comes after he has been raised, when he asks, "Ist nicht die Erde Heiligthum wo unser Mittler wandelt?" (88). In other words, Jesus makes the earth holy by his presence.

As in *Abraham auf Moria*, the one who has experienced or had a vision of heavenly life does not regret returning to earth but returns with a greater sense of the sanctity of the earth and familial relationships. In Lazarus' only solo aria, he first sings of the heavenly harmonies that he heard when he came into bliss; he wants his song of praise to resound with the melodies of angels. Rolle gives him a seven-measure-long rapturous melisma on the word "Gesang" (82–83). Yet more moving than the sound of harps is the tear that flows from the eye of his sister; joining with the others in chorus, he sings of the blessed rapture of reunion with his sisters and brothers. This rapture is beyond both speech and music:

> Mehr! Viel mehr! Kein Harfenklang
> Nennt unser seliges Entzücken.
> Schau her! Es schwimmt in unsern Blicken
> Was keine Sprache nennt, kein Lied dir sang. (84–85)[40]

The life of "noble souls" on earth is continuous with eternal life, for patient suffering "brings us a thousand steps closer to glory." Imagery of seed coming to life and night turning to morning makes death and immortality into a natural process with different stages. The vision of the general resurrection does not include earthly destruction but rather an eternal springtime.

> Auch uns erweckt
> Der Sohn des Vaters, wenn hernieder
> Sein grosser Tag durch alle Himmel schwebt!
> Die Gräber beben,
> Meere rauschen von Leben,
> Das Thal der Leichen blüht,
> Ein ewger Lenz hervor! (105–107)[41]

---

[39] "More, much more will the one who took our sickness onto himself, / who taught us the way to the Father, / yes, who loves us and through whom we are blessed, / much more will he endure one day! Does not every suffering / come from him who is love, indeed completely love?"

[40] "More! Much more! No harp sound / gives name to our blessed rapture. / Look! Swimming in our eyes is that / which no language names and no song sang to you."

[41] "The Son of the Father / awakens us also, when here below / his great day sweeps through all the skies! / The graves shake, / seas rush with life, / the valley of the dead blossoms, / bringing forth an eternal springtime!"

Jesus is again here the one who awakens, but, curiously, another line directly naming Jesus in the printed libretto is changed in Rolle's score. In Niemeyer's *Gedichte*, Jemina and Lazarus sing: "Hochgelobt sey Jesus Christ / Durch den mein Geist unsterblich ist!" ("Highly praised be Jesus Christ, through whom my spirit is immortal!").[42] In Rolle's printed score it reads: "Wo ewger Jubel ihn erhebt / Durch den mein Geist unsterblich ist" ("Where eternal jubilation exalts him, through whom my spirit is immortal", 100–102). Whether Rolle and Niemeyer discussed this alteration cannot be known, but presumably the latter did not object. After all, the more traditional language might have been understood as referring to a substitutionary atonement, which was not in Niemeyer's theology. Jesus was a mediator, a guide, a teacher of the sublime, not a sacrificial lamb.[43]

## 3  *Thirza und ihre Söhne* (1779)

### 3.1  The Story and its Themes

Niemeyer's next drama, set to music by Rolle and first performed in Magdeburg in 1779, was based on a story from the intertestamental book 2 Maccabees concerning a woman with seven sons who all chose to be executed rather than betray their Jewish faith.[44] This and another story of martyrdom from 2 Maccabees were the focus of a section in the fifth volume of Niemeyer's *Charakteristick*. He set the historical context from the time of the Babylonian Captivity, when Jews were living within another culture, leading some to assimilate but others to hold fast to their Jewish practices. They were pushed to a breaking point under Antiochus Epiphanes of Syria, who turned the temple in Jerusalem into a pagan temple and forced Jews to join in ceremonies honoring Dionysius. He forbade circumcision and made a spectacle of two women who had their babies circumcised, casting the women over the city wall. The story of the woman with seven sons began with them being tortured for refusing to eat swine's meat. One by one the sons are executed, each affirming his willingness to die rather than to act against God's law. After the sixth has been killed, the king shows a bit of humanity, as Niemeyer says, and promises the last one favor and honors if he would abandon the law, but he too holds firms and repeats the affirmations of his brothers. In the end the mother also dies, though the mode of death is not described.

One striking element of the affirmations is the belief in life after death, which, as Niemeyer observed, was rare in Old Testament writings. Indeed, it is striking

---

[42] Niemeyer: Gedichte, 113.
[43] For a discussion of German Enlightenment thought concerning the work of Christ, see Karl Aner: Die Theologie der Lessingzeit. Halle: Niemeyer, 1929, esp. 47–50.
[44] Curiously, Arnold Schering, who highlights *Thirza und ihre Söhne* as containing sounds of almost Handelian greatness and scenes comparable to those of Gluck, misidentifies the historical setting as taking place during the time of persecutions of Christians. Arnold Schering: Geschichte des Oratoriums. Leipzig: Breitkopf und Härtel, 1911; reprint: Hildesheim: Olms, 1966, 353–354.

to read the second son's words, "The King of the universe will raise us up to an everlasting renewal of life," (2 Macc 7,9 NRSV) and the mother's encouragement of their sacrifice, saying "The Creator of the world [...] will in his mercy give life and breath back to you again." (7,23) Surely this was one of the factors leading Niemeyer to choose this story for a drama; as we have seen, everlasting life is a major theme in his dramas.

A problem for his contemporaries, however, was the issue of martyrdom. Niemeyer devotes most of the commentary on these stories in 2 Maccabees to the question of the merit of martyrdom. Clearly, he is addressing those who consider religious doctrines or practices—especially Jewish dietary laws—not to be a justifiable reason to sacrifice one's life. Niemeyer struggles with this problem, for he too finds no merit in the dietary laws, and he also thinks that the inclination toward martyrdom can be a kind of sickness or fanaticism. Some have pursued this path on their own in a manner tinged with self-love, he admits, perhaps in the desire for crowns of glory. Others, such as Michael Servetus, are willing to die for what Niemeyer calls a private opinion. He is willing to credit such persons with a certain merit, but he finds it more meritorious to die for universal values such as virtue, innocence, and purity of soul.[45]

The greatest justification for standing firm even for a minor principle or practice is to uphold freedom of conscience. Niemeyer cites his greatly admired professor, Johann August Nösselt, in stating that a martyr has value in making people and rulers sensitive to the fact that conscience is not subject to any human power. Martyrs serve to teach tyrants that nothing can be achieved through external power, and by their sacrifice martyrs serve those who come after them. For example, we can be grateful to John Huss, who had been executed at the Council of Constance (1415), that Luther was not burned at the Diet of Worms (1521).[46]

Steadfastness in the face of tyrannical persecution, then, is the meritorious quality of the one who is convinced that he or she is acting in obedience to God. Niemeyer does not invoke the adiaphoristic controversy, but his position is reminiscent of the time of the Leipzig Interim; during this compromise enacted by rulers, religious practices that were in themselves indifferent became matters of principle when they were a component of a broader suppression of belief. Looking back to Antiochus, Niemeyer could not regard the eating of pork to be significant for its own sake, but to yield on this matter would have caused the tyrant to go on to require another offensive practice. Not stubbornness but the conviction that one belongs to God rather than oneself provides the spiritual greatness necessary to endure suffering. This quality Niemeyer sees most of all in the mother in this story.

---

[45] Niemeyer: Charakteristick, Vol. 5, 564.
[46] Niemeyer: Charakteristick, Vol. 5, 568.

## 3.2 Dramatic Exposition

For his drama, Niemeyer needs to give the mother a name, and he finds this in Klopstock's *Messias*, where she appears in books 11, 13, and 15 with the name Thirza. Klopstock also gives the youngest son the name Jedidoth, which Niemeyer changes to Jedidiah. With these multiple appearances in *Messias*, Thirza and her sons are important witnesses of faith and martyrdom for Klopstock, surely influencing Niemeyer to choose them as subjects of a religious drama.

Act I of *Thirza und ihre Söhne*[47] begins with a victory chorus of Syrians singing to their king Epiphanes in the Jerusalem temple, which now displays a statue of Jupiter. The triumphal song credits Jupiter, the god of thunder, for the victory and acclaims Epiphanes, wishing him a long life. A temple priest then offers prayers and sacrifice to all the gods, naming Apollo and Athena and referring to others by their roles. Afterwards, the chorus praises the gods for giving them courage for the victory in which the blood of their enemies flowed. This would seem to be a unifying event for the Syrians, but Epiphanes is disturbed by those who refuse to join in devotion to these gods. He then reports how he has begun to punish the "proud" woman and her seven sons. Although he seems somewhat unsettled by their equanimity in facing death, he remains confident in the justice of putting to death those who refuse to venerate the Olympian gods.

## 3.3 Chryses

A new character invented by Niemeyer then appears and introduces the element of doubt, though initially it is not an inner conflict within a single person but a conflict in relation to another individual. Chryses, who is called a teacher and confidant of the king, describes the mother as witnessing her son's death not just calmly but even elatedly with a gaze toward heaven. Epiphanes sees in the willingness to die for a cause a desirable trait that could benefit him in his battles, but he still cannot tolerate their repudiation of his gods. Chryses, who taught Epiphanes from his youth, reminds him that he had been educated in wisdom and had dedicated himself to a humane course in life. Hesitant to question the one who is now in authority over him, yet knowing that higher principles are at stake, Chryses asks Epiphanes whether his actions are truly in accord with divine wisdom:

---

[47] Niemeyer's libretto was first published in his *Gedichte* (1778), 117–162. Page references in the text refer to this edition. The libretto was published separately, possibly in 1784, as Thirza und ihre Söhne. Musicalisches Drama. Ausgeführet im Concertsaale zu Magdeburg. Another edition appeared as Thirza und ihre Söhne. Ein religiöses Drama für die Musik Von August Herman Niemeyer, Componirt von Johann Heinrich Rolle, 1786. A handcopied music manuscript with piano accompaniment was made available even earlier for small-scale performances: Johann Heinrich Rolle: Thirza und ihre Söhne, ein musikalisches Drama in Musik gesetzt, als ein Auszug zum Singen beym Klaviere (1781). Sections of the orchestral version, to be found in the Staatsbibliothek Berlin, were reproduced in facsimile in Pyatt, Music and Society, 496–527.

> Hat der Gott der Götter dis Blut gefordert? – geboten diese Rache?
> Lehrt nicht die Weisheit Irrthum dulden?
> Was wären wir, wenn jeden Irrgedanken
> Der Donnerer mit Blitzen rächen wollte? (126)[48]

Chryses reminds Epiphanes that he was born as a human being and is only worthy of the throne as a beneficent, sympathetic ruler. Epiphanes is not persuaded, and the act ends with an impassioned duet, each arguing his own position: the king sees himself as upholding law and order, while Chryses accuses him of punishing the innocent.

The mood shifts dramatically with the beginning of Act II. Now it is not the chorus of Syrians rejoicing triumphantly but a chorus of Israelites pleading mournfully that God may put an end to their afflictions. Significantly, they regard their suffering as a judgment from God rather than the king, perhaps reflecting Niemeyer's view that many Israelites had not remained faithful to the Jewish law when living under occupation. Next Chryses appears and shifts the blame to Epiphanes but is now inwardly conflicted between obedience to his king and his belief in the innocence of the victims. In the text printed in *Gedichte* 1778, this scene includes a report from a Syrian whose duty it was to attend the execution, whereas the libretto printed as the Magdeburg concert version has only Chryses struggling to summon up his own courage.[49] Both versions end the scene with Chryses' solemnly brooding aria, in which Rolle emphasizes the word "Zweifel" ("doubt")[50]:

> Wenn endet dieser Kampf der Seele,
> Wenn werd ich über Sternen
> Des Himmels hohe Weisheit lernen,
> Die durch des Zweifels Hüllen dringt! (133)[51]

After a brief exchange in which Chryses tries once more to persuade Epiphanes to change his decrees, Chryses disappears until the end of Act III. There he discloses to Epiphanes that he had sent a cup of poison to Thirza to save her from a more painful death. His inner struggle has been resolved in favor of serving wisdom rather than a cruel ruler. Thirza recognizes his merciful deeds, which had also included concealing her sons' ashes in an urn surrounded by myrtle leaves, and persuades him that Jehovah will look upon him with mercy. Chryses then realizes that he has found what he has been seeking all his life, and, renouncing the Olympian gods, declares Jehovah as his God. Describing his lifelong search for God as a labyrinth in which he wandered back and forth and as a stream of earthly

---

[48] In the 1784 (p. 9) and the 1786 (p. 11) libretto publications, the last line reads, "Ein Gott mit Blitzen rächen wollte?" Translation: "Did the God of Gods demand this blood? Command this revenge? / Does not wisdom teach tolerance of errors? / What would we be, / if the Thunderer wanted to avenge every erroneous thought with lightning?"
[49] Niemeyer: Gedichte, 131–132; Thirza und ihre Söhne [1784?], 12–13.
[50] Rolle: Thirza und ihre Söhne (1781), 34.
[51] "When does this struggle of the soul end! When will I learn the lofty wisdom above the stars of heaven that penetrates through the mantle of doubt!"

wisdom from which he became even thirstier after drinking, his aria ends with a simple affirmation, "Nun hab ich dich, o dich gefunden / Mein Vater!—Sieh hier ist dein Sohn!" ("Now I have found you, my Father! Behold, here is your son.") Rolle depicts the wandering with long directionless 16th-note runs on the word "Ströme" ("streams") in a 4/4 Andante moderato section that comes to a clear break before the graceful 3/4 Larghetto section expressing the calm of arrival at the journey's end.[52]

As in *Lazarus*, Niemeyer has created a character who undergoes a conversion after a difficult struggle. In this case, the conversion is from false to true religion rather than from disbelief within a religion, but both examine the process of moving from inward turmoil to psychological and spiritual release. While the stories do not fit a prescribed mold for Pietist conversion process, they might still serve the same purpose as earlier conversion narratives. As invented characters, Simon and Chryses were relatable human beings without the sacred aura of biblical figures. Although faced with extraordinary circumstances, their inner conflicts could have been well understood by an 18th-century audience faced with similar crises of faith. In addition, the added characters provide Niemeyer with valuable dramatic elements that enrich and develop the narrative.

## 3.4   Joel

Additional dramatic elements are provided by other invented characters. Human drama, rather than spiritual conflict, is introduced by bringing in an unnamed son of the sixth of Thirza's sons (whom Niemeyer names Joel). Epiphanes tries to appeal to Joel's fatherly devotion by having the boy appear with Joel as the king demands veneration of the gods. Joel's devotion to his God outweighs his paternal feelings, and he trusts that God will protect his son, yet he is not insensitive to his son's plight. In a moving aria he sings of the tears he sheds for his son, compares him to a tender flower and asks who will tend him. Then, addressing God as the protector of the innocent, he gives his son over to God with both joy and trembling ("freudig zitternd", 136). In the original libretto, the boy himself tells tearfully of his mother also falling to the sword in his presence, but in the musical score this narrative is omitted, and the son has only a non-speaking role.

## 3.5   Selima

Another imagined character is Selima, the lover of the seventh son Jedidiah. The preface to the libretto for the concert performance explained that, in addition to contributing to the drama as a whole, the role of Selima was necessary as an additional female role for vocal variety. Indeed, a second female voice makes

---

[52] Rolle: Thirza und ihre Söhne (1781), 82–84.

possible a lovely quartet to end Act II in which each character sings his or her own perspective. Selima's perspective is also necessary to the dramatic development, for she adds the viewpoint of earthly love that fails to comprehend the reason Jedidiah is willing to die and can only see it as rejection of her love. The relationship between Thirza and Selima is reminiscent of that between Mary and Martha in the *Lazarus* drama. Thirza is solely focused on eternal reward, whereas Selima feels abandonment and misery. In an exchange that was omitted from the musical version, Thirza tries to convince Selima that if she truly loved Jedidiah, she would bless his passing into eternity, where she would later be able to be with him forever. In this same omitted passage, we see a glimpse of hesitation in Jedidiah, who sheds tears and asks, "Schuff er nicht mir dieses Herz zur Liebe?" ("Did not Jehovah create my heart for love?", 144). Prior to Selima's entrance, Jedidiah had admitted his weakness and reluctance to be separated from Selima and his mother, praying to God for strength. In the end, he is fully committed to die for Jehovah, whom he addresses with an appellation we encountered from Abraham, "Du Unerforschter, Hocherhabener!" ("Thou unfathomed, highly exalted One!", 146). As the time to separate approaches, Selima does bless Jedidiah and tells him she will be with him "over there" eternally. Still, when she finds Thirza dying in Act III, she loses any sense of God's mercy, now totally alone in the world. To this extent she is rather an unusual character in Niemeyer's dramas, not faithless but unable to grasp higher truths. She is led offstage in despair, unable to join in the final chorus of praise.

### 3.6 Thirza

Thirza is the most steadfast of all the characters, never wavering in her resistance to Epiphanes, even when he offers an opportunity to save the last two sons. Contrary to all expectations of motherly love, she encourages her sons to go to their death as a victory. Like Abraham, Thirza is prepared to give her sons back to God, and she will follow them joyfully. As Jedidiah is taken away, she sings, "Er siegt! Ich seh die Krone in seines Engels Hand" ("He is victorious! I see the crown in the hand of his angel", 147). Like Mary in the *Lazarus* drama, Thirza's steadfastness should not be taken as absence of feeling. She tells Jedidiah how she gave birth to him, nurtured him, and worried when he was in danger. Now she begs him for mercy even as she instructs him to die: "Erbarme dich Jedidiah, mein und stirb!" ("Have mercy on me, Jedidiah, and die!", 142). In the next act, tired and feeling no need to continue living now that her sons are gone, Thirza asks God to have mercy and let her die, a parallel line to the one addressed to Jedidiah. In an aria that lived independently outside the drama, "Der junge Morgen meiner Tage,"[53] she sings of how the innocence of the early morning of her life turned to sadness in the evening, yet God has done all things well ("du hast alles wohlgemacht",

---

[53] This is found in an untitled music manuscript of 98 vocal pieces (1786–1789) in Munich, Bayerische Staatsbibliothek, Mus.ms. 8739, no. 88. URL: https://www.digitale-sammlungen.de/view/bsb00050586 (accessed July 17, 2023).

150). While drinking the poison, she again asks for mercy—for her people, for Selima, and for herself.

Having been told that the poison was offered by Epiphanes, though it was actually sent by Chryses, she is convinced that she has, like her sons, been given the opportunity to die as a martyr. Proclaiming the greatness of Jehovah's name, she senses "an almighty feeling of bliss" flowing through her tired body and rapture that she is worthy to die for her God. Her final line is reminiscent of Jesus' last words: "Herr—Herr—es ist genug!—In deine Hände!" ("Lord, Lord, it is enough! Into thy hands!", 162). Chryses calls her a "hohe Dulderin" (a woman who endures greatly), saying that only one who calls God Jehovah will endure so much, and the chorus ends the drama with a triumphal chorus that parallels the opening victory march of the Syrians.

This patient suffering is for Niemeyer one of the rare virtues that enables a person to overcome pain and stand firm for one's principles. A martyr must be able to overcome human sensibilities, which does not mean that the feelings are any the less strong. In fact, those in whom the more delicate feelings are deadened lose some of the merit of their martyrdom, which consists in facing danger or suffering steadfastly.[54] As in the treatment of Abraham, this is different from Stoicism, at least as Niemeyer sees it, in that virtue does not consist in deadening the senses but in rising above them.

## 4  Mehala (1781)[55]

The last of Niemeyer's musical dramas illustrated the story of Jephthah's daughter from the book of Judges. This belongs to the group of historical books of the Old Testament, and in general, Niemeyer found them to be of less value for Christians, as they tell stories more specific to Jewish history and do not always have clear moral teaching. Niemeyer was able to make distinctions among the books of the Old Testament because he did not regard them all as unified through prefiguring Christ. We have seen the high value he placed on the book of Job and on the poetry of David. He found the religion of the patriarchs to be purer than that of Moses and the law, but the historical books depict a decline from even the standards of Moses. Even though the story of Jephthah follows immediately after the Israelites have repented their worship of other gods, Niemeyer regards this time period as a low point in the level of faithfulness to the God of Abraham and Moses.

---

[54] Niemeyer: Charakteristick, Vol. 5, 561.
[55] Niemeyer's *Mehala* libretto was published in his 1814 volume of poetry, August Hermann Niemeyer: Religiöse Gedichte. Halle: Waisenhaus, 1814, 275–296, though in his introduction he writes that all four of these dramas had had a great reception in the years 1776–1780. Rolle's keyboard arrangement was published in 1784: Johann Heinrich Rolle: Mehala, die Tochter Jephta, ein musikalisches Drama in Musik gesetzt und als Auszug zum Singen beym Klaviere. Leipzig: Breitkopf, 1784. In her dissertation, Janet Best Pyatt reports that *Mehala* was given its premiere in February of 1781; see Pyatt, 412.

## 4.1 Interpreting the Story

Niemeyer's evaluation of Jephthah takes this into account. It might even be objected, he realizes, that the story is unworthy of the Bible. Indeed, over the thousands of years of interpretation, the story has led commentators to struggle for ways to find moral or religious lessons in it. Niemeyer finds value in this and other biblical stories as if a father were reading a book to his children, and the children in this case were the Jews, who were in a state of religious decline. Because of this, Jephthah, as Niemeyer sees it, could be excused for not knowing the difference between acceptable and unacceptable sacrifices. He showed gratitude and trust in God and was a good man of courage who followed religion according to his level of understanding, that is, not as a well-informed Jew would follow Torah, much less a better-informed Christian. But he always had an impression of the true God in a time when others were worshipping idols.

As for Jephthah's vow to sacrifice the first thing that met him on his return home from victory in battle, Niemeyer says that most interpreters are afraid of disrespecting the Bible and thus do not want to criticize either the vow or the deed. Niemeyer sees the vow as against Mosaic prescriptions for sacrifice but stills regards it as proof of Jephthah's religiosity and gratitude toward God. In the section on Jephthah in the third volume of his *Charakteristick*, Niemeyer cites various sources. In doing so, he supports the point that the church fathers agreed that Jephthah's daughter was indeed sacrificed. This being said, he is also aware of an alternative interpretation, whereby the vow becomes a vow of perpetual virginity rather than of actual sacrifice (a version we find in Handel's oratorio). Niemeyer rejects this reinterpretation, saying it is in direct contradiction to the Jewish view of the importance of marriage and childbirth. There was no practice of holy virginity among the Israelites, and if there had been, there would not have been a mourning ceremony when the vow was taken. Thus, the story should be taken at face value.[56]

Nevertheless, Niemeyer still wants to evaluate Jephthah from a moral standpoint. Was he acting out of superstition, as some have charged? Niemeyer sees it rather as a mistaken conscience that places a promise made to God above other duties that may conflict with the promise. In this case it shows serious ignorance of the true concept of God.

---

[56] Niemeyer: Charakteristick, Vol. 3 (1777), 465–468. Despite Niemeyer's assertion that a life of dedicated virginity was contrary to Hebrew custom, a number of Jewish commentators opted for this interpretation. The noted medieval exegete David Kimhi took the daughter's statement that she would mourn for her virginity as an indication that she knew no man, rather than that she was killed. Other Jewish commentators from the Middle Ages through the nineteenth century followed Kimhi's interpretation. See David Marcus: Jephthah and his Vow. Lubbock, TX: Texas Tech Press, 1986, 8–9. Niemeyer's predecessor at the University of Halle, Joachim Lange, also endorsed the position that Jephthah's daughter became a Nazirite, though recognizing that this was not common for young women. Lange: Biblisch-historisches Licht und Recht, 168.

For how unworthily must he be able to think about God if he can imagine that he will do service to him through such an unnatural sacrifice or that [God] will be angry because a father listens to the voice of fatherly feeling—a voice that God himself placed in his heart? Or that he will be angry that he does not keep a careless promise, because it cannot happen without committing an inhuman deed?[57]

Thus, Niemeyer is not sure that Jephthah deserves to be exonerated for staining his hand with the blood of his daughter. Even if he was not informed of particular religious ordinances, and even if the decline of religion was greater than we think, still there were some true servants of God who could have given him guidance. From this standpoint, the action was clearly immoral.

What makes the story so well suited for a dramatic treatment, though, is that Niemeyer cannot let the matter rest there. He still sees a strength of soul motivated by religion in Jephthah's willingness to carry out his vow despite the pain of losing his daughter, even if he misunderstands that religion. Should one not admire Jephthah just as one admires one who gives his life in battle for the fatherland? Niemeyer is tempted to believe that God, even though despising the form of the deed, may have looked at the purity of intention and thus forgiven the act. "How many of our virtues nevertheless need forgiveness!"[58] And who knows whether Abraham may have served as an example for him, even if the stories, as Niemeyer says, have little in common. In the end Niemeyer is willing to credit Jephthah, as did the author of the letter to the Hebrews, as an example of faith (Heb 11,32).

It is really when looking at the figure of the daughter that Niemeyer sees the story's dramatic effectiveness. In an improved edition of *Charakteristick*, Vol. 3, published in 1781, Niemeyer writes that the sight of an innocent flower of springtime bleeding willingly on a sacrificial altar at the hand of her father is a "highly moving drama."[59] Here he cites the first line from the section of Klopstock's *Messias* that mentions the daughter, the more complete text of which is given here in the original and in an English translation from 1813:

> Wie ein Erstling im Frühlingsblumen in duftigen Thälern
> Aufblüht, so erwacht zu dem Leben der Leben, nicht wieder
> Wegzuwelken, die Tochter Jephta's. Zu Silbergetöne
> Ward es, wovon die Lippen der preisenden bebte. Ihr Engel
> Tönt's mit der goldenen Harf' ihr nach, und erhub es auf Flügeln
> Frohbegeisterter Harmonien noch höher gen Himmel.

---

[57] Niemeyer: Charakteristick, Vol. 3, 469: "Denn wie wenig muß der würdig von Gott denken können, der sich einbilden kann, ihm geschehe durch ein so unnatürliches Opfer ein Dienst, oder er werde deswegen zürnen, weil ein Vater der Stimme, die Gott selbst in sein Herz gelegt hat, dem Vatergefühl gehorcht, und ein unvorsichtig Versprechen nicht hält, weil es nicht ohne Begehung einer unmenschlichen That geschehen kann."

[58] Niemeyer: Charakteristick, Vol. 3, 472: "Wie viele unsrer Tugenden bedürfen ohnehin Vergebung!"

[59] August Hermann Niemeyer: Charakteristick der Bibel. Vol. 3. 3rd ed. Halle: Gebauer, 1781, 485.

As expands the first flowers of the spring,
so awaked to life Jephtha's daughter, but never more to fade.
Her tremulous lips in silver sounds sent up her praises,
accompanied by her angel's golden harp, which on the wings
of grateful harmony raised her adoration to Heaven.[60]

We will see Niemeyer using Klopstock's imagery of flowers and angelic harps in his drama, but he also draws on Euripides' *Iphigenia* to observe a component of an engaging drama. It is the willingness of the victim to endure suffering with courage, not the suffering itself, that shows the sublimity of character. "When faced with a completely downtrodden wretched person, we pass by averting our gaze with mere pity; the wretched person who retains some courage up to the last minute gains our respect, and we empathize with that person."[61] With a lengthy paraphrase of Euripides, Niemeyer shows Iphigenia's willingness to die for the fatherland in expectation of a better life in the next world. Yet the biblical story, he asserts, is even more striking in the unexpected acquiescence of the daughter to the father's vow: "If you have opened your mouth, then do to me as you have promised." Further, Niemeyer is moved by the report of the annual period of mourning by the daughter's friends and thinks his own age could benefit from a more respectful regard for the graves of good people.[62]

### 4.2  Developing the Drama

These comments explain why Niemeyer gives Jephthah's daughter a name and uses her as the title character for his oratorio.[63] His story does not begin with an account of the battle or even of Jephthah's vow. Granted, Rolle's overture begins with a fairly martial tone that presumably is intended to convey the victory of Jephthah in battle. But the singing begins in a lilting Larghetto with daughter Mehala, her friend Megiddo, and other Israelite women greeting the sunset and awaiting the joyous embrace of her victorious father. In a recitative Mehala relates how afraid she had been when imagining her father's death in battle. For a while she alternates between the joy of the present and the recollection of nights of anguish.

---

[60] Friedrich Gottlieb Klopstock: Messias. Ein Heldengedicht. Halle: Hemmerde, 1749, XI, 1174; Translation: Klopstock: The Messiah. London: S. A. Oddy, 1813, 322.
[61] Niemeyer: Charakteristick, Vol. 3 (1777), 476: "Vor dem ganz zertretenen Elenden gehn wir bloß mitleidend mit gewandtem Blick vorüber; den Elenden, der noch bis auf den letzten Punct seiner Leiden etwas Muth behält, **achten** wir, und fühlen zugleich mit."
[62] Niemeyer: Charakteristick, Vol. 3 (1777), 476–479.
[63] It is striking how many different names were given to Jephthah's daughter in the many literary and musical treatments of the early modern period: Menulema, Thysia, Seila, Iphis, Miriam, Thaamar, Zebei, and Sulamide, in addition to Mehala. It was rare, however, to put the daughter's name in the title; most of the works have in the title some variation of "Jephthah," "Jephthah's daughter," or "The sacrifice of Jephthah." See Wilbur Owen Sypherd: Jephthah and his Daughter: A Study in Comparative Literature. Newark, DE: University of Delaware, 1948.

## 4  Mehala *(1781)*                                                              173

> Ihr Töchter Israel, was litt mein Herz, dacht ich im blutigen Gefilde der Schlacht den Vater mir! Todt lag die Schöpfung vor meinem Blick! Die Morgenthräne fand der Abend nicht getrocknet; Seufzer drängten die Freude weg von meiner Brust; dann schwebten Todesgestalten vorüber—Blutbedeckt fiel er, dumpf scholl der Boden, wo er sank, und ich erwachte! Gott! Wie lohnst du mich durch dieses Fest der Wonne![64]

Then the chorus of women sing that they too regard Jephthah as their father because he has freed the people of Judea. March-like music can then be heard, arousing the expectation of his arrival, and the chorus sings "Hail to the victor" while the instruments play fast scales and arpeggios (15–17).[65] One woman sings excitedly of freedom with turns and fast scales and then expresses Niemeyer's integrating perspective of religion along with Klopstock's image of silver tones: "O Freyheit! Silberton dem Ohr, Licht dem Verstand, und hoher Flug zu denken, dem Herzen groß Gefühl" ("Oh, freedom! Silver tones to the ear, light to the understanding, and high flight to thinking, great feeling to the heart", 17–19).

Jephthah then enters with fanfare that is abruptly ended when he sees Mehala and cries out in dismay. Not understanding, Mehala proceeds to sing affectionately while greeting him with palm branches and dancing. Jephthah then painfully explains what he had sworn, confesses to a wavering commitment but fears a curse upon the land if he does not fulfill his promise. Mehala, understanding the consequences, is willing to be sacrificed, asking only for a few days to enjoy the valley of flowers (reference to Klopstock) with the friends of her youth. Interestingly, with allusion to Euripides, it is for the fatherland she sees herself as sacrificing her life. Significantly, there is no reference to bewailing her virginity, only to shedding tears of separation from her father.

> Doch laß—o du, den ich noch nie vergebens bat—um eins mich flehn—um Leben nicht—um wenig Tage nur, mit den Gespielen meiner Jugend mich im Blumenthal zu letzten, Abschiedsthränen dir ungesehn zu weinen, mich dem großen Tod fürs Vaterland zu weyhen. Dann kehr ich wieder, und Jephta sammelt mich zu seinen Vätern.[66]

Her friend Megiddo then pleads with Jephthah to spare Mehala, and if God is angry, all Israel will submit to his rage. The chorus then repeats this plea, and the first act ends.

The second act opens with Jephthah wandering deep in thought among the trees in front of his house. He reflects on how much happier the anonymous and

---

[64] Rolle: Mehala, 8: "You daughters of Israel, how my heart suffered when I thought of my father in the bloody field of battle. Creation lay dead before my gaze! The tears of the morning did not dry by evening. Sighs pushed the joy away from my breast; then shapes of death hovered over; covered in blood he fell, the ground rumbled where he sank, and I awoke! God! How you reward me through this festival of joy!" The text is slightly different in Niemeyer: Religiöse Gedichte, 277.

[65] Page numbers in this section refer to Rolle: Mehala.

[66] Rolle: Mehala, 23; Niemeyer: Religiöse Gedichte, 283: "O you, from whom I have never made a request in vain, I plead for one thing—not for life, but only for a few days to enjoy the valley of flowers with the companions of my youth, to shed tears of departure unseen by you, to dedicate myself to a great death for the fatherland. Then I will return, and Jephthah will gather me to his ancestors."

poor are, while fame and success have brought him great unhappiness. This also is reminiscent of Euripides, where Agamemnon says, "What an advantage humble birth possesses! For it is easy for her sons to weep and tell out their sorrows; while to the high-born man come these same sorrows, but we have dignity throned o'er our life and are the people's slaves."[67] Megiddo arrives to say that they are ready to bring the sacrifice to the altar if he so commands, but she demands that he say whether he is a father. He tells himself that to be a hero he must not surrender all his children for the sake of one. Mehala and Jephthah then sing a graceful duet with Mehala expressing her willingness despite the darkness of the grave and Jephthah tearfully blessing her for dying for motherland. Then they picture her in a joyous afterlife, even if tears run down the angels' harps. Only at the line about tears running down the harps do the melodic lines turn chromatic with juxtaposed intervals of major or minor seconds rather than the thirds that predominate in the rest of the duet. (34) They sing that she will be blessed by future generations while Jephthah will be cursed. Megiddo sings "Grausamer Vater!" ("Cruel father!"), to which Mehala responds, "Gut und fromm ist er!" ("He is good and faithful!", 35–36). and asks Megiddo to take care of him in his old age and console him. She requests that the chorus sing her a last song but not one that will soften her intention. The song they sing welcomes her into the heavenly ranks where she meets Deborah, the mother of Israel, and the choir of the blessed greets her as a heroine. They continue to sing of Mehala as a rose that has blossomed and then withered, but suddenly a new character rushes into the scene: Abiathar asks why the feast of sacrifice, as it is neither Sabbath nor New Moon. Seeing Mehala, he rejoices that he has come in time, having heard the call from afar.

Abiathar bemoans what has become of the religion of Abraham that sons and daughters would be sacrificed to a God of love. An atrocity has been turned into a duty. He calls for slumbering conscience to be awakened; the God of love is not reconciled by burning rage. Jephthah, not yet convinced, asks Abiathar whether he will reconcile the Lord when he takes revenge for not carrying out the oath. Abiathar replies that God is not a bloodthirsty human, and he has never listened to foolish promises. What God wants is not Mehala's blood but her heart, though committing a whole life is harder than giving oneself to death. Mehala then sings to the God of love and offers her tears as a sacrifice, committing her beating heart to heavenly virtue. She wants to sing a song of thanks to Abiathar, but he redirects her song to Jehovah, to truth, to holy religion. In the final chorus, the choir asks the daughter of God, dressed in the light of Truth, to heal the land and guide them through the darkness of life.

One could easily think that they were singing to daughter Mehala, but it is actually Truth that is now being called a daughter of God the Father. The father-daughter relationship is a central theme of the drama. Megiddo's haunting question "Are you a father?" implicitly calls on Jephthah to recognize the validity

---

[67] Euripides: Iphigenia in Aulis, lines 446ff. In: The Plays of Euripides. Vol. 2. Trans. by Edward P. Coleridge. London: George Bell, 1907, 404.

of his feelings toward his daughter. She senses his ambivalence and tries to get him to admit his fatherly feelings. However, he sees that as weakness and urges himself to be a hero for the larger cause of his whole country. Niemeyer's comment about the Bible story as if meant for a father to read to children seems relevant here. Relationships of parent and child are examined, and parenthood is extended beyond immediate blood relationships. All the Israelite women see Jephthah as father, and he is conscious of responsibility to all of them. Again, this calls to mind Agamemnon's conviction that the fate of more than his own daughter is at stake: "they will slay my daughters in Argos as well as you and me, if I disregard the goddess's behests."[68] Further, Mehala asks Megiddo to take care of Jephthah in his old age after she is gone. It may be too much of a stretch to think that Niemeyer had in mind the Halle orphanage when thinking of extended family relationships, but it is surely appropriate to point out that his greatest claim to fame was as an educator. As much as he was drawn to poetry and drama, the goal was to teach moral character through inspiring reverence and religious feeling.

His manner of fleshing out the story engages the audience by showing the inner conflicts and feelings of the main characters. Mehala has been tormented by bad dreams of losing her father in battle. Even while she sings her joyous song of victory, she is haunted by these memories. We see Jephthah struggling with his dilemma, and at that point Niemeyer does not undermine the general belief that God would punish the failure to carry out his vow. The entrance of Abiathar then seems to be a *deus ex machina* that resolves the dilemma but lessens the dramatic effect of the story. For this, he is in good company with Euripides, but Waczkat regards the abrupt resolution of conflict as a weakness of the drama that runs counter to Niemeyer's own ideas about religious drama.[69] Ultimately, of course, the main goal is religious rather than dramatic, and from a theological perspective, the ending is perhaps the only one feasible for an enlightened Protestant who was fundamentally convinced of the reasonableness of Christianity and the goodness of creation and of the moral universe.

## 5 *Die Feyer des Todes Jesu* (1783)

The final dramatic text by Niemeyer is generally categorized as a Passion rather than a musical drama, and because Rolle's music has been lost, it has received little attention. While we cannot, therefore, discuss the dramatic effect of the music, the libretto merits examination for further insight into Niemeyer's religious views. In fact, when Niemeyer republished his oratorios in 1814, he recognized that music styles and tastes had changed significantly in the decades after Rolle, but he hoped that his texts would remain worthy of attention.[70]

---

[68] Euripides: Iphigenia in Aulis, 432, ca. line 260.
[69] Waczkat: Rolles musikalische Dramen, 244.
[70] Menne: August Hermann Niemeyer, ix–x.

In the case of *Die Feyer des Todes Jesu*, Rolle's music was never published, but the libretto appeared as a single publication around 1783 with an indication on the title page that Rolle had written the music.[71] Structurally there is little to differentiate it from his other musical dramas, and in his 1814 volume he includes it with the other works we have discussed in a section under the heading "Oratorien."[72] This later publication does differ, though, in including seven congregational hymns and the introductory statement that the hymns are intended for use in church. A further difference is that the church version is not divided into two parts as is the original. Whether Rolle's composition was presented as a concert like the other dramas is unclear. There are also many textual emendations in the later publication, though they appear to make little difference in the content. The earlier libretto will form the basis of our study, as it is closer in time to the other works we have examined.

In contrast to most Passions, Niemeyer's is set not in Jesus' last days but on the first anniversary of his death at a gathering of his closest friends. This avoids the dilemma of presenting Jesus as a singing or speaking character and yet allows his words to be heard as recalled clearly by those who were present in his last hours. Jesus' words, though, are embedded within the emotional recollection of their experience. As in his other dramas, Niemeyer looks at the feelings of the characters and their emotional and spiritual conflicts. This commemoration of Jesus' death evokes a deep sense of both gratitude and sadness. In his opening monologue, the apostle John observes, "Wie wechselt heute tiefer Schmerz / Mit himmlischer Entzückung!" ("How this deep sorrow / alternates today with heavenly rapture!", 3). Mary, mother of Jesus, expresses the pain of every human mother who has lost a child. She says thus that no day has passed since his death when she has not relived the horrible event and felt the sword that ripped her heart with a "noch nie geheilte, unheilbare Wunde" ("not yet healed, irreparable wound", 4). Still, she finds a certain peace and expectation of eternal healing through the remembrance of his suffering in company with those who can retell the story.

John proceeds to recount the Last Supper and Jesus' assurance that he would see his disciples again in the Father's kingdom. Peter recalls Jesus' agony in Gethsemane and yet his loving attitude toward those who failed to keep watch with him. Still struggling with pangs of conscience for his denial of Jesus that night, Peter is even more confident that Jesus sees into his heart and returns his love.

Jesus' qualities of love, patience, and willingness to suffer are the themes of the drama. John explains that Jesus wanted to experience the fate of humanity through suffering, even though he was completely pure and innocent. The lesson to be drawn is to follow his example by enduring one's tribulations with the same patience and willingness to submit to God's will. James urges the gathering to

---

[71] August Herrmann [sic] Niemeyer: Die Feyer des Todes Jesu. Leipzig: Breitkopf, n.d.
[72] Niemeyer: Religiöse Gedichte, 297–322. Also included in this section is another lengthy poetic work that he calls a Requiem, which he hopes will find a composer and will become the Protestant equivalent of the Catholic Requiem Mass. He gives leeway to the potential composer to revise the organization of choruses, arias, and recitatives, but the text is clearly closer to an oratorio than to any liturgical funeral service. See August Hermann Niemeyer: Am Gedächtnißfeste der Todten. In: Niemeyer: Religiöse Gedichte, 323–334.

stand firm against the forces of the world and imitate the example of the one who sacrificed himself for truth and for his brethren. The first act ends with the disciples and choruses affirming their commitment to hold fast to Jesus even if tyrants threaten them with persecution and death.

The second act continues the story of the route to Golgatha. John asks why his people's souls are not softened by Pilate's recognition of Jesus' innocence and by the "himmlische Geduld" ("heavenly patience") visible in Jesus' face: "Aber sie—sie fühlen nicht!" ("But they—they do not feel!", 12). Mary Magdalene describes his suffering, the burden of carrying the cross and his sadness that no bystander would assist.[73] She then tells of her lapsed life and vain search for peace before she lay at Jesus' feet and was received with empathy, mercy, and forgiveness. In describing the moment of Jesus' death, John and Mary Magdalene tell of his bodily expiration, but Mary sees more:

> Nun schlummerte die Hülle
> Von Staub am Kreuz—nun war er hingewandelt
> Zu seligen Gefilden ew'gen Friedens! (18)[74]

John then joins in seeing Jesus' death as a brief slumber from which he awoke in triumph and returned to impart peace to his followers before going to be with God. He then envisions the throngs of those yet unborn who will gather around the cross and find courage and refreshment there. John and Mary then join in a duet dedicating themselves to be faithful to Jesus, serve him in humility through good deeds, and suffer like him if required.

The entire cast and chorus end the drama with a song of praise to Jesus, who now is crowned with honor and glory, and to "dem, der dich vollendet hat, der über allen Himmeln wohnt!" ("the one who has completed you, who dwells above all heavens!", 21). This theme of completion is striking in its recurrence throughout the text. John twice calls Jesus the "Vollendeter" ("the one who has been completed"). This conveys a passive sense, as if to say that God is working his purposes through Jesus, but elsewhere he is called the "Vollender," the one who completes in an active sense. Early in the drama John seems to be citing his own gospel (John 17,4) with the lines:

> Vollendet ist, mein Vater, nun die Bahn,
> Vollbracht dein Werk, ich komme, Herrlichkeit
> Von dir, Gerechter, zu empfahn. (6)[75]

---

[73] No mention is made here of Simon of Cyrene, who, according to the gospels, was ordered to help Jesus carry the cross. Perhaps the fact that Simon was not a willing volunteer leads Niemeyer to ignore him.
[74] "From then on the frame slumbered / from dust on the cross; from that point he was transported / to the blessed fields of eternal peace!"
[75] "Now, my Father, the course is completed; / your work is accomplished; / I come to receive glory from you, Righteous One."

Then James takes up the theme: "O selig, wer vollendet hat / Wie du des Lebens Pilgerpfad" ("Oh, blessed is the one who, like you, has completed the pilgrim path of life", 6). A search of Niemeyer's *Geistliche Lieder* reveals other uses of a form of "vollenden" to refer to Jesus' work. In a poem for the celebration of the Lord's Supper, the final strophe refers to Jesus as the victor, the finisher ("Vollender") in the struggle against death. In the Requiem, the chorus sings praise to the "Vollender," and a poem for Ascension Day is entitled "Dem vollendeten Erlöser."[76] Another word Niemeyer uses frequently for Jesus is "Dulder," a word that is not easily translated; it also has both an active sense, as one who exercises patience, and a passive sense, as one who endures suffering.

The theological implication of these unusual terms is not entirely clear, but Niemeyer seems in this and his other dramas to view obedience to God's sovereign will as the main obligation of one who is to follow a path of godliness. God's reasons are unknowable, but the one who is humble, patient, and obedient will be rewarded with joy in eternal life. The themes of death and suffering dominate Niemeyer's dramas, but the end is always a glorious victory over forces of evil and death. The one certainty for Niemeyer is that the souls of the faithful will unite with God and one another in eternity.

## 6  Pietism and Niemeyer's Musical Views

In an article for the International Pietism Congress of 2001, Andreas Waczkat raised the question of the relationship between Rolle's religious dramas and Pietism.[77] For his study he reported not only on Niemeyer's librettos but also those of Samuel Patzke, who, together with Niemeyer and Rolle, belonged to the literary society of Magdeburg that had been founded in the 1760s. Patzke's librettos were more numerous and also more varied than those of Niemeyer, drawing on both classical and biblical sources. Having begun his studies in Frankfurt, Patzke completed his theological studies in Halle and later became pastor of the Heilige-Geist-Kirche in Magdeburg. His religious dramas, then, emerged from a similar theological background as those of Niemeyer. Waczkat identifies as elements common to Patzke and Niemeyer the significant roles assigned to secondary characters and the focus on conversion of one of these characters. To this extent, Waczkat sees in these dramas an affinity to Pietism that would explain their prominence in Moravian repertoire, but still Rolle's musical style seems not to accord with Pietist practice. The strophic arias that are identified with Pietist music are lacking in Rolle, as are chorales. Waczkat regards Rolle's compositional method, with its instrumental interjections, as influenced by the melodramatic style

---

[76] Niemeyer: Geistliche Lieder, 42, 44, 328–330.
[77] Andreas Waczkat: Die religiösen musikalischen Dramen Johann Heinrich Rolles. Stoffe, Personenzeichung und Rezeption. In: Interdisziplinäre Pietismusforschungen: Beiträge zum Ersten Internationalen Kongress für Pietismusforschung 2001. Ed. by Udo Sträter. Halle: Niemeyer, 2005, 453–463.

of his time, having nothing in common with the softly flowing melodies associated with the Pietists. To talk of a Pietist musical style may be wrong-headed, he rightly concludes, for the style of music is secondary to what Waczkat calls a "submersion of the self" ("Selbstversenkung").

In a citation we encountered earlier, we saw how Niemeyer expressed his appreciation of all types of music. The decades that had passed since Pietists had first objected to elaborate church music had brought new musical styles. The musical context in which Niemeyer lived was no longer that of the Baroque cantata, and the sacred musical dramas were intended for a different setting. Neither church music nor private devotion but a public concert, they needed to suit the musical taste of the cultured circles of the time. Clearly, Rolle's music accomplished this, and yet it also succeeded in evoking the religious feelings that were central to Niemeyer's theology.

Despite the changes in theology and music since the early 18th century, Niemeyer's general thoughts on sacred music for congregational use are remarkably similar to those of his Pietist predecessors.

> A hymn is not a ditty, religious drama is not comic opera and also not high opera, though it comes close to this. Even in the most cheerful aria, I would like to hear to a certain extent that it is religious music. Those hymns that are put with tasteless devotion to melodies of jesting songs, to which one might dance, if necessary, are unbearable. A certain dignity must be spread over everything concerning religion. A wise person laughs and smiles, but it is not the laugh of the fool. The person for whom religion is uppermost does not lack any joy; he drinks each joy so purely, so unalloyed, but it never becomes a drunken giddy pleasure. I do not want to make solemnity and seriousness into more general characteristics of religious music, because both strain our souls too much. But I would demand dignity from each of their works; in the cheeriest, most delightful songs of creation, I would like to hear that the singer feels the Omnipresent One, but in such a way that this feeling does not stem the effusion of joy but makes every sentiment more flowing, every joy more inward. Devotion would have to be the dominant affect where the text is a prayer or conversation with God; religious music would have to be a tamer of all intense passions and to pour the high peace of heaven over the soul. Because it is music of the people, the simplicity of the song, which is united with the simplicity of the heart, is its proper characteristic. Effortlessness and comprehensibility of the melody, harmonic pace, rejection of higher art where it is applied at the expense of simplicity, not too sparing in word painting, from which the player can always keep enough distance—these are all, it seems to me, not unfitting demands for the composer of religious works.[78]

---

[78] Niemeyer: Abraham auf Moria, 54–56. "Das geistliche Lied ist kein Liedchen, das religiöse Drama ist keine komische Oper, auch keine höhere Oper, ob es sich dieser gleich nähert. Selbst in der fröhlichsten Arie möcht ich gern einigermaßen hören, daß es religiöse Musik sey. Unerträglich sind die geistlichen Lieder, die man mit sehr geschmackloser Andacht auf Melodien zu Scherzliedern gepaßt, und zu denen man zur Noth tanzen könnte. Ueber alles, was die Religion angeht, muß eine gewisse Würde verbreitet seyn. Der Weise lacht und lächelt, aber es ist nicht die Lache des Thoren: wem die Religion das höchste ist, dem mangelt keiner Freude, er trinkt jede so rein, so ungetrübt, aber sie wird nie trunkne Taumellust. Ich will nicht einmal Feyerlichkeit und Ernst zum allgemeineren Charakter der religiösen Musik machen, weil beydes unsre Seele zu sehr anspannt. Aber **Würde** möcht' ich von jeder ihrer Arbeiten fordern; im heitersten, wonnevollsten Schöpfungsgesange möcht' ichs hören, daß der Sänger den Allgegenwärtigen fühlte, aber so, daß eben dies Gefühl der Freude vollen Erguß nicht hemmte, sondern strömender jede Empfindung, inniger jede Freude machte. **Andacht** müste besonders da der herrschende Affekt seyn, wo

Niemeyer's openness to the musical styles of his day did not entail an abandonment of the musical guidelines of his Pietist predecessors. A dignified style without the worldly connotations of dance music, simplicity that is accessible to the congregation, a text that inspires devotion, and joy that comes from the soul rather than the passions are all values that Francke, Lange, and Rambach shared with Niemeyer.

## 7    Summary

Niemeyer's dramas have a similar purpose as his volumes of biblical character studies. By depicting those who overcame human struggles and crises to become models of faith, Niemeyer sought to inspire his contemporaries to attain the same level of godly religion. Themes of love, trust, faith, constancy, patience, and obedience pervade the dramas. Characters in each drama are confronted with a dilemma that causes inner conflict and doubt; secondary characters in the dramas serve to represent these inner conflicts outwardly. Through Rolle's setting of Niemeyer's text, the audience can also experience the emotional tension by musical means. In each case, the tension is resolved in favor of faith and hope; visions of heaven affirm the belief in life after death, and music serves effectively to convey a sense of heavenly rapture. While these inward struggles between faith and doubt share elements of a Pietist conversion experience, the Pietist themes of sin, repentance, and atonement are missing. Depth of feeling and religious sensitivity are the primary qualities that lead Niemeyer's characters to overcome crises of faith.

---

der Text Gebet oder Sprache mit Gott wäre; die religiöse Musik müste Besänftigerin jeder heftigeren Leidenschaft werden; müste hohen Frieden des Himmels über die Seele gießen. Da sie Volksmusik ist, so wäre Einfalt des Gesanges, die sich mit des Herzens Einfalt vereinte, recht eigentlich charakteristisch für sie. Leichtigkeit und Faßlichkeit der Melodie, harmonischer Gang, Verleugnung der höheren Kunst, wo sie auf Unkosten der Simplicität angebracht werden soll, nicht zu sehr gesparte Mahlerey, die sich immer vom Spielenden weit genug entfernt halten kann—lauter, dünkt mich, nicht unbillige Forderungen an den Komponisten religiöser Arbeiten."

Postscript

# Into the Nineteenth Century

The story of biblical interpretation and music among Halle Pietists reaches a fitting end point with Niemeyer's religious dramas. We have taken some glimpses into his publications of the 19th century, but the connection between Bible and music was no longer so directly in his focus at this time. His biblical dramas did live on to some extent through the musical setting of *Abraham* by Franz Danzi (1807), the *Abraham* adaptation by Ignaz Ritter von Seyfried (1818), and, most notably, the setting of *Lazarus* by Franz Schubert (1820).[1] These compositions were connected to Niemeyer only through the texts, however, not through his underlying theology. For a theological connection, we should look to the thought of Friedrich Schleiermacher, the most influential Protestant theologian of the nineteenth century.

Schleiermacher's Pietist background has long been recognized as one of the influences on his theology. Growing up as the son of a Reformed minister, he received his early education from Moravians and for a while adhered to their mold. In his teen years, however, he began to read works of Kant, Goethe, and others, and sought to break away from the restraints of Moravian teachings. Leaving the Moravians to attend the university of Halle, Schleiermacher turned his attention to philosophy, although, succumbing to his father's wishes and the practical need for employment, he took theological exams and became a clergyman. After some years of tutoring and preaching, he returned to Halle as professor of theology in 1804, staying there until 1807. Most of his career, however, was spent in Berlin as preacher, university professor, and member of the Royal Prussian Academy of Sciences.

Much has been written about Schleiermacher's views on aesthetics and music, both from a philosophical and a theological viewpoint.[2] The most accessible source for his theology of music is the Christmas Eve dialogue in which the limitation and rigidity of religious language is contrasted with the "speechless joy" of music.[3] This fits with the well-known summary of his systematic theology, i.e., that religion is neither a knowing nor a doing but a feeling. While the meaning of "feeling" is

---

[1] See Blanken: Franz Schuberts *Lazarus*, esp. 142–45.
[2] To attempt a complete list of relevant articles would be overwhelming, especially if German-language publications were included. A worthwhile recent study in English is Philip Edward Stoltzfus: Theology as performance. Music, aesthetics, and God in western thought. New York: T & T Clark International, 2006.
[3] Friedrich Schleiermacher: Die Weihnachtsfeier. Ein Gespräch. Halle: Schimmelpfennig, 1806. Various English translations are available, all beginning with the words "Christmas Eve."

developed more thoroughly in his theology than in the thinking of earlier Halle theologians, the centrality of internal subjective appropriation of religious teachings was a theme for all those we have studied. To be sure, Schleiermacher was also influenced by Romanticism,[4] which shared a subjective approach to religion. To determine the extent to which Pietism led to Romanticism would be a topic for another study, but in the case of Schleiermacher, the two blended easily.[5]

In matters more specifically touching on church music, recent research on Schleiermacher's song sheets offers valuable insights into his views on music in worship.[6] A comparison of his work on hymnody with that of Niemeyer might be worthwhile. One author has suggested that Niemeyer may have shaped Schleiermacher's thinking on liturgical matters in Schleiermacher's student years, but that in later years there may have been a reciprocal relationship. Christoph Albrecht finds in Niemeyer's textbook on liturgics some themes that also appear in Schleiermacher's views: simplicity of worship and worship in spirit and truth.[7] Albrecht observes that Niemeyer began his section on liturgics with the heading, "Simplicity of Christian Worship of God."[8] When Schleiermacher writes of worshipping in spirit and truth, Albrecht traces this to Niemeyer's appeal to clergy to come closer to worshipping in spirit and truth by abandoning old customs that were carried over from pre-Reformation times.[9] While these themes are common to both men, they can only suggest, not demonstrate, a dependence of Schleiermacher on Niemeyer. We have seen the importance for Francke and others of the Johannine verse on worshipping in spirit and truth. Pointing out the importance that Niemeyer placed on singing, Albrecht recognizes that this is not unique to Niemeyer but still thinks his lectures may have instilled in Schleiermacher a respect for hymnody. Other possible influences noted by Albrecht are Niemeyer's disapproval of singing scriptures and connecting Holy Communion to confession.

Interestingly, Albrecht is even more convinced of a reverse influence, i.e., from Schleiermacher to Niemeyer, in later editions of Niemeyer's liturgics. In the 1827 edition, for instance, Niemeyer develops his theoretical part more fully, not regarding simplicity as the basis of liturgical practice but rather the consciousness of dependence on a Supreme Being. Although not the same wording as Schleiermacher's "feeling of absolute dependence," it is too similar to be mere coincidence. Certainly, such an appropriation of Schleiermacher's thinking is possible, as by this time Schleiermacher had surpassed his former teacher and colleague in depth of thinking and in widespread recognition of the significance of his writings.

---

[4] See Jack Forstman: A Romantic Triangle. Schleiermacher and Early German Romanticism. Missoula, MT: Scholars Press, 1977.
[5] Cf. Eaghll: From Pietism to Romanticism, 107–119.
[6] Bernhard Schmidt: Schleiermachers Liederblätter 1817: Edition, Analyse und Kommentar eines einzigartigen Phänomens. Berlin: De Gruyter, 2008.
[7] Christoph Albrecht: Schleiermachers Liturgik. Göttingen: Vandenhoeck & Ruprecht, 1963, 107–108.
[8] August Hermann Niemeyer: Handbuch für christliche Religionslehrer. Vol. 2: Homiletik, Pastoralwissenschaft und Liturgik. 2nd ed. Halle: Waisenhaus, 1794, 311.
[9] Niemeyer: Handbuch, 344.

Furthermore, we have at least one confirmation of the connection between the two men in an entry in Niemeyer's diary that he visited Schleiermacher in Berlin in April of 1821.[10] More substantively, there is a direct citation by Niemeyer of a paragraph from an 1804 Gutachten by Schleiermacher concerning hymn selection.[11]

Niemeyer in this section on liturgics and Schleiermacher in his Gutachten shared a concern to make hymn singing a more meaningful component of worship. Both sought to avoid didactic hymns in favor of hymns that would inspire devotion, and both were wary of overloading the service with so much singing that the effect would be diminished. They were sensitive to different levels of education and culture, recognizing that different styles of music may suit different demographic situations, particularly the difference between rural and urban churches. Theatrical or operatic music, however, was considered inappropriate for church use by both thinkers.

Despite the groundbreaking shifts in biblical interpretation among the thinkers we have studied, this concern for devotional hymnody, congregational involvement, and simplicity of musical form was consistent from early Pietists through Niemeyer and Schleiermacher. Also consistent was the priority of personal engagement over doctrinal assent, of heart over mind. Each of our writers contrasted the outward forms of liturgical observance with worshipping "in spirit and in truth." As a result, considerable ambivalence was expressed about the value of public worship in the imperfect state of the church. Although Semler seemed to arrive at a separation of individual faith from institutional structures, even he saw the importance of the church.

While there is undeniably a strand of individualism and subjectivity in Pietism that grows even thicker as it evolves into Romanticism, the theologians of Halle, including Schleiermacher, always intertwined individualism with commitment to the church and subjectivity with responsibility to the body of Christ. In the preface to his 1814 *Religiöse Gedichte*, Niemeyer wrestled with the problem of including in his hymnal poetry that sprang from the personal feelings of an individual poet. Yet, he answered, religious poetry has a social purpose: "It wants to unite the community of worshippers of God and confessors of the Savior in song and prayer and to generalize the sentiments [Empfindungen] of the individual, stirring them through language and song."[12] Schleiermacher, likewise, though best known for the theological subjectivity of feeling, was a preacher who sought to elevate the religious sensitivities of worshipping congregations. In an article titled "Schleiermacher on the Necessity of the Church," Eugene Schlesinger acknowledged the seeming paradox:

---

[10] Diary of August Hermann Niemeyer. Archiv der Franckeschen Stiftungen, Halle, AFSt/N A.H.Niemeyer 2 : 12.

[11] August Hermann Niemeyer: Handbuch für christliche Religionslehrer. Zweyter Theil: Homiletik, Katechetik, Pastoralwissenschaft und Liturgik. Revised 6th ed. Halle: Waisenhaus, 1827, 377. The reference is to Friedrich Schleiermacher: Zwei unvorgreifliche Gutachten in Sachen des protestantischen Kirchenwesens zunächst in Beziehung auf den preußischen Staat. Berlin: Realschulbuchhandlung, 1804, 110.

[12] Niemeyer: Religiöse Gedichte, xxv.

> Two seemingly contradictory strands run through Friedrich Schleiermacher's thought. On the one hand, Schleiermacher represents a turn to interiority, to individual subjectivity, to an eschewal of the outward. On the other hand, he unflinchingly asserts the corporate nature of the Christian life and the necessity of the church for redemption.[13]

It is sometimes forgotten, notes Schlesinger, that Schleiermacher was a churchman as well as a theologian. At the same time, Schleiermacher, like Niemeyer before him, saw the value of musical offerings outside the church for forms of music that were of a higher level of artistry than was appropriate for congregational worship. He recognized that oratorios, while dealing with religious matters, generally included virtuosic arias characterized by trills and runs that could disturb devotion and step beyond the nature of a service of worship.[14] Accordingly, he became a strong supporter of a non-ecclesial choral organization founded to cultivate sacred music in its artistic forms, the Berlin Singakademie, in which he himself participated. In the poetic theories of Klopstock and Niemeyer we observed a similar separation of simpler forms suited for public worship and higher artistic forms for persons of more refined aesthetic sensitivity. Semler's distinction between private religion and the outward institutional organization represents another way of distinguishing between a general societal common ground and a more advanced spiritual individual. It is fair to ask whether these various distinctions represented a devaluing of the church and a move toward secularization. Our thinkers themselves would have seen it from the opposite perspective, however: given the weaknesses and failures of organized religion, they hoped to serve the religious needs of those who found spiritual connection through the arts. Martin Fritz, writing about Niemeyer's oratorio libretti, does indeed see in them an emancipation of the burger elite from the dogmatic restraints of the official church. He cautions, however, that this aesthetic reshaping is not a form of secularization but rather "a theological program in the service of powerful religious experience."[15] Whether these later Halle theologians were paving the way for *Kunstreligion* would have to be a question for another study, but their indebtedness to their Pietist predecessors is undeniable in their commitment to find more meaningful ways of worshipping in spirit and in truth.

---

[13] Eugene R. Schlesinger: Schleiermacher on the Necessity of the Church. In: The Journal of Theological Studies, New Series 66, April 2015, Issue 1, 235–236.
[14] Friedrich Schleiermacher: Die praktische Theologie nach den Grundsätzen der evangelischen Kirche. Ed. by Jacob Frerichs. Berlin: Reimer, 1850, 173–174.
[15] Martin Fritz: Musikandacht: Über Herkunft und Bedeutung eines Elements bürgerlicher Religionskultur. In: Zeitschrift für Theologie und Kirche 111, March 2014, Issue 1, 34.

# Summary

The theme common to all the theologians discussed in this study is that worship should occur "in spirit and in truth." For them as academicians, "truth" meant that it be in accord with the teachings of the church. While the Pietists criticized the intellectual approach to theology in Lutheran Orthodoxy, they did not fundamentally disagree with Lutheran doctrine. There were, to be sure, differences in soteriology and eschatology that led to disputes between the two camps, but Francke and the other Halle theologians saw themselves as reformers within Lutheranism, not as separatists forming another religious community. Whether or not historians evaluate their theology as a deviation from orthodoxy, they regarded their efforts as a continuation of Luther's reformation of the church.

"Spirit" was the more problematic criterion for worship. If pastors were not filled with the spirit and congregants sang with their mouths and not their hearts, did worship truly happen? Was music of any value when it did not penetrate beyond the ears? How could spirit-filled worship take place in a congregation comprised of many unconverted persons? Could true worship occur only among the regenerate? If a spirit-filled heart was what mattered, was audible singing even necessary? And was a community of believers necessary if God's spirit could enter the heart of the individual?

While there is validity in describing Pietist theology as individualistic and subjective, the communitarian impulse was just as strong. Often accused of forming little churches within the church by holding gatherings for Bible study and singing, they regarded such gatherings as supplements rather than replacements for corporate public worship. Viewing the church of their own day as falling far short of the ideal Christian community, they often looked to the early Church or to the Church Triumphant for their image of the Church. Despite a disparaging attitude toward the visible church, they nevertheless encouraged true believers to participate in public worship.

Sometimes this encouragement may seem half-hearted and give an appearance of inconsistency. August Hermann Francke stated clearly that one should attend services, even if they were insufficient and tainted by the presence of hypocrites. When writing about the sanctuaries of the ancient Hebrews, Francke said they had been superseded by the sanctuary of the heart, citing the verse in John 4 that I have taken as a theme of this book, that those who worship must do so in spirit and in truth. It is through music that the community of worshippers is best experienced. In both an audible and a metaphorical sense, music creates a harmony that strengthens community. In some of Francke's psalm commentaries, music appears to be only a metaphor for inward praise of God, but taken on the whole, there can be no doubt that he advocated singing as an important element of corporate worship.

Joachim Lange's advocacy of music as a means of praising God is less ambiguous than Francke's. For Lange, music has a divine source with power to influence the human spirit. The songs of the Hebrews resulted from a spirit of prophecy, and the Holy Spirit worked through the community for orderly and harmonious worship. Their musical instruments were not metaphors for a more spiritual reference but had spiritual value in themselves. By viewing scripture as a unified prophetic scheme, Lange could see the joyous celebrations of the Hebrews as prefigurings of future heavenly rejoicing. He also recognized that physical spaces, whether the tent of meeting for David or the churches of his own day, could provide a special sense of God's presence. Congregational worship is important, and the musical portion should not be neglected in favor of the sermon. Nevertheless, in keeping with Pietist theology, the music should be serious and simple and should issue forth from a sanctified heart. When music is not directed toward a spiritual or moral purpose, it is sinful and an abuse of a good thing.

Again with Johann Jakob Rambach, we find the conviction that music is valid only when it comes out of faith and only for a spiritual purpose. He agreed with Lange in rejecting a category of indifferent moral activities that might justify dancing and theater. Also, in their view of the unity of scripture within a prophetic scheme, Rambach and Lange were in agreement. Furthermore, Rambach's work in writing hymns for church and home and editing hymnals should leave no doubt that corporate worship with hymn singing was central to his pastoral theology. However, it was the content of the hymns that mattered most to him, not the power of music. He was more attuned to the aesthetics of poetry than of music. His interpretations of Old Testament references to music are often, like Francke's, metaphorical. While he appreciated the orderliness of Hebrew worship, he did not place much value on their music. For him, music had natural powers of affecting emotions, but it was not endowed with divine power.

The transition from the core period of Pietism in Halle to Neology or New Protestantism entailed some perspectives that were radically new, but many Pietist propensities remained. What was new was that the Bible was no longer to be read as a unified whole or as verbally inspired by God. This was stated more boldly by Johann Salomo Semler than by Siegmund Jakob Baumgarten, but both approached the Bible as a text to be interpreted in the context of its time and place in history. The tools for such interpretation were accessible to all, regardless of their state of grace. The typological reading of the Old Testament as prefiguring Christ and the New Testament was abandoned by both theologians, and Semler even rejected the biblical canon, especially the book of Revelation. He found no value in those parts of the Old Testament that pertained specifically to the Jewish people if they could not apply to all people universally. What Baumgarten and Semler held in common with Francke, Lange, and Rambach was the priority of the experience of faith over doctrine, of inward over outward religion. They all attributed to the psalmist David a special awareness of divine truth and valued his psalms as having lasting significance. Whether singing the psalms of David or any other songs, though, the devotional intent of the singer was most important. Even more than Francke, Baumgarten and Semler emphasized the subjective side of faith without much attention to the institutional church. For them, the Christian message was universal, meant for all people everywhere. By broadening their viewpoint beyond the visible church, they moved, ironically, toward a more individualistic religious stance.

For Semler, individualism entailed a distinction between public and private religion, whereas for August Hermann Niemeyer it meant an approach to the Bible that examined individual lives as examples of faith and morality. His portrayals of biblical persons with all their faults as well as their fidelity were intended to inspire not only churchgoers but also skeptics. His oratorios were explicitly directed toward the general public, though perhaps a more sophisticated audience than a church congregation. This is not to say that he was unconcerned with congregational worship; rather, he felt it was not achieving its potential for arousing religious feelings and communicating the sublime. This could be better accomplished, under the circumstances, outside the church with a receptive audience. Even more than previously, doctrine faded into the background when Niemeyer exalted poetry and music as the closest relatives to religion. Like his predecessors who insisted on singing from the heart, Niemeyer demanded that poets write from a soul that is senstive to the depths of religious experience. Neither poetry nor music need be complex or based on mastery of technical skill; simple, unaffected songs may best convey the sense of the divine.

Overall, the Halle theologians from Francke to Niemeyer held an ambivalent position regarding church music. In general, they preferred simple hymnody, but they did not reject choral or instrumental music. Musical style or form was not a major concern. For all of them, the inward, subjective response to the gospel was such a high priority that the outward observance of liturgical worship drew little of their attention. Their own religious feelings had been nourished in small devotional gatherings of believers, and they found such nourishment lacking in church services with random attendees and uninspired leaders. Nevertheless, they held to a vision of a church—even if only to be realized in the Church Triumphant—in which all would sing in musical harmony and harmony of spirit to the glory of God.

# Bibliography

## Primary Sources

Aken, Adolph Christoph von: Glaube und Sitten Davids, des andern Königes im Volke Gottes. Leipzig, Stockholm: Kiesewetter, 1746.
Baumgarten, Siegmund Jacob: Auslegung der Briefe Pauli an die Galater, Epheser, Philipper, Colosser, Philemon und Thessalonicher. Ed. by Johann Salomon Semler. Halle: Gebauer, 1767.
———: Erbauliche Erklärung der Psalmen. 2 Vols. Ed. by Johann Salomon Semler. Halle, Gebauer, 1759.
———: Evangelische Glaubenslehre. Vol. 3. Ed. by Johann Salomon Semler. Halle: Gebauer, 1766.
———: Unterricht von Auslegung der heiligen Schrift. Halle: Bauer, 1742.
———: Unterricht vom rechtmässigen Verhalten eines Christen, oder Theologische Moral. Halle: Bauer, 1738.
Chandler, Samuel: A Critical History of the Life of David. 2 Vols. London: Buckland and Coote, 1766; German translation: Kritische Lebensgeschichte Davids. Bremen: Cramer, 1777–1780.
Delany, Patrick: An Historical Account of the Life and Reign of David, King of Israel. London: Osborn, 1740; German translation: Historische Untersuchung des Lebens und der Regierung Davids des Königes von Israel. Hannover: Förster, 1748–1749.
Euripides: The Plays of Euripides. Trans. by Edward P. Coleridge. London: George Bell, 1907.
Francke, August Hermann: Erklärung der Psalmen Davids. Vol. 1. Halle: Waisenhaus, 1730; Vol. 2. Halle: Waisenhaus, 1731.
———: Idea Studiosi Theologiae, oder Abbildung eines der Theologie Beflissenen. Halle: Waisenhaus, 1712.
———: Kurtze Anweisung Zur wahren, lautern und Apostolischen Erkenntniß Jesu Christi. Halle: Waisenhaus, 1714.
———: Schriften zur biblischen Hermeneutik. Vol. 1. Ed. by Erhard Peschke. Berlin: De Gruyter, 2003.
———: Werke in Auswahl. Ed. by Erhard Peschke. Berlin: Evangelische Verlagsanstalt, 1969.
Freylinghausen, Johann Anastasius: Geistreiches Gesangbuch: Edition und Kommentar. Ed. by Dianne Marie McMullen and Wolfgang Miersemann. Tübingen, Halle: Franckesche Stiftungen, Niemeyer, 2004–2020.

Klopstock, Friedrich Gottlieb: Messias. Ein Heldengedicht. Halle: Hemmerde, 1749; English Translation: F. G. Klopstock: The Messiah. London: S. A. Oddy, 1813.

Lange, Joachim: Antibarbarus Orthodoxiæ Dogmatico-Hermeneuticus, Sive Systema Dogmatum Evangelicorum. Halle: Meyer, 1711.

— — —: Apocalyptisches Licht und Recht, das ist richtige und erbauliche Erklärung des prophetischen Buchs der heiligen Offenbahrung Johannis. Halle: Franck, 1730.

— — —: Apostolisches Licht und Recht, Das ist Richtige und erbauliche Erklärung Der sämtlichen Apostolischen Briefe. Halle: Waisenhaus, 1729.

— — —: Biblisch-historisches Licht und Recht, Das ist, Richtige und Erbauliche Erklärung Der sämmtlichen Historischen Bücher Des Alten Testaments, Von dem Buche Josuä an bis auf das Büchlein Esther, Mit hinzugethanem Buche Hiobs. Halle, Leipzig: [n.p.], 1734.

— — —: Davidisch-Salomonisches Licht und Recht: oder Richtige und Erbauliche Erklärung Der geistreichen Psalmen Davids, Wie auch der lehrreichen Sprüche, auch des Predigers und Des Hohenliedes Salomons. Dazu kömmt Die Auslegung Des Propheten Daniels. Halle: [n.p.], 1737.

— — —: Disputatio Exegetico-Dogmatica De Experientia Spirituali: Quam ex Epist. Ad Philipp. C. 1. V. 9, 10. Demonstratam. Halle: Henckel, 1710.

— — —: Evangelisches Licht und Recht, Oder Richtige und Erbauliche Erklärung der heiligen Vier Evangelisten, und der Apostel=Geschichte. 2nd ed. Halle, Leipzig: [n.p.], 1736.

— — —: Historia Ecclesiastica Vet. Testamenti A Mundo Condito Per Septem Periodos Usque Ad Christum Natum. Halle: Waisenhaus, 1718.

— — —: Mosaisches Licht und Recht, Das ist, Richtige und Erbauliche Erklärung Der fünf Bücher Mosis. Halle, Leipzig: Walther, 1732.

— — —: Prophetisches Licht und Recht, Oder Richtige und erbauliche Erklärung der Propheten. Mit einer Einleitung in die Offenbahrung Johannis zum hermeneutischen Schlüssel In die schweresten Stellen der Psalmen Davids und der Propheten: und mit einem Anhange von der allgemeinen Gnade in Christo. Halle: Francke, 1738.

— — —: Die richtige Mittel=Straße / zwischen den Abwegen der Absonderung von der euserlichen Gemeinschafft der Kirchen. Halle: Renger, 1712.

— — —: Der richtigen Mittel=Straße zwischen den Irrthümern und Abwegen Anderer Theil. Halle: Renger, 1712.

— — —: Der richtigen Mittel=Straße Zwischen den Irrthümern und Abwegen Vierter und letzter Theil / In der Lehre Christus in uns zur Heiligung. Halle: Renger, 1714.

Leben, Charakter und Verdienste Johann August Nösselts. Nebst einer Sammlung Nösseltscher Aufsätze und Fragmente. Ed. by August Hermann Niemeyer. Halle: Waisenhaus, 1809.

Löscher, Valentin Ernst: The Complete Timotheus Verinus. Trans. by James L. Langebartels. Milwaukee, WI: Northwestern Publishing, 1998.

Luther, Martin: Werke. Deutsche Bibel. 15 Vols. Weimar 1906–1961 [abb. WA DB].
Niemeyer, August Hermann: Abraham auf Moria. Ein religiöses Drama für die Musik. Leipzig: Weygand, 1777.
— — —: Charakteristick der Bibel. Vol. 1. Halle: Gebauer, 1775; 4th improved ed. Halle: Gebauer, 1780. Vol. 2. Halle: Gebauer, 1776. Vol. 3. Halle: Gebauer, 1777; expanded ed. Schaffhausen, 1779; 3rd ed. Halle: Gebauer, 1781. Vol. 4. Halle: Gebauer, 1779. Vol. 5. Halle: Gebauer, 1782.
— — —: Die Feyer des Todes Jesu. Leipzig: Breitkopf, n.d.
— — —: Gedichte. Leipzig: Weygand, 1778.
— — —: Geistliche Lieder, Oratorien und vermischte Gedichte. Halle: Waisenhaus, 1820.
— — —: Handbuch für christliche Religionslehrer. Vol. 2: Homiletik, Pastoralwissenschaft und Liturgik. 2nd ed. Halle: Waisenhaus, 1794; revised 6th ed. Halle: Waisenhaus, 1827.
— — —: Religiöse Gedichte. Halle: Waisenhaus, 1814.
— — —: Thirza und ihre Söhne. Musikalisches Drama. Aufgeführt im Concertsaale zu Magdeburg [1784?].
— — —: Timotheus: Zur Erweckung und Beförderung der Andacht nachdenkender Christen. Part 2. Leipzig: Weidmann, 1789.
— — —: Die Universität Halle nach ihrem Einfluß auf gelehrte und praktische Theologie in ihrem ersten Jahrhundert, seit der Kirchenverbesserung dem dritten. Halle: Waisenhaus, 1817.
Rambach, Johann Jakob: Ausführliche und gründliche Erklärung der Epistel Pauli an die Römer. Ed. by Ernst Friedrich Neubauer. Bremen: Sauermann, 1738.
— — —: Ausführliche und gründliche Erläuterung über seine eigene Institvtiones Hermenevticae Sacrae. Ed. by Ernst Friedrich Neubauer. Giessen: Krieger, 1738.
— — —: Christliches und Biblisches Exempel-Büchlein für Kinder. Part 2. 3rd ed. Leipzig: Friderici, 1742.
— — —: Christus in Mose, oder Betrachtungen über die vornehmsten Weissagungen und Vorbilder in den fünf Büchern Mosis auf Christum. Ed. by Johann Philipp Fresenius. Frankfurt/Main, Leipzig: Spring, 1736.
— — —: Collegivm Historiae Ecclesiasticae Veteris Testamenti, Oder Ausführlicher und gründlicher Discurs über die Kirchen-Historie des alten Testaments. Ed. by Ernst Friedrich Neubauer. Frankfurt/Main: Möller, 1737.
— — —: Erkenntniß der Wahrheit zur Gottseligkeit, oder Predigten über verschiedene Evangelische Texte. Halle: Waisenhaus, 1727.
— — —: Evangelische Betrachtungen Uber die Sonn= und Fest=Tags=Evangelia Des gantzen Jahrs. Halle: Waysenhaus, 1730.
— — —: Geistliche Poesien. Halle: Neue Buchhandlung, 1720.
— — —: Gründliche Erklärung des Propheten Esaiä, darin nach einer Einleitung, so wol in die Propheten überhaupt, als in den Esaiam insonderheit, alle Theile desselben ordentlich zergliedert und aus der Philologie und Hermeneutic erkläret. Ed. by Ernst Friedrich Neubauer. Züllichau: Frommann, 1741.

———: Institvtiones Hermenevticae Sacrae. 2nd ed. Jena: Hartung, 1725.
———: Moral=Theologie oder Christliche Sitten=Lehre. Frankfurt/Main: von Sand, 1738.
———: Poetische Fest=Gedancken Von den höchsten Wohlthaten Gottes. 2nd ed. Jena: Ritter, 1727.
———: Richtige und Erbauliche Erklärung der Ep. Pauli an die Colosser. Giessen: Krieger, 1740.
———: Theologische Betrachtungen über einige Auserlesene und vortreffliche Materien der Dogmatischen, Polemischen, Moralischen u.s.f. Gottes-Gelahrtheit. Ed. by Adam Lebrecht Müller. Jena: Ritter, 1739.
Rolle, Johann Heinrich: Abraham auf Moria: Musikalisches Drama. Ed. by Norbert Klose. Haale: Renaissance-Musikverlag, 2002.
———: Lazarus, oder die Feyer der Auferstehung, ein musikalisches Drama, in Musik gesetzt, und als ein Auszug zum Singen beym Klaviere herausgegeben. Leipzig: Breitkopf, 1779.
———: Mehala, die Tochter Jephta, ein musikalisches Drama in Musik gesetzt und als Auszug zum Singen beym Klaviere. Leipzig: Breitkopf, 1784.
———: Thirza und ihre Söhne, ein musikalisches Drama in Musik gesetzt, als ein Auszug zum Singen beym Klaviere. [Magdeburg] 1781.
Scheibel, Gottfried Ephraim: Zufällige Gedancken Von der Kirchen-Music. Wie Sie heutiges Tages beschaffen ist. Frankfurt/Main: by author, 1721; trans. by Joyce Irwin: Random Thoughts about Church Music in our Day 1721. In: Bach's Changing World. Voices in the Community. Ed. by Carol K. Baron. Rochester, NY: University of Rochester Press, 2006, 227–249.
Schleiermacher, Friedrich: Die praktische Theologie nach den Grundsätzen der evangelischen Kirche. Ed. by Jacob Frerichs. Berlin: Reimer, 1850.
———: Die Weihnachtsfeier. Ein Gespräch. Halle: Schimmelpfennig, 1806.
———: Zwei unvorgreifliche Gutachten in Sachen des protestantischen Kirchenwesens zunächst in Beziehung auf den preußischen Staat. Berlin: Realschulbuchhandlung, 1804.
Schmidlin, Johannes: Singendes und Spielendes Vergnügen Reiner Andacht, Oder Geistreiche Gesänge, Nach der Wahl des Besten gesammlet. Zürich: Bürgklisch, 1752.
Semler, Johann Salomo: Ascetische Vorlesungen, zur Beförderung einer vernünftigen Anwendung der christlichen Religion. Halle: Hemmerde, 1772.
———: Christliche freye Untersuchung über die so genannte Offenbarung Johannes, aus der nachgelassenen Handschrift eines fränkischen Gelehrten. Halle: Hendel, 1769.
———: Ueber historische, geselschaftliche und moralische Religion der Christen. Leipzig: Beer, 1786.
Theologische Facultæt zu Wittenberg: Bedencken über das zu Glauche an Halle 1703. im Wäysen=Hause daselbst edierte Gesang=Buch. Frankfurt/Main, Leipzig: Zimmermann, 1716.

Vitringa, Campegius: Aanleyding tot het rechte Verstant van den Tempel, die de propheet Ezechiel gesien en beschreven heeft. Franeker: Gyselaar, 1687.
— — —: Commentarius in librum prophetiarum Jesaiae. Leeuwarden: Halma, Part 1: 1714; Part 2: 1720.
Vockerodt, Gottfried: Mißbrauch der freyen Künste, insonderheit der Music. Frankfurt/Main: Zunner, 1697.

## Secondary Sources

Albrecht, Christoph: Schleiermachers Liturgik. Theorie und Praxis des Gottesdienstes bei Schleiermacher und ihre geistesgeschichtlichen Zusammenhänge. Göttingen: Vandenhoeck & Ruprecht, 1963.
Alter Adam und neue Kreatur. Pietismus und Anthropologie. Beiträge zum II. Internationalen Kongress für Pietismusforschung. Ed. by Udo Sträter. Tübingen: Niemeyer, 2009.
Aner, Karl: Die Theologie der Lessingzeit. Halle: Niemeyer, 1929.
Anttila, Miikka E.: Luther's Theology of Music: Spiritual Beauty and Pleasure. Berlin: De Gruyter, 2013.
Bayreuther, Rainer: Pietismus, Orthodoxie, pietistisches Lied und Kunstmusik. Eine Verhältnisbestimmung. In: Pietismus und Liedkultur. Ed. by Gudrun Busch and Wolfgang Miersemann. Tübingen: Niemeyer, 2002, 129–142.
Berlin, Isaiah: The Roots of Romanticism. Ed. by Henry Hardy. 2nd ed. Princeton: Princeton University Press, 2013.
Besser, Beate: Art. "Hallesches Gesangbuch 1704". In: Komponisten und Liederdichter des Evangelischen Gesangbuchs. Ed. by Wolfgang Herbst. Göttingen: Vandenhoeck & Ruprecht, 1999, 127–130.
Biographisch-bibliographisches Kirchenlexikon. Vol. 7. Ed. by Friedrich Wilhelm Bautz and Traugott Bautz. Herzberg: Traugott Bautz, 1994.
Blanken, Christine: Franz Schuberts *Lazarus* und das Wiener Oratorium zu Beginn des 19. Jahrhunderts. Stuttgart: Steiner, 2002.
Bukofzer, Manfred: Music in the Baroque Era. From Monteverdi to Bach. New York: W. W. Norton, 1947.
Bunners, Christian: Musik. In: Geschichte des Pietismus. Vol. 4: Glaubenswelt und Lebenswelten. Ed. by Hartmut Lehmann. Göttingen: Vandenhoeck & Ruprecht, 2004, 428–455.
— — —: Philipp Jakob Spener und die Kirchenmusik. In: Philipp Jakob Spener— Leben, Werk, Bedeutung: Bilanz der Forschung nach 300 Jahren. Ed. by Dorothea Wendebourg. Tübingen: Niemeyer, 2007, 241–265.
Busch, Gudrun: "Der Geist hilft unsrer Schwachheit auf". Das Geist=reiche Gesang=Buch Johann Anastasius Freylinghausens von 1704 auf dem Wege zur "Erweckung". In: Alter Adam und neue Kreatur. Pietismus und Anthropologie. Beiträge zum II. Internationalen Kongress für Pietismusforschung. Vol. 2. Ed. by Udo Sträter. Tübingen: Niemeyer, 2009, 621–644.

―――: "Singt dem Herrn nah und fern": 300 Jahre Freylinghausensches Gesangbuch. Tübingen: Niemeyer, 2008.
Damrau, Peter: Tears That Make the Heart Shine? "Godly Sadness" in Pietism. In: Edinburgh German Yearbook. Issue 6: Sadness and Melancholy in German-Language Literature and Culture. Ed. by Mary Cosgrove and Anna Richards. Rochester, NY: Camden House, 2012, 19–33.
Dannenbaum, Rolf: Joachim Lange als Wortführer des Halleschen Pietismus gegen die Orthodoxie. Diss. phil. Universität Göttingen 1951.
De Boor, Friedrich: Von den privaten "Singestunden" im Glauchaer Pfarrhaus (1698) zu den öffentlichen "Ermahnungs=Stunden" im Waisenhaus 1703. Forschungsbericht und Quellenüberblick. In: Pietismus und Liedkultur. Ed. by Gudrun Busch and Wolfgang Miersemann. Tübingen 2002, 1–46.
Eaghll, Tenzan: From Pietism to Romanticism: The Early Life and Work of Friedrich Schleiermacher. In: The Pietist Impulse in Christianity. Ed. by Christian T. Collins Winn et al. Eugene, OR: Pickwick, 2011, 107–119.
Forstman, Jack: A Romantic Triangle: Schleiermacher and Early German Romanticism. Missoula, MT: Scholars Press, 1977.
Fritz, Martin: Musikandacht: Über Herkunft und Bedeutung eines Elements bürgerlicher Religionskultur. In: Zeitschrift für Theologie und Kirche 111, March 2014, Issue 1, 28–55.
Gastrow, Paul: Joh. Salomo Semler in seiner Bedeutung für die Theologie mit besonderer Berücksichtigung seines Streites mit G. E. Lessing. Giessen: Töpelmann, 1905.
Geck, Martin: Ph. J. Spener und die Kirchenusik. In: Musik und Kirche 31, 1961, 97–106, 172–184.
"Geist=reicher" Gesang: Halle und das pietistische Lied. Ed. by Gudrun Busch and Wolfgang Miersemann. Tübingen: Niemeyer, 1997.
Gerdmar, Anders: Roots of Theological Anti-Semitism: German Biblical Interpretation and the Jews, from Herder and Semler to Kittel and Bultmann. Leiden: Brill, 2009.
Gignilliat, Mark S.: A Brief History of Old Testament Criticism from Benedict Spinoza to Brevard Childs. Grand Rapids, MI: Zondervan, 2012.
Grimm, Jacob and Wilhelm Grimm: Deutsches Wörterbuch. Leipzig: Hirzel, 1854–1961.
Grote, Simon: The Emergence of Modern Aesthetic Theory: Religion and Morality in Enlightenment Germany and Scotland. Cambridge, UK: Cambridge University Press, 2017.
―――: Pietistische "Aisthesis" und moralische Erziehung bei Alexander Gottlieb Baumgarten. In: Aufklärung 20, 2008, 175–198.
Harnisch, Ulrike: Die "ungeistlichen und fast üppigen Melodeyen" des Gesangbuches von Johann Anastasius Freylinghausen, Halle 1704. In: Musikkonzepte: Konzepte der Musikwissenschaft. Ed. by Kathrin Ebert-Ruf. Vol. 2: Freie Referate. Kassel: Bärenreiter, 2000, 246–252.

Heidrich, Jürgen: Der Meier-Mattheson Disput. Eine Polemik zur deutschen protestantischen Kirchenkantate in der ersten Hälfte des 18. Jahrhunderts. Göttingen: Vandenhoeck & Ruprecht, 1995.

Heigel, Julian: Die Legitimation der Kantate mithilfe des hallesch-pietistischen Affektkonzepts. In: Die Kantate als Katalysator: Zur Karriere eines musikalisch-literarischen Strukturtypus um und nach 1700. Ed. by Wolfgang Hirschmann and Dirk Rose. Berlin: De Gruyter, 2018, 202–212.

— — —: "Vergnügen und Erbauung". Johann Jakob Rambachs Kantatentexte und ihre Vertonungen. Halle: Franckesche Stiftungen, 2014.

Herbst, Wolfgang: Pietismus und Dadaismus. Das "Geheimniß=volle Triumph-Lied" aus Gottfried Arnolds zweitem Teil der *Göttlichen Liebesfunken* von 1701. In: Jahrbuch für Liturgik und Hymnologie 56, 2017, 186–239.

Hirsch, Emanuel: Geschichte der neuern evangelischen Theologie im Zusammenhang mit den allgemeinen Bewegungen des europäischen Denkens. Vol. 2. Gütersloh: Bertelsmann, 1951.

Hofmann, Hans-Ulrich: Luther und die Johannes-Apokalypse. Dargestellt im Rahmen der Auslegungsgeschichte des letzten Buches der Bibel und im Zusammenhang der theologischen Entwicklung des Reformators. Tübingen: J. C. B. Mohr, 1982.

Hornig, Gottfried: Die Anfänge der historisch-kritischen Theologie: Johann Salomo Semlers Schriftverständnis und seine Stellung zu Luther. Göttingen: Vandenhoeck & Ruprecht, 1961.

— — —: Johann Salomo Semler: Studien zu Leben und Werk des Hallenser Aufklärungstheologen. Tübingen: Niemeyer, 1996.

Hug, Walter: Johann Jacob Rambach (1693–1735). Religionspädagoge zwischen den Zeiten. Stuttgart: Kohlhammer, 2003.

Irwin, Joyce L.: Dancing in Bach's Time: Sin or Permissible Pleasure? In: Bach Perspectives, 2018, Issue 12, 17–35.

— — —: German Pietists and Church Music in the Baroque Age. In: Church History 54, March 1985, Issue 1, 29–40.

— — —: Neither Voice nor Heart Alone: German Lutheran Theology of Music in the Age of the Baroque. New York: Peter Lang, 1993; reprint: Eugene, OR: Wipf & Stock, 2018.

Johann Jakob Rambach (1693–1735): Praktischer Theologe und Schriftausleger. Ed. by Helge Stadelmann and Peter Zimmerling. Leipzig: Evangelische Verlagsanstalt, 2019.

Kang, Chi-Won: Frömmigkeit und Gelehrsamkeit: Die Reform des Theologiestudiums im lutherischen Pietismus des 17. und des frühen 18. Jahrhunderts. Giessen: Brunnen, 2001.

Kevorkian, Tanya: Pietists and Music. In: A Companion to German Pietism, 1660–1800. Ed. by Douglas H. Shantz. Leiden: Brill, 2015, 171–200.

Knothe, Paul: Siegmund Jakob Baumgarten und seine Stellung in der Aufklärungstheologie. In: Zeitschrift für Kirchengeschichte 46, 1928, Issue 9, 491–536.

Koski, Suvi-Päivi: "Und sungen das lied Mosis deß Knechts Gottes/ und das lied deß Lamms – Apoc. XV:3": Zur Theologie des *Geist=reichen Gesang=Buches* (Halle 1704) von Johann Anastasius Freylinghausen. In: "Geist=reicher" Gesang: Halle und das pietistische Lied. Ed. by Gudrun Busch and Wolfgang Miersemann. Tübingen: Niemeyer, 1997, 171–196.

–––: Zur theologischen Anthropologie der Freylinghausenschen Gesangbücher. In: Alter Adam und neue Kreatur. Pietismus und Anthropologie. Beiträge zum II. Internationalen Kongress für Pietismusforschung. Ed. by Udo Sträter. Tübingen: Niemeyer, 2009, 597–610.

Krauter-Dierolf, Heike: Die Eschatologie Philipp Jakob Speners. Der Streit mit der lutherischen Orthodoxie um die "Hoffnung besserer Zeiten". Tübingen: Mohr-Siebeck, 2005.

Leaver, Robin A.: J. S. Bach and Scripture: Glosses from the Calov Bible Commentary. St. Louis, MO: Concordia, 1985.

Lüder, Andreas: Historie und Dogmatik. Ein Beitrag zur Genese und Entfaltung von Johann Salomo Semlers Verständnis des Alten Testaments. Berlin, New York: De Gruyter, 1995.

Lüdke, Frank: Johann Jakob Rambach in Halle und Gießen: Spätblüte des Pietismus an deutschen Theologischen Fakultäten. In: Johann Jakob Rambach (1693–1735): Praktischer Theologe und Schriftausleger. Ed. by Helge Stadelmann and Peter Zimmerling. Leipzig 2019, 11–20.

Marcus, David: Jephthah and his Vow. Lubbock, TX: Texas Tech Press, 1986.

McMullen, Dianne Marie. The *Geistreiches Gesangbuch* of Johann Anastasius Freylinghausen (1670–1739): A German Pietist Hymnal. Diss. phil. The University of Michigan, 1987.

–––: Melodien geistlicher Lieder und ihre kontroverse Diskussion zur Bach-Zeit: Pietistische kontra orthodox-lutherische Auffassungen im Umkreis des *Geist=reichen Gesang=buches* (Halle 1704) von Johann Anastasius Freylinghausen. In: "Geist=reicher" Gesang: Halle und das pietistische Lied. Ed. by Gudrun Busch and Wolfgang Miersemann. Tübingen: Niemeyer 1997, 197–210.

McMullen, Dianne and Wolfgang Miersemann: "Ungeistliche" und "leichtsinnige" Weisen? Zur Eigenart "Hallischer Melodien" anhand ausgewählter Beispiele. In: Singen, Beten, Musizieren: Theologische Grundlagen der Kirchenmusik in Nord- und Mitteldeutschland zwischen Reformation und Pietismus (1530–1750). Ed. by Jochen M. Arnold et al. Göttingen: V&R unipress, 2014, 211–31.

Menck, Peter: Die Erziehung der Jugend zur Ehre Gottes und zum Nutzen des Nächsten: Die Pädagogik August Hermann Franckes. Tübingen: Niemeyer, 2001.

Menne, Karl: August Hermann Niemeyer: Sein Leben und Wirken. Halle: Niemeyer, 1928.

Muller, Richard A.: J. J. Rambach and the Dogmatics of Scholastic Pietism. In: Consensus 16, 1990, Issue 2, 7–27.

Nannini, Alessandro: The Language of Affects. From "Pathologia Sacra" to "Pathologica Aesthetica". In: Gefühl und Norm: Religion und Gefühlskulturen im 18. Jahrhundert. Beiträge zum V. Internationalen Kongress für Pietismusforschung 2018. Vol. 1. Ed. by Daniel Cyranka et al. Halle: Franckesche Stiftungen, 2021, 177–190.

Peschke, Erhard: Studien zur Theologie August Hermann Franckes. Berlin: Evangelische Verlagsanstalt, Vol. 1: 1964; Vol. 2: 1966.

Peters, Mark A.: Marian Theology in Printed Cantata Librettos for the German Lutheran Church, 1704–1754. In: Yale Journal of Music & Religion 3, 2017, Issue 1, 93–118 [Art. 6].

Pietism and Community in Europe and North America, 1650–1850. Ed. by Jonathan Strom. Leiden: Brill, 2010.

Pietismus und Liedkultur. Ed. by Gudrun Busch and Wolfgang Miersemann. Tübingen: Niemeyer, 2002.

Pyatt, Janet Best: Music and Society in eighteenth-century Germany: The music dramas of Johann Heinrich Rolle (1716–1785). Diss. phil. Duke, 1991.

Sattler, Gary R.: God's Glory, Neighbor's Good: A Brief Introduction to the Life and Writings of August Hermann Francke. Chicago, IL: Covenant Press, 1982.

Scheitler, Irmgard: Der Streit um die Mitteldinge. Menschenbild und Musikauffassung bei Gottfried Vockerodt und seinen Gegnern. In: Alter Adam und neue Kreatur. Pietismus und Anthropologie. Beiträge zum II. Internationalen Kongress für Pietismusforschung. Ed. by Udo Sträter. Tübingen: Niemeyer, 2009, 513–530.

Schering, Arnold: Geschichte des Oratoriums. Leipzig: Breitkopf & Härtel, 1911; reprint: Hildesheim: Olms, 1966.

Schlesinger, Eugene R.: Schleiermacher on the Necessity of the Church. In: The Journal of Theological Studies, New Series 66, April 2015, Issue 1, 235–256.

Schloemann, Martin: Siegmund Jakob Baumgarten: System und Geschichte in der Theologie des Übergangs zum Neuprotestantismus. Göttingen: Vandenhoeck & Ruprecht, 1974.

Schmidt, Bernhard: Schleiermachers Liederblätter 1817: Edition, Analyse und Kommentar eines einzigartigen Phänomens. Berlin: De Gruyter, 2008.

Schmidt, Eckart David: "Lazarus, oder die Feyer der Auferstehung": Die Erzählung von der Auferstehung des Lazarus im Johannesevangelium und ihre Interpretation durch den Dramatiker August Hermann Niemeyer und den Komponisten Franz Schubert. In: Theologische Quartalschrift 196, 2016, Issue 2, 161–183.

Schmidt, Martin: Der Pietismus als theologische Erscheinung. Gesammelte Studien zur Geschichte des Pietismus. Vol. 2. Göttingen: Vandenhoeck & Ruprecht, 1984.

Schröter, Marianne: Siegmund Jacob Baumgarten. *Unterricht von Auslegung der heiligen Schrift* (1742). In: Handbuch der Bibelhermeneutiken Von

Origenes bis zur Gegenwart. Ed. by Oda Wischmeyer. Berlin, Boston: De Gruyter, 2016, 639–649.

Singen, beten, musizieren: Theologische Grundlagen der Kirchenmusik in Nord- und Mitteldeutschland zwischen Reformation und Pietismus 1530–1750. Ed. by Jochen M. Arnold et al. Göttingen: V&R unipress, 2014.

Smither, Howard E.: A History of the Oratorio. Vol. 3: The Oratorio in the Classical Era. Chapel Hill, NC: University of North Carolina Press, 1979.

Sorkin, David: Reclaiming Theology for the Enlightenment: The Case of Siegmund Jakob Baumgarten, 1706–1757. In: Central European History 36, 2003, Issue 4, 503–530.

Stadelmann, Helge: Die Juden "hertzlich lieben": Johann Jacob Rambach und die Zukunft des jüdischen Volkes. In: Christen, Juden und die Zukunft Israels: Beiträge zur Israellehre aus Geschichte und Theologie. Ed. by Berthold Schwarz and Helge Stadelmann. Frankfurt/Main: Lang, 2009, 213–234.

Stoeffler, F. Ernest: German Pietism During the Eighteenth Century. Leiden: Brill, 1973.

Stolt, Birgit: "Laßt uns fröhlich springen!" Gefühlswelt und Gefühlsnavigierung in Luthers Reformationsarbeit. Berlin: Weidler, 2012.

Stoltzfus, Philip Edward: Theology as performance. Music, aesthetics, and God in western thought. New York: T & T Clark International, 2006.

Sträter, Udo: Halle als ein Zentrum des Pietismus. In: Musikkonzepte – Konzepte der Musikwissenschaft. Vol. 1: Bericht über den Internationalen Kongress der Gesellschaft für Musikforschung Halle (Saale) 1998. Ed. by Kathrin Eberl and Wolfgang Ruf. Kassel: Bärenreiter, 2000, 214–225.

Strom, Jonathan: German Pietism and the Problem of Conversion. University Park, PA: The Pennsylvania State University Press, 2018.

Strube, Werner: Schönes und Erhabenes: Zur Vorgeschichte und Etablierung der wichtigsten Einteilung ästhetischer Qualitäten. In: Archiv für Begriffsgeschichte 47, 2005, 25–59.

Swarat, Uwe: Der Bund eines guten Gewissens mit Gott: Die Theologie des Chorals "Ich bin getauft auf deinen Namen" von Johann Jakob Rambach. In: Johann Jakob Rambach (1693–1735): Praktischer Theologe und Schriftausleger. Ed. by Helge Stadelmann and Peter Zimmerling. Leipzig: Evangelische Verlagsanstalt, 2019, 203–227.

Sypherd, Wilbur Owen: Jephthah and his Daughter. A Study in Comparative Literature. Newark, DE: University of Delaware, 1948.

Tholuck, August: Geschichte des Rationalismus. Vol. 1: Geschichte des Pietismus und des ersten Stadiums der Aufklärung. Berlin: Wiegandt and Grieben, 1865.

Waczkat, Andreas: Johann Heinrich Rolles musikalische Dramen. Theorie, Werkbestand und Überlieferung einer Gattung im Kontext bürgerlicher Empfindsamkeit. Berlin: Ortus Musikverlag, 2007.

–––: Die religiösen musikalischen Dramen Johann Heinrich Rolles. Stoffe, Personenzeichung und Rezeption. In: Interdisziplinäre Pietismusforschungen:

Beiträge zum Ersten Internationalen Kongress für Pietismusforschung 2001. Vol. 4. Ed. by Udo Sträter. Halle: Niemeyer, 2005, 453–463.

Wissemann-Garbe, Daniela: Johann Jakob Rambach in hymnologischer Sicht. In: Johann Jakob Rambach (1693–1735): Praktischer Theologe und Schriftausleger. Ed. by Helge Stadelmann and Peter Zimmerling. Leipzig: Evangelische Verlagsanstalt, 2019, 173–201.

Yoder, Peter James: Pietism and the Sacraments: The Life and Theology of August Hermann Francke. University Park, PA: The Pennsylvania State University Press, 2021.

Zeim, Martin: Die pietistische Lyrik Johann Jacob Rambachs. In: Pietismus und Neuzeit 18, 1992, 95–117.

Zierer, Klaus: On the Historical Oblivion of August Hermann Niemeyer, A Classic Author on Education. In: The Journal of Educational Thought (JET) / Revue de la Pensée Éducative 43, Winter 2009, Issue 3, 197–222.

# Index of Names

Biblical personages are identified with the abbreviation "bib."

## A

Abraham (bib.)   20, 74, 126, 131, 145, 147–154, 168–169, 171, 174
Amos (bib.)   6
Anton, Paul   3
Arndt, Johann   1
Arnold, Gottfried   10
Asaph (bib.)   48, 72, 108–109
Augustine of Hippo   24, 83, 89, 119

## B

Bach, Carl Philipp Emanuel   145
Bach, Johann Sebastian   1, 23, 87, 95
Baumgarten, Alexander Gottlieb   85, 101
Baumgarten, Siegmund Jakob   3, 101–113, 115, 120–121, 186–187
Bayle, Pierre   128, 130
Becker, Cornelius   10
Bezaleel (bib.)   40, 134
Breithaupt, Joachim Justus   3
Brockes, Barthold Heinrich   89
Buddeus, Johann Franz   101
Burke, Edmund   127
Buxtehude, Dietrich   1

## C

Catullus (Roman poet)   85
Chandler, Samuel   128, 130
Chemnitz, Martin   17
Cocceius, Johannes   37, 60
Cramer, Johann Andreas   143

## D

Dannhauer, Johann Conrad   84
Danzi, Franz   147, 181
David (bib., psalmist)   8, 11, 15–16, 19–20, 27, 38, 40, 42, 46–50, 53–54, 60, 65, 69–74, 79, 81, 111, 115–116, 128–133, 135, 169, 186
Deborah (bib.)   11, 77, 174
Delany, Patrick   128, 130

## E

Ernst Ludwig, Landgrave of Hesse   68
Euripides (Greek playwright)   126, 172–175

## F

Francke, August Hermann   1, 3, 6–8, 13–33, 37, 60, 65, 67, 70, 84–85, 88, 90, 102, 105, 110, 112, 121, 125, 180, 182, 185–187
Francke, Gotthilf August   14, 67, 101
Freylinghausen, Johann Anastasius   1, 6–12, 13, 27, 54, 102

## G

Gellert, Christian Fürchtegott   121, 143
Gerhard, Johann   17
Gerhardt, Paul   6, 10, 143
Großgebauer, Theophilus   6

## H

Handel, Georg Friedrich   137, 170
Hannah (bib.)   38, 44–45, 77

Hasse, Johann   137
Heman (bib.)   48, 72
Homer (Greek poet)   126
Hunold, Christian Friedrich (Menantes)   87
Huss, John   164

**I**
Isaac (bib.)   15, 145, 150–154, 159

**J**
Jeduthun (bib.)   48, 72
Jephthah (bib.)   169–175
Job (bib.)   80, 126–128, 154, 169
John (bib., evangelist)   17, 29, 57, 123, 136, 154, 176–177
Josephus   146
Jubal (bib.)   6, 38–39, 49, 69, 125

**K**
Kimhi, David   170
Klopstock, Friedrich Gottlieb   121, 126–127, 137, 139–140, 142–143, 147, 155, 161, 165, 171, 173, 184

**L**
Lange, Joachim   2–3, 35–65, 67–70, 73–74, 76, 84, 89–90, 101–102, 104–105, 110, 120, 125, 170, 180, 186
Lange, Johann Christian   92
Lavater, Johann Kaspar   143
Lazarus (bib.)   154–163, 167–168, 181
Longinus (Greek author)   126
Löscher, Valentin Ernst   37
Luther, Martin   10, 29–30, 38, 40, 54, 56, 58, 73–74, 76, 81, 84, 113, 164, 185

**M**
Martha (bib., sister of Lazarus)   95, 124, 155–159, 161, 168
Mary (bib., mother of Jesus)   45, 77–79, 92, 123, 176–177

Mary (bib., sister of Lazarus)   124, 155–159, 161, 168
Metastasio, Pietro   145
Michaelis, Johann Heinrich   3
Milton, John   122, 126, 140
Miriam (bib.)   11, 23, 38–40, 49
Moses (bib.)   11–12, 17–18, 23, 39–40, 49, 50–51, 72, 77, 105, 115, 125, 169

**N**
Neander, Joachim   143
Neubauer, Ernst Friedrich   67–68, 73, 75
Neumark, Georg   143
Niemeyer, August Hermann   3, 119, 121–184, 187
Nösselt, Johann August   118–119, 121, 164

**O**
Osiander, Andreas   17
Ovid (Roman poet)   85

**P**
Patzke, Samuel   178
Paul (bib., apostle)   11, 15, 25–26, 31, 42, 50, 53, 55, 58, 61, 74, 84–85, 94, 109, 111
Pergolesi, Giovanni Battista   137
Petersen, Johann Wilhelm   92
Pfaff, Christoph Matthäus   101
Philo (Greek philosopher)   40
Pindar (Greek poet)   126
Plato   116
Porst, Johann   1
Pythagoras   116

**R**
Rambach, Johann Jakob   3, 36, 67–99, 101–102, 120–121, 125, 180, 186
Ramler, Karl Wilhelm   137
Richardson, Samuel   121
Rist, Johann   10

## Index of Names

Rolle, Johann Heinrich 145–180 passim
Rousseau, Jean-Jacques 122

### S
Samuel (bib., prophet) 20, 38, 44–46, 49, 133–134
Sarah (bib., wife of Abraham) 147, 149–150, 152
Saul (bib., king of Israel) 45–47, 69–70, 81, 129, 133
Scheibel, Gottfried Ephraim 84, 87
Schleiermacher, Friedrich 4, 181–184
Schubert, Franz 154, 181
Semler, Johann Salomo 3, 112–121, 125–126, 128, 131, 183–184, 186–187
Seneca 116
Servetus, Michael 164
Seyfried, Ignaz Ritter von 147, 181
Sophocles (Greek playwright) 126
Spangenberg, Cyriacus 11
Spener, Philipp Jakob 1, 4–6, 8, 37, 57, 84
Sulzer, Johann Georg 145

### T
Tasso, Torquato 126
Tindal, Matthew 130

### V
Vitringa, Campegius 37–38, 57, 60, 74, 102, 120
Vockerodt, Gottfried 9, 64

### W
Wolff, Christian 3, 59, 67, 101–102

### Y
Young, Edward 121

### Z
Zachariah (bib.) 77
Ziegler, Johann Gotthilf 87–88
Zinzendorf, Nikolaus Ludwig Graf von 1

# Index of Biblical References

Entries are to complete chapters; numbers following colons are to page numbers in text. The order of the biblical passages follows their order in the Lutheran Bible.

Genesis 4:   38–39, 49, 69, 125
Genesis 15:   39
Genesis 22:   147
Genesis 24:   15
Exodus 15:   40, 45
Exodus 33:   151
Leviticus 25:   41
Numbers 10:   42
Deuteronomy 32:   11, 51
1 Samuel 2:   44–45
1 Samuel 3:   45
1 Samuel 10:   69
1 Samuel 16:   35, 46, 69
1 Samuel 18:   70
1 Samuel 19:   46
2 Samuel 23:   71
1 Kings 15:   129
2 Kings 3–4:   46, 134
1 Chronicles 23:   42
1 Chronicles 25:   42–43
2 Chronicles 5:   23–24, 43
2 Chronicles 29:   42
Nehemiah 8:   93
Job 1:   154
Job 26:   127
Job 36:   127
Job 37:   127
Job 38:   127
Job 42:   154
Psalm 2:   71
Psalm 8:   107, 115–116, 131
Psalm 15:   116
Psalm 19:   116
Psalm 24:   131
Psalm 26:   50
Psalm 27:   16, 18
Psalm 29:   27, 106
Psalm 32:   129
Psalm 33:   26–27, 50–51, 107, 111
Psalm 41:   71
Psalm 42:   103
Psalm 44:   20
Psalm 46:   25, 27
Psalm 47:   19–22, 31, 79, 105–106, 131
Psalm 50:   108
Psalm 51:   129
Psalm 55:   71
Psalm 57:   79
Psalm 61:   28
Psalm 64:   15
Psalm 67:   30
Psalm 68:   79, 131
Psalm 71:   79
Psalm 81:   19, 22, 109–110
Psalm 89:   11
Psalm 92:   24, 51, 79, 111
Psalm 96:   18, 50–51, 112
Psalm 98:   51, 112
Psalm 101:   11
Psalm 103:   52, 129
Psalm 106:   60, 79
Psalm 108:   79
Psalm 110:   73
Psalm 112:   115
Psalm 113:   53, 59
Psalm 114:   53, 59
Psalm 115:   53, 59
Psalm 116:   45, 53, 59
Psalm 117:   53, 59

Psalm 118:   53, 59
Psalm 119:   15
Psalm 133:   24, 53
Psalm 136:   53
Psalm 139:   131
Psalm 144:   52
Psalm 145:   52, 79
Psalm 146:   52
Psalm 147:   52
Psalm 148:   52
Psalm 149:   51–52, 112
Psalm 150:   28, 50, 52, 79, 108
Song of Solomon 7:   12
Isaiah 1:   74–75
Isaiah 4:   75
Isaiah 6:   52, 98
Isaiah 26:   11
Isaiah 42:   51, 111
Isaiah 61:   74
Isaiah 66:   75
Jeremiah 31:   11
Daniel 3:   86
Daniel 7:   52
Amos 5:   6, 26, 77
Haggai 2:   18
Wisdom 10:   11
Sirach 47:   11
Sirach 50:   30
2 Maccabees:   163–164
Matthew 4:   21
Matthew 5:   103
Matthew 13:   12
Matthew 18:   26, 86
Matthew 23:   86
Matthew 24:   37
Matthew 26:   53
Mark 14:   53
Luke 1:   44
Luke 2:   21, 52
Luke 9:   31
Luke 24:   11
John 1:   161
John 4:   16, 18, 116, 182, 185
John 11:   160

John 13:   71
John 14:   136
John 17:   177
John 18:   29
Acts 1–2:   23–24
Acts 4:   43, 71
Romans 8:   52
Romans 9:   74
Romans 10:   74
Romans 11:   74
Romans 14:   61
1 Corinthians 10:   61
1 Corinthians 12:   4, 25–26
1 Corinthians 13:   55
1 Corinthians 14:   26, 72
1 Corinthians 15:   43, 94
2 Corinthians 3:   19
Ephesians 2:   16
Ephesians 4:   25, 72
Ephesians 5:   4, 11, 25, 42, 50,
    53–54, 56, 58, 74, 76, 78, 109–110
Ephesians 6:   55
Philippians 1:   84
Philippians 4:   31–32
Colossians 3:   11, 25, 42, 50, 53–56,
    58, 69, 74, 76–77, 79, 110
Titus 1:   86
Hebrews 10:   15
Hebrews 11:   16, 171
James 5:   79
1 Peter 3:   21
Revelation 4:   28, 59
Revelation 5:   27–29, 43, 50–52,
    57–59, 111–112
Revelation 8:   41
Revelation 9:   41
Revelation 10:   37, 41–42
Revelation 11:   41–42
Revelation 14:   27, 37, 42–43, 51, 58,
    59, 111, 112
Revelation 15:   27, 40, 42–43, 51,
    112
Revelation 18:   58
Revelation 19:   51, 58–59